After Holy Cross, Only Notre Dame

After Holy Cross, Only Notre Dame

◆

The Life of Brother Gatian
(Urbain Monsimer)

George Klawitter

iUniverse, Inc.
New York Lincoln Shanghai

After Holy Cross, Only Notre Dame
The Life of Brother Gatian (Urbain Monsimer)

iUniverse, Inc.

For information address:
iUniverse, Inc.
2021 Pine Lake Road, Suite 100
Lincoln, NE 68512
www.iuniverse.com

ISBN: 0-595-29830-3

Printed in the United States of America

For my parents

George and Caroline Klawitter

Contents

Preface

This book could not have been written without the groundwork of Denis Bruneau, Marie Josephe Tourneux, and Yves Guilmineau. For fifteen years, Denis Bruneau has devoted careful attention to Brother Gatian and has published two monographs about the young man whose grand niece married M. Bruneau's own brother in 1936. Mme. Tourneux has worked patiently to trace the Monsimer family tree from the seventeenth century to the present day. The research by M. Guilmineau has given us valuable information on the Mottais family and the home in which Brother André Mottais was born.

This book examines the life of the talented Gatian, the finest linguist among the pioneer brothers in America. His writings in French are superb and his writings in English amazingly good for a teenager. Basil Moreau, his superior in Le Mans, wrote beautifully in French, and his circular letters are rich in creative spiritual insights, but he knew little English. Edward Sorin, Gatian's superior in America, wrote basic French, occasionally purple, and his circular letters are full of pious jargon. The Holy Cross patriarch in America, Brother Vincent, wrote fair French prose, and Brother Theodule's is downright bad. Neither man mastered English. These were all good men, but if they are measured for their abilities to write, Gatian and Moreau are the best stylists, and only Gatian was equally facile in two languages. His sense of syntax, his large vocabulary, his sensitivity to tone, his ability to paint a scene with vivid details, all demonstrate a young man of eminent linguistic gifts.

This life of Gatian will present a challenge to any readers who expect a traditional biography because I have included an extended introduction on the founders of Holy Cross. The two male giants in the history of Holy Cross have always been Jacques Dujarié and Basil Moreau, but what if a third man were so important that without him Dujarié's brothers would have fallen into the footnotes of history and Moreau's mixed community would never have seen the light of day? What if this man were schooled in religious spirituality more formally than Dujarié and supervised more classrooms than Moreau ever set foot in? What if such a man had a humility so ingrained that after fifteen years of running the day-to-day operations of a religious organization, he accepted demotion and the humblest of tasks because he knew that the future of his brothers depended upon his unconditional submission? What if such a man has been sidelined more or less in the history of Holy Cross while Dujarié and Moreau have advanced in stature and renown, the latter well into the process of canonization? Such a man, we would say, deserves resurrection: his indefatigable energy, his uncanny foresight, and his overpowering virtue need to be better acknowledged than they are. This man was Brother André Mottais.

Brother André is the almost forgotten founder of the Congregation of Holy Cross. His importance not only in saving the Brothers of St. Joseph, but in forming hundreds of young men, including Gatian, should never again be underestimated. André was the life blood of the brothers: it was his energy and perseverance that insured Urbain Monsimer a Community that would transform the little boy into the audacious Brother Gatian. Never again should André or Gatian be buried in archives or footnotes. Both deserve a place in Holy Cross history, the founder for his unstinting service, the disciple for his intrepid attachment to religion.

I wanted to investigate the spirituality of the three founders of the Congregation of Holy Cross so that their influence on Gatian can be clearly understood. Without an appreciation of Dujarié's courage, we could not appreciate Gatian's brash personality. Without knowing André's sense of a brother's vocation, we would be at a loss to know Gatian's sense of community. Without understanding Moreau's asceticism, we could never understand Gatian's inflexible adherence to rules. But the respective charisms of all three founders contributed to Gatian's mental breakdown, because the two priests and the religious brother gave him ideals that he could not reconcile to the tremendous energy that welled up within him. The priestly courage of Dujarié rose up against the humility of André, and both clashed against Moreau's rigidity. The oak that Moreau nurtured in Gatian snapped in the wind that was Dujarié and washed away in the river that was André Mottais.

And then, of course, there was Sorin, Gatian's superior and nemesis for nine years in America, a priest unable to separate Notre Dame from Holy Cross. He thought that the success of his institution indicated the success of his Congregation, and thus he sometimes compromised his moral sense to further the school he had woven inextricably around himself. When Gatian complained in the 1840's that discipline at Notre Dame was lax and undercutting the work of the teachers, Sorin counselled kindness lest he lose students and their tuition dollars, but in the 1850's when Notre Dame's financial base was more secure, he cracked down on students with an excessive ferocity. When he sensed money slipping from his grasp, he sacrificed principle to save his institution.

After Sorin left Sainte Croix (Holy Cross) in France and settled in Indiana, he gradually began to live only for Notre Dame, a process that Americans laud as his being "Americanized," but he sacrificed Holy Cross roots in Le Mans so that his own college in Indiana could thrive. "After Holy Cross, only Notre Dame" came to be not a chronology, but first a decision, and then a mindset. This attitude was both his greatest asset and his greatest defect. In the process, he used people. Gatian was brash enough to confront him, and Sorin broke him. Had Gatian stayed under Moreau's more patient eye in France, he may have thrived in Holy Cross for fifty years. Instead, he died bitter and broken far from the land and work he had initially welcomed in America as a boy of fourteen.

In the writing of this book, I received gracious help from many people. Special thanks must be tendered to Holy Cross archivist Robert Antonelli, CSC, for his help in assembling material on Brother André Mottais, and to Mrs. Jackie Dougherty who could always be counted on for help at the Indiana Province Archives, Notre Dame. Brother John Kuhn, CSC, of the Midwest Brothers Province Archives, has encouraged this project, and Sister Georgia Costin, CSC, has been an inspiration for it. Brother Philip Armstrong, CSC, and James T. Burtchaell, CSC, read the manuscript and offered valuable advice. Special thanks go to St. Edward's University, especially President George Martin, Executive Vice-President Sister Donna Jurick, SSND, and Vice-President for the Undergraduate College J.D. Lewis for the sabbatical leave that afforded me the time to finish my research and to write this life of Brother Gatian.

Brother Gatian: Time Line

April 3, 1826	Birth at Préau, Saulges, France
February 17, 1837	Death of James Dujarié, founder of the Brothers of St. Joseph
March 1, 1837	Fundamental Pact joining Brothers of St. Joseph and the auxiliary priests
August 13, 1939	Urbain enters Brothers of St. Joseph in Le Mans
August 5, 1841	Gatian leaves for America
September 13, 1841	Gatian arrives at New York City
October 10, 1841	Gatian arrives at Vincennes, Indiana
October 14, 1841	Gatian settles at St. Peter's, Black Oak Ridge, Indiana
November 16, 1842	Gatian leaves for Notre Dame
November 27, 1842	Gatian arrives at Notre Dame
February 27, 1843	Brother Vincent arrives from St. Peter's, Black Oak Ridge
July 12, 1845	Anselm drowns in the Ohio River at Madison
February 14, 1849	Gatian leaves for Brooklyn
February 20, 1849	Gatian arrives in New York City
April [ ], 1849	Gatian returns to Notre Dame
January 7, 1850	Gatian restrained at Notre Dame
February 28, 1850	St. Joseph Company leaves for California
July [ ], 1850	St. Joseph Company arrives in Placerville, California
October [?], 1850	Urbain leaves the Congregation of Holy Cross
January [ ], 1851	Urbain in Dry Town, Calavaras County, California

March [ ], 1851	Urbain in Kelsey, California
August [ ], 1851	Urbain relocates to Shasta City, California
June, 1854	Urbain in Kelsey, California
May 5, 1860	Urbain leaves for New York City from San Francisco
July 27, 1860	Urbain dies at Préau, Saulges, France

Introduction

Part I:
Jacques Dujarié, the First Founder:
"A more heroic action"

It would be difficult to name anyone more heroic in the history of Holy Cross than Jacques Dujarié. Born in halcyon days at Rennes-en-Grenouilles on November 9, 1767, a generation before the French Revolution, he enjoyed a happy childhood. His parents raised four children and owned over a hundred and twenty-five acres of land. Educated by a courageous parish priest, Abbé Guerin de la Roussardière, who would one day refuse to take the oath of clerical submission demanded by the Revolution, Dujarié learned early the lesson of digging in for his beliefs. Roussardière served as pastor at Sainte-Marie-du-Bois from the time Dujarié was five until he was twenty. After receiving a rudimentary education in the priest's home, Dujarié in 1778 went at the age of eleven to a formal school at Lassy, about five miles from his home. After three years, he entered the seminary in Le Mans and studied under the Vincentians before transferring to a school in Ernée closer to his home. After two years at Ernée, he went to the minor seminary at Domfront, an excellent school run by the Eudists. In 1787 at the age of twenty, he received tonsure in Le Mans and was given a stipend to cover his expenses for the major seminary in Angers where he would study until the Revolution would close the school in 1792 and force him to go into hiding. He thus had an excellent education and was not at all hindered by poor training when he eventually did get ordained. He has often paled by comparison with Holy Cross's third founder, Basil Moreau, in formal educational training, but in reality, Dujarié was well educated.

The French system of schools during the reign of Louis XVI was under the direction of the church. When Louis was crowned in 1775, he ruled a country that boasted a strong sense of education, so strong, in fact, that the Revolution itself did not obliterate a widespread appreciation for study. In fact, in 1800, near the end of the revolutionary period, the literacy rate in France was higher than it was in the United States in the late twentieth century.[1] The Revolution may have destroyed the church's control of the schools, but it never exterminated the common people's desire to read and write. Eighteenth century France not only produced philosophical giants like Rousseau and Voltaire, it also produced an educated populace that endured throughout and beyond the Reign of Terror. Along the way, there were tragic losses of brilliant thinkers like the chemist Lavoisier and the gentle botanist-lawyer Malesherbes, both guillotined (the latter for his legal defense of the king), but the Revolution never attempted to obliterate education. It was no Khmer Rouge. Much of the most provocative, albeit radical, thinking went on in Jacobin and Girondin political clubs where stellar rhetoric was appreciated and fresh thinking prized. There was, of course, an obliteration of logic once the ideologues let their rabid chauvinism and personal ambitions control their brains and tongues, but in the earliest days of the clubs, sound reason triumphed over injured feeling more often than not. In all the turmoil before and during the Revolution, the French value for knowledge afforded the farm boy Dujarié a superb fourteen years of formal education, after his informal schooling in the rectory at St. Marie-du-Bois, and before his college was closed.

But that tragic closure at Angers happened in 1792, well into the heat of the Revolution. What did the seminarian Dujarié think in 1789 when the king convened the Estates General? He must have been keenly interested in a legislative approach that had not been tried in France for almost two hundred years. The French parlements in the seventeenth and eighteenth centuries had been more advisory than legislative. Who, after all, would be able to legislate for the great Sun King, Louis XIV? But the last of such advisory bodies convened at Versailles in 1688. When Louis XVI agreed to know the mind of his people in 1789, he solicited from each of the three estates (nobles, clergy, commoners) their real concerns. From all over France came the "cahiers de doléances," the gripe sheets that listed the complaints of high and low. Naively, Louis really believed that the Estates General would be an excellent device for his government. It proved to be a disaster. The three estates were not equal, and soon the commoners resented the privileging of the nobles and the clergy. On important ceremonial occasions, for example, the top two estates would process with festive pomp into a hall by its front entrance, while the lowest estate scrambled in by a side door. Soon the commoners requested double voting count so their power would be equal to the voting block of the upper estates, but when they could not achieve this goal, they argued for a fusion of all three estates into one legislative body. Gradually some members of the upper estates drifted into the lowest estate, and by late June, 1789, the fusion of the three estates was accomplished. Meanwhile, the king had been distracted by the death of his oldest son, the dauphin, and could not stop the outbursts of patriotic manipulation that resulted in passionate scenarios like the Tennis Court Oath, taken on June 22 away from the formal meeting hall that Louis had designated for the Estates.

Dujarié may or may not have had an opinion on these events at Versailles, as long as the Assembly seemed to be under the graces of the king, but in July when Parisian patriots invaded the Bastille, he must have sensed the ominous thrill that both shocked and enlivened France. Although there were but seven prisoners in the whole Bastille (the mob was actually after gunpowder), hack journalists made much of the mass liberation of prisoners, and graphic illustrators caught the imagination with vivid portrayals of the prison's supposed atrocities. Once the Bastille had become an important symbol of the common people's power, Dujarié could not have failed to be aware of further events: e.g., the National Assembly's picking itself up and moving from Versailles to Paris, away from the king and his court. In August came *The Declaration of the Rights of Man*, printed and disseminated across the country, and in October, the Parisian mob, abetted by the National Guard, invaded Versailles and forced the royal family to go to Paris. Louis was stripped of his title "King of France" and made to accept the title "King of the French." This was only the beginning of his demotion, a demotion that would end before his execution with his being addressed as "Louis Capet," a name he resented because he said he never used it. Jacques Dujarié, at age twenty-one, could not have been pleased with these affronts to established authority: he was, after all, a thriving student of the church, and the church was based on obedience to established authority. The king was God's anointed, and Dujarié was in service to God—he could not countenance the deposition of God's anointed king. Still Dujarié remained in Angers, and there was no indication in 1789 that the seminary was in real danger.

With the death of Mirabeau in April, 1790, the Constituent Assembly lost a man who believed strongly that France still needed some kind of a king. Gradually the concept faded, and its erosion was helped by the aborted flight of the royal family in June, 1790. Arrested at Varennes, the king and queen were brought back to Paris. Riding in their coach were two representatives of the people, one of whom, Pétion, the illegally elected mayor of Paris, took the occasion to flirt with the king's sister and later boasted of his masculine appeal in terms that indicate his rude vulgarity.[2] Finally, in January, 1791, the oath of submission to the civil constitution was required of all clergy. It meant that henceforth the church would be answerable to the government alone. All bishops, for example, would be selected by civil authorities, and no allegiance was any longer owed to the pope. At the Angers seminary, not a single priest took the juring oath. The bishop of Angers also refused the oath and was replaced by a constitutional bishop. On March 18, 1792, the night before the new bishop was to arrive, the Sulpician faculty gathered all the seminarians in the chapel for a final meditation: the text was "the sins of the people call down upon them evil pastors."[3] Within days only ten of two hundred and forty clerics remained in the seminary. The ten soon left as well. The magnificent college was emptied, and Jacques Dujarié returned to Sainte-Marie-du-Bois.

When many think of the French Revolution, they tend to append the year 1789 to it and the year 1793 to the Reign of Terror. Thus it seems a revolution no longer than the American Revolution or the American Civil War, but actually the French Revolution carried itself along in waves that decreed persecution of clergy periodically over a period of thirteen years. The church in France was not free to breathe until Napoleon's 1802 Concordat. Thus when Dujarié left Angers in 1792, he was simply at the beginning of a long stretch of years during which he would often be at risk of execution. The pastor at his birth parish in Rennes-en-Grenouilles, Abbé Migoret-Lamberdière, for example, was executed on January 21, 1794, along with fourteen priests and four nuns.[4] Among them was the pastor of Brother Gatian's grandfather's parish. At that time Dujarié, not yet a priest, worked as a weaver. Finally in 1795, Dujarié went to complete his secret training for ordination under Jacquet de la Haye, a priest in hiding at Trôo. On December 26, 1795, he was ordained in Paris at an undisclosed location by Bishop de Maillé, who himself hid out in various areas of the city, sometimes disguised as a soldier. Dujarié began a life on the run.

By this time, France had suffered a massacre at the Tuilleries (August 10, 1792), which was blamed wrongly on the king, and another massacre in the Paris prisons one month later by a mob that slaughtered indiscriminately, even killing boys who had been imprisoned for petty delinquency in Bicêtre at the request of their parents. One of the boys killed was twelve years old. The year 1793 brought further bloodshed to good and bad: the king was executed in January and Marat was assassinated in his bath by Charlotte Corday, who came in from Argentan for the express purpose of killing him. She rode regally in the tumbril to her death, holding her head high and standing the entire route. The queen was guillotined in October, her young son left to pine in filthy captivity until he too died in 1795. Finally with the execution of Robespierre and the leaders of the Reign of Terror, some of the worst horror left the country. As Jacques Dujarié was ordained a priest, Paris was beginning to look at its recent history and realize that a small minority had destroyed justice and propriety. The noise continued, however, if only to cover some of the shame. France was still learning to live without a royal family, and the country struggled with the presence of two sets of clergy: those who had sworn the clerical oath to the government and those who did not. The former ministered openly in the churches while the latter ministered in barns and cellars hidden from the eyes of those who would betray them to authorities. Among the hidden was Jacques Dujarié.

After his ordination in Paris, Dujarié returned to Ruillé where he celebrated his first Mass in a cellar on the Aubry farm known as Fosse-Garnier.[5] Assigned to the area around Ruillé, Dujarié ministered under cover for seven years. Even as the country inched toward the Concordat, priests were still in danger of execution or exile, and were it not for the courage of the local people who hid him, Dujarié himself might have died as a very young man. Many Holy Cross religious have, of course, been in danger over the years, e.g., the missionaries in Bengal at the time of partition, men and women interned during World War II in the Philippines, young Holy Cross Brothers in Rwanda at the close of the twentieth-century, but few have lived under threat of their lives as long as Jacques Dujarié had. When he came to found the two religious congregations that he did, he brought to his work a courage and humility he might not have had were it not for the years when he feared for his life. The man was purified by fire.

In his first years serving openly at Ruillé, Dujarié saw the lack of care for the poor, and so he enlisted the help of a few peasant girls whom he housed on the outskirts of town in a house he built himself with stones from the surrounding fields. If non-juring clergy before the Revolution knew privilege and ease, few of them did after the Revolution. Of course, before 1789 there were two levels of clergy, and only the bishops and top administrators enjoyed wealth and power. Talleyrand, for example, was a bishop in name only: he hardly knew how to say Mass, but he certainly knew how to use power. Many rural priests were as dirt poor as their peasant parishioners. But virtue does not always reside in the poor. Poverty stricken priests in 1792 faced the same dilemma as rich priests: swear the oath, please the Assembly, lose the respect of many parishioners (especially in rural areas), or refuse the oath, go into hiding, retain a sense of integrity. The choice was not easy. Many clerics got caught up in the revolutionary spirit and recognized that privilege was not a good thing for churchmen: in order to reform a corrupt church, they hoped to capitalize on the economic leveling that the patriots purportedly espoused. Luckily for many of the juring, they were able to renounce their constitutional oath after 1802 and save their ecclesiastical careers. Their brothers in the non-juring clergy, caught in the cogs of the Revolution, were not so lucky: thousands were forced to emigrate or had their day with the guillotine.

Jacques Dujarié had religious convictions that kept him faithful, and he had good luck to evade capture. Settled in Ruillé after the Concordat, he directed his pious women to begin their work of ministry to the poor. They thrived under his direction. He then was asked by local clergy to found a group of dedicated men. This task he undertook in 1820, and they thrived too, but not as steadily as his Sisters of Providence: the sisters had gotten a twenty year head start over the brothers and were in sound financial shape by the time the 1830 Revolution once again threatened to ravage France. In 1827 Father Dujarié had agreed with Father Gabriel Deshayes to amalgamate the Brothers of St. Joseph with two congregations that Deshayes had founded. Nothing came of the agreement, but the proposed merger, coming only seven years after Dujarié's first recruits to the brothers at Ruillé, shows just how precarious Dujarié's administrative grip was early on. Then the Brothers of St. Joseph were hit hard in 1830 and struggled to stay afloat under Dujarié's eye until they finally realized their only hope lay in younger management.

Their savior was one of their first members, André Mottais. André's first biographer, Philéas Vanier, called André "co-founder of his Congregation" because "he exercised all the functions: he accepted all responsibilities."[6] Although under Dujarié there were four brother "directors" of the Ruillé community, the second, third, and fourth were not associate directors but director assistants to André. He alone was master of novices, presided over religious exercises, gave all permissions, gave spiritual direction, supervised the schools, and kept general good order among the scores of men who came into the Brothers of St. Joseph. Of the thirty-six letters we still have by André, many of the earliest are directed to individual brothers out in the schools, showing that he executed much of the work Dujarié would have done, health permitting. For example, on June 22, 1826, he wrote to Brother Adrian:[7]

My dear brother,

Our Father [Dujarié] is happy that you are settled at Hardanges. He is aware as well as I am of the inconveniences that the parish priest experiences in regard to his health. The Lord sends tribulations to his elect in order to enrich the immortal crown that He prepares for them.

You can buy four handkerchiefs and two pair of stockings. Our good father gives his permission. He sends his regards and asks that you extend his to the priest at Hardanges.

I'm obliging you, my dear brother, to follow as much as possible the Rule Book for the schools, because those of our brothers who use most of what it prescribes are also those who succeed the most in their classes. Strive to teach yourself by teaching others to become a good school teacher, a pious and fervent religious, having no other desire but to sanctify yourself and those that Divine Providence has entrusted to you. Be careful above all about neglecting the sacraments.

If you are not aware of the death of Brother Jerome, I'll tell you about it. Do for the repose of his soul all that you had to do for the repose of Brother John Mary's. Good-by, my dear brother. Pray for me.[8]

The death of the two young religious, Jerome at age 24 and John Mary at age 25, must have been a blow to Dujarié and the fledgling community, but André's attention is on the living: Adrian has responsibilities and André reminds him of his duties.

It is to André too that we owe an early list of all the schools opened and closed by the Brothers of St. Joseph. In April of 1831 he notes that from 1820 to 1829 the little community grew by leaps and bounds up to fifty schools, most of them manned by one or two brothers. One hundred and two brothers attended the annual retreat at Ruillé in the summer of 1829. That was not the entire community because a few brothers did not show up for the retreat. It certainly was a huge number of men, therefore, who had responded to Dujarié and André in the first nine years of the organization. Of the one hundred and five members, André notes, eighty percent wore the religious habit. But then numbers began to decline. The crisis prompted André and Dujarié to formulate an important document at the September retreat of 1831. It is a kind of pact that the two founders hoped "will lead us to peaceful days and true freedom by which our Institute will be able to appear in its former glory." The document contains ten stipulations to which all brothers were to agree under pain of sin:

1. to live attached to our holy Institute.

2. to sustain each other until death.

3. to remain united in the body of the Congregation and the Community as long as possible, following the same practices and rules that we have practiced up to now.

4. and in case we have to dissolve, to remain united in heart and affections, sustaining and assisting each other reciprocally.

5. to assemble as a body in community as time and place permit.

6. We Brothers of Saint Joseph will continue our submission to and depen-
    dence on Father Dujarié, our founder and superior general who, assisted
    by four Brothers of his council who are presently Brother André Pierre
    Mottais (Chief Director), Brother Léonard Francis Guittoyer (Second
    Director), Brother Henry Michael Taupin (Third Director), and Brother
    Vincent Ferier John Pieau. Whether or not it is possible to reunite them,
    he will give us orders for all of them, following the circumstances below.

7. Conforming to the dispositions of the preceding article, he will be able to
    innovate and abrogate in our rules and customs everything he judges nec-
    essary for the time and circumstances.

8. Round our superior we have our rallying point.

9. And if we have the misfortune to lose him, we will rally around the
    bishop of Le Mans.

10. If one of the members of the council is lost, the superior with his remain-
    ing counselors will elect another.[9]

That the pact stipulates Dujarié as the sole founder of the group is in keeping
with accepted form at the time: as important as André was to the success of the
group during the previous eleven years, protocol would preclude a layman's
assuming parity with a priest.

There are only twenty-one signatures on the 1831 pact, indicating that within
the previous two years, the group had lost about eighty percent of its membership.[10] At the same retreat twenty men took a public vow of obedience, conse-
crating themselves "to the education of children." Some of the items in the pact
are desperate, the result of men determined not to let a good thing die. Most
touching perhaps is the fourth resolution: if they did not harbor in their hearts
the real possibility of dissolution, they never would have included a resolution
that would govern their affection for each other if the community really did come
to disband. Clearly here were men who, under Dujarié's direction, had been
happy together for years and wanted some shred of their life together to remain,
even if it meant only occasional gestures of good will. In the back of their minds
may have been the threat of suppression of religious communities such as happened after the Revolution. What were the feelings of men sent away from companions they had lived with for years? France periodically visited the fate on its
religious, most recently in 1903 when anticlerical laws shut down all monasteries
and emptied the monks into the world. The trappists today at La Grande Trappe
in Normandy keep on exhibit photographs of those sad times. Some Holy Cross
religious in 1903 emigrated to America rather than be secularized. Brother Louis

Gazagne, for example, fled and taught many years in the United States, ending his career at St. Edward High School in Lakewood, Ohio, in the 1960s. The pact signed at Ruillé in 1831 foresaw the eventuality of dissolution by attrition, and the faithful remnant wanted to hold some hope of happy reunions that would be similar to the reunions of war veterans: high on reminiscence.

The pervasive political paranoia was still present in France as Brother André demonstrates in a letter dated June 20, 1832. There he chronicles a search of the Ruillé house by armed national guards:

> On the 20th of June, 1832, about 10:30 in the morning the parish house and the two sentriesties of Ruillé-sur-Loir were invaded by the police and armed national guards; sentries were placed at all exits, and a great number of the guards searched the houses and gardens. The king's prosecutor and the magistrate from St. Calais, accompanied by the mayor of Ruillé, entered and visited all the rooms and furnishings. They recorded all the information in detail and repeated the same. The three houses, our superior, the Brothers and Sisters were not found at fault and were left to answer the questions of those gentlemen and open the doors for them so that they might rummage around everywhere. When their visits were ended, these gentlemen departed, and we lived on in tranquility as was ordinary. The Sisters were visited first, our Father superior next, and the Brothers last.[11]

Such activities indicate the impetuousness of local police two generations after the Revolution had turned in on itself and eliminated many of the very leaders who had led it to glory in 1789.

On August 31, 1835, Dujarié turned over his brothers to Basil Moreau, and Brother André's leadership role soon began to wane. Although he continued on as novice master at Le Mans, we have no more business letters written by him once the Brothers of St. Joseph were turned over to Moreau. His last administrative letter was dated June 28, 1835, a memo acknowledging receipt of fifty francs from the Sisters of Providence. Then for three years André's pen is silent, until 1838 when he writes a touching memorial on the life of Dujarié. Two more years pass and he writes the first of five fascinating letters about his new life as a missionary in northern Africa. In 1840 he is but forty years old. He will die four years later. Gatian knew him less than a year.

The qualities that Dujarié had demonstrated to his brothers were survival skills that served them well in their many troubles. Dujarié was intrepid, and he attracted to his Brothers of St. Joseph many men of great potential. Well educated himself, he instilled in the brothers a thirst for education that they were unfortunately rarely able to satisfy because of the demands for teachers in parish schools. When he finally had to relinquish control of them, he turned them over to Basil Moreau, who characterized Dujarié's sacrifice as "one of the most meritorious deeds of his entire life, and I defy anyone to find a more heroic action than that."[12] Dujarié himself recognized the need for stamina. In a letter to a sick brother, he wrote:

> Your poor health worries me and your distaste for your religious vocation bothers me still more. I am sure that this has a great deal to do with your illness. My dear child, you must revive your courage and reject all those thoughts which would incite you to abandon your holy state.[13]

A man of great patience and infinite goodness, Dujarié was very solicitous when he dealt with any of his men. In his final months at Le Mans, he delighted in being with the school children in the school yard where he would give them candy.

In Gatian we will find the same wonderful strength that Dujarié had. Not always right, Gatian was stubborn enough to fight for his will, much as Dujarié learned to do. Dujarié the survivor helped form Gatian the survivor, even though the two never met, because there was a continuity of strength from Dujarié through the remnant of his Brothers of St. Joseph who survived to become Brothers of Holy Cross. The latter men would train Urbain when he showed up, an energetic boy of thirteen, to become a brother in Le Mans. Like Urbain, Dujarié had a touch of paranoia in him: who could blame the priest after living for seven years always looking over his shoulder for someone who might betray him to his death? Finally, Dujarié did not stand for rank: when he started his Brothers of St. Joseph, they were egalitarian. Not one to enjoy much if any semblance of clerical privilege, Dujarié wanted in his men a sense of *egalité* as well as *fraternité*. The only hint of status in his community was the council of four brothers who advised him in administrative matters, but these men (André, Vincent, Leonard, and Henry) had day jobs and worked as hard in teaching as any of the other brothers. This quality of Dujarié, we will see, would not endure: as France got farther and farther from its Revolution, the church accepted back some of the hierarchical privileges that had been on the brink of extinction. In some ways, the Revolution did not go far enough.

Part II:
Brother André Mottais, The Second Founder:
"Remove my name every time it appears"

Born André Pierre Mottais in Larchamp, fifty miles northwest of Le Mans, the man who was destined to help forge Holy Cross came of solid farming stock.[1] His parents, Jean Mottais and Jeanne Blot, were married May 14, 1793, seven years before André's birth. The father was born in 1768 and the mother in 1773, making them 24 and 20 at the time of their marriage in the bloodiest year of the French Revolution.[2] Jeanne Blot and Jean Mottais had four children that we know of: Jean François (born September 16, 1794), André Pierre (February 21, 1800), Jeanne Julienne (August 10, 1805), and Joseph (June 17, 1811). For generations the Mottais family lived at Pontperrin, a farm-estate in Mayenne near the town of Larchamp, fifteen miles east of Fougères. The property had been in the family since the sixteenth century. Before the French Revolution it comprised over two hundred and fifty acres. Today it has a single manor house owned by the de Blic family, who also own four surrounding farms. The Mottais farm-estate is located just southeast of Larchamp, off the intersection of Route 799 and Route 523, and its name "Pontperrin" suggests that the family property may have been named for a bridge over a small river on the eastern edge of the property.

The Mottais home remains standing today, three stories tall, with chimneys at either end of the building. Its weathered brick indicates a family of some wealth. Stone steps lead up to an entrance on the second level, suggesting that originally the lowest level was probably used for storage. The living quarters would then be confined to the two upper levels, and the orderly placement of the windows suggests two or four rooms per floor, the middle level for living and dining, the top floor for sleeping. A barn next to the house is equally old and is still used by the de Blic family. Its walls are twenty feet high, and its roof peaks to thirty feet. At one end a high shuttered window indicates a grain loft. The other end appends a smaller building still used as living quarters.

André Pierre Mottais, therefore, came from a family with deep roots in the area going back several hundred years. As the second son, he was not christened with the name of his father, grandfather, and great-grandfather, nor would he have inherited the family farm. Born in the winter of 1800, André was welcomed into a country chronicled by a new calendar: Revolutionary France records André's birth as 2 Ventose in the year 8 (February 21, 1800). His birth announcement in the Larchamp parish records begins, "Today, the second Ventose," indicating that the Revolutionary Calendar was duly regarded as official in small French towns. In its fourteenth year (1805), however, the calendar would revert to the Gregorian style. The parish church in Larchamp dominates the town and remains much as André would have known it. The bell tower is the highest structure in the area, its old dark stone already hundreds of years old when André was carried into the church to be baptized. The baptistry, where the Mottais family had their son baptized in February, 1800, is a separate little room at the back right of the church, a small room that can accommodate a dozen people. The stone font in which he was ritually brought into the Larchamp faith community is still used today to welcome the infants of the parish into their ancient religion. The interior of the church is dark, although some stained-glass windows let in welcome light. The foot-thick walls would give a little boy the sense of a fortress, affording him security in his religion, albeit tinged with gloom.

The school André attended in Larchamp has only recently been torn down, but André, like the sons of other farm owners, would have learned the basics of reading, writing, and numbers before working full time on the family farm, awaiting whatever destiny would come his way. Did he enjoy farm work? We have no record left of his early life on the farm, but later letters written from Africa demonstrate a keen sense of farming. We presume that this virtuous young man worked with a willing back and a cheerful heart, but at some point there resonated in him a call at the age of twenty to leave his family and travel south to the little town of Ruillé where Dujarié was beginning to gather young men into his Bothers of St. Joseph. André would have walked, or perhaps ridden in a cart, south to Ernée, then further south to Laval, the largest city he would have seen in his life so far. Then he probably would have headed southeast to Sablé and farther to la Flèche where he would have encountered the Loir River—not the mighty Loire of famed chateaux, but the little Loir that runs east-west joining the Sarthe River (from Le Mans) just north of Angers. From la Flèche, André may simply have headed east, following the little Loir as it rambled toward him, past le Lude, Château-du-Loir, and la Chartre-sur-le-Loir to little Ruillé-sur-le-Loir, where the pastor of the parish either expected him (possibly apprised of his arrival by letter) or was pleasantly surprised by the young farmer's appearance.

Jacques Dujarié had been nudged by Bishop Pidoll of Le Mans as early as 1818 to begin a community of brothers who would teach in rural schools because Dujarié's community of Providence Sisters had been a growing success during the previous decade. By 1820 the Curé of Ruillé had begun to accept young men into his rectory. The first, Pierre Hureau, arrived on July 15, the second, Louis Duchêne (Dujarié's nephew), on August 20. The former left a year later but returned for six years in 1824. The latter left in 1825. Dujarié's third arrival was a prize: André Pierre Mottais arrived on October 22, 1820, persevered, and eventually became the first brother to profess perpetual vows of poverty, chastity, obedience, and stability (August 25, 1836). These young recruits slept in Dujarié's attic with the rats, and as the numbers of young men grew, the brothers flowed over into the laundry room, the bakehouse, the barn, and even the stable.[4] Three months after André arrived, Dujarié told him to start a school at Ruillé. Such was Dujarié's impression of André's promise and talents: the young man had just come from a farm and had no training as a teacher. Then, since Dujarié felt he did not know how to train male religious, in spite of his successful guidance of the Providence women, the priest consulted Abbé de Lamennais, founder of a successful community of brothers, who advised him to study the spiritual practices of the Christian Brothers. Their founder, John Baptist de la Salle, had had noteworthy success with a burgeoning community of religious teachers. Thus a few months after André had started his little school in Ruillé, Dujarié sent him north to Le Mans where the young man had to be reviewed for military conscription, was exempted, and then lived for five months in 1821 with a priest named Lamare and took classes from the Christian Brothers.[5]

The experience with Lamare was a kind of active novitiate by which André blended the pious direction of his priest-mentor with the practical classroom know-how of his Christian Brother directors. In fact, as we read between the lines of André's praise for Father Lamare, we can discern the origins of André's own life-long sense of piety. Lamare was a man of fixed routine, André tells us in his 1833 sketch of the man: he slept no more than five hours a night, prayed two hours before Mass, and left promptly for St. Julian's Cathedral at 6:30. After lunch, the priest heard confessions, sometimes on the eve of great feasts until midnight, breaking away only for a hurried supper. He ate little, subsisting on soup and vegetables, and he never touched wine. During meals he was usually interrupted by poor people at the door begging alms: he never turned them away and listened to all their troubles. In these acts of a saintly man, it is easy to see what André himself picked up for his own life in religion: he became an indefatigable supervisor of new teachers, both in their training at Ruillé and in their little parish schools around the region, and he was a prayerful man whose good sense rooted in him a firm and unwavering belief in the viability of the Brothers of St. Joseph, even in their darkest hours. He was as practical as Lamare, and eventually, once his supervisory duties were taken away from him, he exhibited the same calm and ascetic piety that Lamare had exhibited when André was a malleable twenty-one year old young man.

The books that Lamare gave André to read in that five month period tell us much about what André valued. First there was the life of Vincent de Paul and a history of his foundations. Here André would have seen witness of the great charitable works of the hospitalers. Secondly, Alphonsus Liguori's book on the love of God which André characterizes as the work of a "faithful soul." Thirdly, that bedrock of religious meditation right up into the twentieth century, Thomas à Kempis' *Imitation of Christ*. Fourthly, the New Testament, and finally the *Exercises of the Presence of God*. Most of André's reading, therefore, was of the quieting kind, just the sort of material he needed to balance the intellectual foot race he was running with the Christian Brothers, learning all he could to help him return credibly to Ruillé as a master-teacher of those young men, many of them teenagers, who would be sent out by Dujarié to teach in schools with even less of the rushed preparation that André received in Le Mans. The practice among religious communities in the nineteenth and twentieth centuries of sending out young men and women with astonishingly little formal preparation to run a classroom endured for over a hundred years, yet many of these religious did surprisingly fine educational work. Many, of course, failed themselves and their students who were often almost as old as their religious teachers. André later questioned the wisdom of this practice, but under the protection of Lamare, he was well prepared to assimilate a hasty education from the Christian Brothers, and André recalls with great appreciation Lamare's "wise counsels during my critical troubles."[6]

André does not specify what these troubles were, nor does he specify when they occurred. They may have arisen while he lived with Lamare, but as he kept in contact with the old man for another dozen years until Lamare's death in 1833, he may be referring to any number of crises that arose in the little community at Ruillé. A maxim sent to him by Lamare is most telling: "Let us work always while we are on earth; we will rest when we are in heaven."[7] André became a workaholic, yet he credits Lamare with "level headedness and humor that still charm me when I remember them."[8] These twin qualities of common sense and humor would make André a highly valuable member of Dujarié's band of men. In fact, it is not farfetched to conclude that without such qualities, André might have folded like scores of other young men. Undoubtedly, he arrived at Ruillé with a sound virtue instilled by his Larchamp family, but Dujarié's foresight and Lamare's wisdom helped André root his potential into the soil of a solid religious spirituality. It is often a wonder that one or two single influences can determine a human being's formation: a generous and wise novice master can make all the difference in the world when adolescents make crucial decisions about their destinies.

When André returned to Ruillé at the end of November, 1821,[9] with Brother Stephen,[10] who had apparently been sent to Le Mans to retrieve him, the two men were met by Dujarié outside of Ruillé at the foot of a wayside cross and vested with a religious habit designed by the bishop[11] The habit was simple:

> It was decided that they would wear a kind of black robe or soutane without a train, buttoning down to the waist and buttoned inside from the waist to the bottom, of ordinary cloth, and descending to six inches from the ground; a hat flat in the middle, that is, five and a half inches, and the edge three and a half inches; a small black and white collar, a cloth skullcap, and short pants. Several weeks after, a white band was added to the collar with two branches, resting on the top of the chest, and sewn together halfway. Each branch was about two inches wide, and the length from the neck to the end was about four inches.[12]

At this time in Ruillé there were five brothers, the first recruit (Pierre Hureau) having left in June. Only two were given the habit, possibly because they were considered "novices." In December four more recruits would arrive, the same month that Dujarié sent André away for a second time, this time to Paris to live for six months (until June, 1822) at the Christian Brothers' novitiate.[13] In all, André spent almost a year in training (five months in Le Mans and six months in Paris), not a bad educational experience when one compares it to what was afforded most of the Brothers of St. Joseph.

It is difficult to establish precisely how many men came and went at Ruillé in the early years. Record keeping was good but not precise. For example, the *Chronicles* note that in 1822 twenty men arrived and three left, but the "Matricule Generale" assembled by Brother Bernard Gervais in the twentieth century lists for 1822 only fifteen arrivals and no departures. It could be that men who stayed for only a few days were not officially recorded. If a young man came, for example, just to test the waters, so to speak, he may have been regarded as an overnight visitor rather than as someone serious about devoting his life to religion. In 1823 one man is listed as arriving in April and leaving sometime that same year, but we do not know how long he stayed. It is not until 1824 that the "Matricule Generale" lists a young man (Jean-Pierre Chabrun) who arrives at age fifteen, takes the name Brother Alexis, and leaves two days later. We must remember that for the last half of 1821 and the first half of 1822, André was not in Ruillé and record keeping was probably in the hands of the over-extended Dujarié. When André did get back to Ruillé, he was totally responsible for the instruction of the young men who came, one as young as twelve, to be Brothers of St. Joseph. As for those men who went into the field, the *Chronicles* note: "Those of these novices who had grace of state studied in their establishments and little by little they made themselves useful teachers."[14]

The loose federation of men that constituted the Brothers of St. Joseph was united by a single vow (obedience) which they could take annually. The formula was simple and read in part: "I submit fully to the rules and statues of the said Congregation, promising to observe them exactly; and consequently I renew for one year the vow of obedience to the superior of the said Congregation."[15] This vow was enough to hold the group together: defections in the first decade of the Brothers of St. Joseph numbered 171 out of a membership of 241. There were, of course, never 241 members at any one time in those first ten years. The peak enrollment was 106 in 1827.

Defections were either unusually low for this fledgling community or under-reported. Either way, they had to be expected: when young people decide to change the course of their lives, they often have second thoughts. André had his own temptations to leave: not at Ruillé where Dujarié kept him busy and impor-tant, but rather in Le Mans where he was a little fish in a big pond. A note by André in the *Chronicles* maintains that without the encouragement of Lamare, he might have abandoned the Brothers of St. Joseph. One incident in particular is very important. A seminarian André counted as a friend came to the carriage which was about to carry André back to Ruillé. The seminarian "made the last efforts to make him lose his vocation in forcing him to change his determination, but Brother André saw the snare which the demon held out to him, rejected his perfidious advice, and entered the cart on the field, detesting the conduct of this pretended friend."[16] What exactly was the friend's advice? It was apparently not the first time he had attempted to influence André's vocation. Did he want André to become a seminarian in Le Mans? André's strong reaction and references to "the snare which the devil held out to him" and "perfidious advice" and "pre-tended friend" suggest something more sinister because, after all, the temptation to enter a seminary is not "perfidious." It is a rather noble calling. The last minute appeal, the dramatic appearance at the carriage, all suggest that the friend did not want to lose André's company and, suspect or not, he wanted whatever bonds they had to continue. The scenario can be recollected by any number of religious who made similar decisions against last ditch temptations of whatever nature.

Of the thirty-seven letters we have by André Mottais, all but two of the first thirty were written at Ruillé, and most of them concern business relating to administration of the Brothers of St. Joseph. In the first letter, to Brother Adrian at Hardanges,[17] André gives sparse directions for settling in: the brother's belongings will soon be sent to him, and the pastor owes the community for books and supplies. The brother is to bring the money to Ruillé in one week. Apparently to assuage Adrian's fear of being separated from the community, André tells him that Hardanges is not far away from the town where Brother Francis teaches:[18] "You can see each other from time to time."[19] What little affection we can discern here is cradled in business. Eight months later, in another letter to Adrian, the formality is still evident: "I'm obliging you, my dear brother, to follow as much as possible the Rule Book for the schools, because those of our brothers who use most of what it prescribes are also those who succeed the most in their classes." The advice is almost formulaic, and one wonders what comfort it would have brought to a young man living with a parish priest who is, we are told, in bad health. Adrian was only three years younger than André and had been sent out to teach within seven months of his arrival at Ruillé. He received a teaching license one month before André's first letter to him, one of the fortunate young men sent out to teach with an actual license.[20] Such a license, easily obtainable by simply showing the local authorities a letter of obedience from Dujarié,[21] would have been a sign of willingness to teach rather than an ability to teach.

Appointed by Dujarié to serve the little group as novice master, spiritual director, and supervisor of instruction both in Ruillé and out in all the parish schools, André must have been disheartened at times by the rate of turnover among his young brothers. Of the first fifty men to come to Ruillé, thirty-eight eventually left or were dismissed. Only twelve persevered to die either in the Brothers of St. Joseph or the Brothers of Holy Cross. But as is still true today, the work that André did in affording young men an opportunity to live a prayerful life and acquire the rudiments of a teaching career must have at times convinced him that parishes were much enriched by the lay men who returned to their homes better for their having lived in a religious community for however short a time. In the first of André's circular letters (dated July 17, 1826), André reminds all the men to think somberly of the coming retreat as it may be the last for some of them: two men had died since the previous year's retreat, the first two men lost to death within a community which already had over eighty-five members.[22] As early as 1825, André each year visited all the schools, even the most remote ones, scattered across fifteen departments.[23] Dujarié thought the visitations would be a good thing, but he himself attempted to make the visits only twice and gave up both times soon after he left Ruillé because of his health,[24] delegating the trips to André who travelled on foot because most of the roads could not be used by carriages.[25]

André was a careful supervisor and very particular in what he expected of his young teachers. Among his early letters is an inventory of goods for the school at Milly. Every door, window, and stick of furniture is inventoried. Even the number of bolts and hooks in the shutters is set down. Linens are inventoried down to dishrags. In the dormitory are four little beds for the brothers. The library has fifty-five books. The date of the inventory is May, 1829, near the end of the first year the brothers ran the school. Two years later Milly is thriving and André pronounces it "the best and most agreeable in our Congregation."[26] One can imagine the joy and pride the men and students must have felt when the Brother Supervisor made a visit: since he would inquire after every imaginable detail pertinent to good teaching, everyone would be on his best behavior. The establishment at Milly was not founded without problems, however. In a letter dated November 11, 1929, André indicates step by step what had to be done via the mayor and the local prefect in order to get the brothers sanctioned for the Milly school. The process began in September, 1828, with a request from the mayor to the prefect. Five months later the project was approved by the commune and three copies of the contract were requested. They were sent within three days to the mayor who signed them and forwarded them to the prefect who refused the documents because they were written on the wrong kind of paper. Two months later the community still waited for approval to teach at Milly, but the brothers were already working there: a letter from André to Brother Stanislaus in September, 1830, indicates brothers had been in Milly for a year teaching 110 students.

As foundations increased and money matters grew complicated, Bishop Carron of Le Mans thought it necessary to disentangle the finances of the Providence Sisters and the Brothers of St. Joseph. The sisters, established by Dujarié a generation before the brothers, were solid financially and legally, but the brothers continued to struggle for the legal recognition that would facilitate their financial health. To understand the dynamics of this variance, one needs to appreciate the character of the mother superior of the Sisters of Providence at the time. The sisters began their history more amorphously than the Brothers, as a group of a half dozen pious girls living two miles from Dujarié. Financed in part by a loan from Marie Lair, the first woman Dujarié asked to teach the local children in 1804, the establishment encountered problems when the woman proved to be mentally unstable and irascible. It took years to get rid of her. Meanwhile, Dujarié's pious women saw to the needs of the local poor and trudged into Ruillé every Sunday to receive spiritual guidance from their director. By 1811 they numbered ten, and Dujarié relied on a superior named Sister Félicité (her family name is lost) who lasted but a short time before she left the group. In 1813 more stability came with the arrival of Madeleine Beucher who directed the group for seven years, until the saintly Zoé du Roscoät was elected first Superior General (1820). When Zoé arrived, the sisters numbered eighteen. Four years later she died, having been with the Sisters of Providence only a short time but leaving an indelible mark on their history. A woman of great virtue and sweet personality, she came from an aristocratic background that heightened the generosity of her selfless dedication to Dujarié and his little community. Her successor was decidedly different: Perrine Lecor was a Breton peasant who grew up on an isolated peninsula in northern France and spoke only Breton, no French, until the age of twenty. Madame du Roscoät had hired her as a teaching-aide back in Brittany, and Perrine followed Madame to Ruillé, succeeding her as Mother General in 1822. Where Mother Marie-Madeleine was diplomatic, Mother Marie Lecor was brusque. Where the former venerated Dujarié, the latter confronted and circumvented him, not afraid to recognize that the aging priest was losing his ability to direct. Marie-Madeleine had put the person of the founder primary in her concerns, but Marie Lecor barged ahead with Providence as her single concern. Before being elected Mother General, Marie Lecor judged herself to have "a cold temperament,"[27] to be undereducated, and to be without virtue. The Cattas dub Mother Marie-Madeleine the "Angel of Providence." Mother Marie Lecor, to the contrary, was anything but an angel.

Thus when the separation of finances surfaces in 1831 as a necessity in the eyes of Bishop Carron, it is against the backdrop of a tough Mother General, the only one that most of the brothers would have known because the gentle one had died in the second year of the brothers' foundation. André would have known Mother Marie-Madeleine, but she died when there were but a dozen brothers in Dujarié's new little religious group of men. What the brothers therefore had to deal with for most of their religious lives was the strong minded Breton Mother Marie Lecor. If the separation of finances was effected in an atmosphere of paranoia and gloom, the onus lies on Marie Lecor who wanted what was best for her sisters and was not particularly concerned about the future of the brothers, whose future was darkened by more defections than arrivals in the three years previous to the financial separation. Some of the bad feelings must, of course, be traced to Dujarié himself. He had alienated himself from Marie Lecor by refusing to deal with her. On one occasion when she visited his rectory to see him, half a block from the Providence motherhouse he had built for the sisters, he refused to see her, and when she then wrote him a letter, he sent it back unopened.[28] The pettiness that grew over several years between two very strong personalities nowhere reflects itself in André Mottais who, as primary director of the brothers, was in a position to become as rancorous as the other two players in the scenario but who remained, like Bishop Carron, fair and above the fray.

André was no match for Marie Lecor's grit, and Dujarié, plagued by gout, often confined to bed, no longer enjoyed the deference of the mother general, her council, or the sisters in the hinterlands who barely knew him. If anything good can be said for Marie Lecor, it is that she exerted a tremendous amount of power at a time when women were quite powerless both in the church and in society generally. Once she found her foothold, there was no stopping her, and the last thing she wanted was any financial co-dependence with a group of men who had declined in numbers for two years and showed no signs of any restructuring. Moreau was waiting in the wings, but Dujarié was still in charge, and Marie Lecor wanted less and less to do with him. She should be admired surely for her tenacity in promoting the sisters, but the bad chemistry between her and Dujarié was as much her fault as his. The old man expected things to go on as they always had under his kind and generous eye: she looked to the future and saw a wonderful opportunity for women to assume their own direction. What she thought of André Mottais we do not know. She probably considered him a well intentioned and harmless drudge who was linked more inextricably to Dujarié by gender and domesticity than she was. Her energies were employed to cut off Dujarié: André was simply one of his adjuncts. Enjoying the ear of the bishop, she was unstoppable.

The document in André's handwriting for the financial separation of the two communities is dated April 21, 1831, which would be the final day of the bishop's three-day visit to Ruillé. André sets out in detail the brothers' financial status from November, 1826, up to the day of the document. He notes that the peak enrollment came at the annual August retreat in 1829 (almost 105 men by his count) from sixty-six foundations, but "since that happy time the number of Brothers, and establishments, has declined a lot."[29] He does not here specify reasons for the decline, but various historians have attributed it to two reasons: the political unrest leading up to the July, 1830, mini-revolution when old embers from 1789 were rekindled for another revolutionary outburst, and the lack of a solid formation for the young brothers before they were sent out to teach in parish schools. André then lists twenty-five schools taken on since 1826 (some of which were operated by the brothers for only one school year) and fifty-three schools which had either paid or failed to pay annual salaries. Some items include benefactors who bankrolled the schools: e.g., the Duchess of Tourzelle who gave 900 francs a year for the Larchamp school and M. de la Porte who gave 10,000 francs to construct classrooms at Sablé and repair the brothers' house. One of the most poignant entries lists the Ruillé boarding school that was under André's direct supervision and existed legally under his name, not Dujarié's, so the brothers could count on some property: it was sold for 7000 francs to a contractor employed by Moreau to build Holy Cross in Le Mans. Although it has always been known that Moreau was involved in the spiritual guidance of the brothers as preacher and confessor as early as 1823,[30] that is, within three years of the first vocations at Ruillé, it has generally been assumed that Moreau's involvement with the brothers' physical properties did not begin until 1835.[31]

The brothers were not exactly dirt poor at the separation from the Sisters of Providence. They owned and enjoyed the income from the Grand Saint-Joseph (eventually sold for 11,900 francs), the Ruillé boarding school, several vineyards, and some farm property.[32] The *Chronicles* note that the boarding school brought in revenue from its twenty boarders, and the salaries of brother carpenters were significant. Moreover, various benefactors continued to be generous.[33] The sisters, of course, had developed their Ruillé motherhouse rather grandly, some of the work being done by the brothers. The women were, however, established sixteen years earlier than the brothers and had as their leader for nine years that intrepid mother general who fought aggressively for her sisters.

About this time someone (probably André) came up with an idea for the brothers to swear an oath of allegiance to the community (and to Dujarié). The oath is mentioned in a letter to Brother Adrian dated July 20, 1831, and was conceived as a way to show support for the elderly priest, support much needed after his clashes with the mother general. It is dated September, 1831, indicating that it was probably administered and signed during the annual retreat, that one time of year when all the brothers were expected to come to Ruillé. It is signed by only twenty men, but some whose signatures do not appear on the document did sign a vow formula binding them to a vow of obedience to Dujarié for one year. The oath of allegiance is striking for several reasons. First of all, it is in André's hand and therefore indicates his primary workmanship. Secondly, it swears mutual fidelity, even if the institute should dissolve. The bonds forged by many of these men over a decade were considered valuable enough and enriching enough that the men would want to remain mutual even if they were no longer financially or organizationally a unit. Thirdly, the document lists four directors (up from three of previous years), all but one of whom would die in the community.[34] Thus the brothers did enjoy some measure of self-governance even if Dujarié remained ostensibly their superior.

The next few years for André were relatively quiet, although the decline in numbers continued, membership hovering around sixty brothers: not a bad enrollment, but nothing like the 100-plus enjoyed from 1826 to 1829. André may have come to realize that the vocation fields had been reaped for the region: there are only so many vocations to any one profession that can be gathered from one demographic area. The few letters we have from him for 1832 and 1833 concern business matters with the Providence sisters. In the summer of 1834, however, André wrote the first of three remarkable letters that had enormous impact on the future of his brothers.

In a letter marked "private" to the bishop in Le Mans just before the beginning of the 1834 August retreat, André points out that the community is being demoralized by one of the four directors, Brother Henry, who does not follow the rules and gives permissions indiscriminately to those who wish to circumvent André. Secondly, the community has been trying to sustain two novitiates, one at Ruillé and another at Esclimont, and the latter is draining them with little hope of attracting many recruits in that region. Thirdly, the matter of Dujarié's ability to direct is becoming problematic: the elderly priest weakens both physically and mentally. André closes with eleven points he would like the bishop to discuss face to face with three of the four brother directors (omitting only Brother Henry from the interview). The eleven items are substantial and include matters of property as well as matters of administration and formation. Recognizing that Dujarié's group of brothers was disintegrating, in spite of all the effort that Dujarié and André had put into revitalizing the group at each summer retreat, André asks the bishop to push Dujarié for reforms.[35] Among the eleven points he makes to the bishop is the need for an administrative structure with specific attention given to the number of officers for the brothers. More importantly, André asks for a chaplain for the brothers at Ruillé, admitting for the first time in print that Dujarié is unable to minister to the spiritual needs of his own community. André closes his letter by saying that "with these matters on the table for the Bishop, it will be impossible for our Father to refuse to deal with them."[36] The implication is that Dujarié has been approached about the crisis, but the aged priest has been unwilling to face reality and deal with it. With this letter André puts two mechanisms in operation: the rescue of the brothers and his own eventual replacement as leader. There is no mention of Moreau in the letter, only a remark that a chaplain is needed for the brothers at Ruillé. We do not know if this letter actually resulted in an interview with the bishop. Thus six years before Urbain Monsimer would arrive in Le Mans to join the brothers, Brother André Mottais took some of the most important steps of his life.

A lengthier letter to the bishop three months later has a more upbeat tone than André's previous letter. In fact, the November letter is downright jubilant.

In the course of this letter André uses Moreau's name twice, so even if the bishop had not already been thinking of Moreau as a replacement for Dujarié, he may very well have been nudged in that direction by this letter.

The existence of the Brothers of Saint Joseph being quite precarious up to this time, I feel the need to set forth the means which my mind considers proper in order to consolidate, enlarge and make perfect its real end. These means involve the creation of three societies in one. The first would be the priests under the title of the Sacred Heart of Jesus; they would exercise the duties and tasks of the superiorship in the Congregation: thus the Brothers of Saint Joseph with that support would have clear and firm direction and government. The goal of the entire Society would be to be an asylum for people in all conditions, to put them at the service of God, to work for his glory, to work for their own salvation and that of their neighbor, while holding themselves away from the dangers of the world. The secondary goal would be to give a Christian education, one suitable under all conditions of our times, and for all classes of society.

The Institute of three societies in one, or of the Holy Family, could establish houses everywhere in a manner that I am going to explain. The priests of the Sacred Heart would maintain houses where, at the same time, they would have a novitiate for the Brothers of Saint Joseph and a normal school in which to train lay school masters, these however living in separate quarters. The Brothers of Saint Joseph would continue to expand in the villages and countryside, several Brothers together or alone in the pastors' houses; they would live dependent on the Order or Institute. The lay teachers, once formed, would be free to establish themselves and live as they wished, except that they would be given and ever receive protection, good advice and counsel, and any of them who found themselves closer to the spirit of the Order as a whole, by their zeal, good morals, piety or celibacy, could form a branch with a rule, one like or shortened from the rule of the Brothers of Saint Joseph or a short form of the rule of Sacred Heart priests. This rule of the priests of the Sacred Heart would be a reflection of the teachings and conduct of Jesus Christ, of Saint Joseph and the very holy Virgin. But since a while later they would have more extensive functions to fulfill (such as I will explain later), they would accept the rule of Saint Ignatius for the Jesuits, whatever is suited to their condition or perhaps even the same rule in its entirety.

The priests of the Sacred Heart of Jesus, aside from the functions which have just been enumerated, will themselves maintain boarding schools or colleges for the upper class. There they would teach Latin, rhetoric, etc. They would also do the work of diocesan missionaries; they would conduct annual retreats for the Brothers of Saint Joseph and the masters of the lay schools, in the houses of the novitiate and the normal schools during the vacations. They would be able to do the same for people in the outside world and even in their houses like the one in Brittany. The three societies in one would have to contribute to this, at least by their prayers and alms. To help the souls in Purgatory would always be the object of their zeal; to this end they would gain a number of indulgences each month; that is, every member would strive to gain such indulgences in harmony with the practice of their duties. Briefly put: it is the Holy Family, the name the Congregation bears.[37]

André elaborates a totally new idea for the brothers: he suggests that they be amalgamated into a new tripartite community of priests, brothers, and laymen. André obviously does not consider the brothers to be "lay men" in the canonical sense and envisages them as ecclesiastically somewhere between priests and lay men. The new community will be named for the Holy Family, and there is ample evidence in the letter that André considers the priests will be the elite members: he reserves to them the instruction of children of the "upper class"[38] while the brothers will continue to work with poor and ordinary children. He does allow for some fluidity among the priests, brothers, and lay men in that "the two lesser societies would be able to rise into the society of the Sacred Heart,"[39] but the elevation, André cautions, would have to be watched carefully because few men would be capable of moving upward.

As tasteless as this hierarchy of higher and lower vocations is to many today, what is remarkable in André's plan is that the vision for a mixed community of priests and Brothers of St. Joseph attributed to Moreau actually originated with André. We cannot say, however, that the plan was entirely André's since he mentions in the letter to the bishop that he has discussed his new idea with one other person: Moreau. If the two men had a conversation in which they probably reviewed the problems of Dujarié's brothers, Moreau may have mentioned that he was starting a group of priests who would serve as auxiliaries to the diocese. André may then have mused in private on amalgamating Moreau's priests and Dujarié's brothers, thus germinating the Congregation of Holy Cross.

Such an explanation, however, leaves an important person out of the process: Dujarié himself had planned on starting a group of priests devoted to parish missions as early as 1823, eleven years before André's letter to Bishop Bouvier. Dujarié even planned to dedicate his auxiliary priests to the Sacred Heart. André would have known about all of these plans since he was Dujarié's right-hand man during all the years that Dujarié dreamed of his association of auxiliary priests.[40] Although Dujarié never founded such a group, his plans were intended to bind priests to his brothers and sisters. Once the sisters were out of the picture (by 1831), André could dream of a different tripartite community, a dream he confided first to Moreau and then to Bouvier. André was not given credit for his plan, however, for over a hundred years. Finally in the 1940's, Philéas Vanier,

CSC, archivist for the Congregation of Holy Cross, wrote a note to Albert F. Cousineau, Superior General at the time:

> The confidential letter of Brother André (November 14, 1834) greatly influenced Father Moreau in the organization of the Community; this is a very important point to study, which can explain many things; it should be done without taking sides, slowly, etc. Please excuse the candor of this remark.[41]

It is obvious from this note by Vanier that André's plan had fallen into the cracks of history.

Moreau's original plan (in 1831) was for an association of auxiliary priests alone. With the death of Bishop Carron in 1833 and the accession of Bouvier, Moreau had as his new prelate a man who had himself long recognized the value of an auxiliary group of priests in the diocese.[42] It was not, however, until June, 1835, a year after André had written to the bishop, that Moreau formalized his plans to found an association of auxiliary priests. Two months later he took on the direction of the Brothers of St. Joseph in a touching ceremony at Ruillé when Dujarié officially ceded authority over the brothers. Immediately, Moreau began to clean house: he dismissed some brothers and insisted all teachers keep careful financial records. Older brothers who were showing signs of ebbing academic fervor were shifted into manual labor.[44]

André began to lose power. When Moreau went to spend three days at La Chesnaie consulting with the founder of the Brothers of Ploërmel, Moreau took Brother Leonard Guittoger with him, not André,[45] and when Moreau opened his new boarding school at Saint-Croix in November, 1836, it was Brother Vincent who was put in charge, not André.[46] Catta suggests that Vincent was chosen because he had a teaching license,[47] but André's license predates Vincent's by one year. Of course, André may very well have been left behind in Ruillé to look after the boarding school there in its waning years, but when Moreau moved the novitiate to Sainte-Croix, there were but five or six students left in the Ruillé boarding school.[48] Yet when Moreau called upon the brothers to signify their fidelity to his organization by pronouncing vows, it was André who came forward first at the end of the 1836 retreat, surely not just because of his seniority, but also because he had worked hard in 1833, 1834, and 1835 to keep the brothers viable as Dujarié slipped farther and farther away from an ability to inspire and lead. The vows would show his unfaltering faith in Moreau's leadership because they were the first perpetual vows pronounced in the community.

In his third and final letter to Bouvier, cosigned by Leonard and Vincent, André begs the bishop for a secret meeting without Dujarié's being aware of it. André is concerned that the rules he has been designing for the brothers would irk Dujarié because the old priest was not in on their making. This April letter makes no mention of Moreau and gives every indication that the brothers were convinced they themselves could salvage the community. But four months later they were turned over to Moreau's control. André's final memo as head director is dated June 28, 1835. It is a simple notice that he has received fifty francs that the Sisters of Providence owed for one year of rent. His days as the central administrator are about to end.

Why did Moreau demote André Mottais? Thomas Maddix has analyzed at length Moreau's understanding of a brother's vocation and concluded that it differed radically from Dujarié's understanding. Under Dujarié, all brothers were equal and shared one apostolate, the evangelization of children.[49] When Moreau shifted some brothers out of the classroom into manual labor, he created two tiers of membership in the brothers. Some of the men, in fact, may have welcomed the opportunity to leave a profession for which they had no taste or talent, an opportunity that allowed them to remain within the religious society doing some other kind of work. It was, nevertheless, a big shift in the basic dynamics of the brother's vocation and worked against the very sense of democracy that Dujarié and André had fostered. Under Moreau, men who could not handle classroom duties were shifted to manual labor: hierarchy was thus born in the Brothers of St. Joseph. Did André confront Moreau on this shift in paradigm? Did Moreau react negatively to any questioning of his decisions and sideline André? We do not know. What we do know is that once Moreau assumed control of the brothers, André begins to fade from administration, in spite of his fifteen years' experience, in spite of his being a man of enormous talent and virtue in the prime of his life. Moreau was one year younger than André (they were born in the same month one year apart), yet in 1836 one's star continues to rise and the other's starts to fall.

As the brothers began to look to Moreau to save their community, it is curious that we have no record of letters from André to Moreau. Brother Leonard, however, did write to Moreau in June, 1835, and Moreau responded with an offer of the house in Le Mans "which would be perfectly suited for you, and where I would gladly set you up, in preference to another foundation which I plan to get underway."[50] It is obvious that Moreau is eager not only to assume direction of the brothers but also to move them to his own territory. He adds, "Nevertheless, I want to wait some time yet out of consideration for your own interests, and you can inform Brother André accordingly." A reader today wonders why Moreau was not communicating these very important sentiments to André himself who, as primary director, was really the person who should have been consulted. The tone of "you can inform Brother André accordingly" is slightly ominous, indicating that Moreau may have had little concern for the primary director's prerogative. Finally, Moreau delivers a coup: "If you speak to the Bishop, tell him only that I would consider to revive and develop you, provided that I am given full freedom of action." By "full freedom of action," Moreau could mean freedom from restrictions by the bishop or diocesan authorities, but the phrase could also be the triumphant call of a person who already senses victory. There is no deference in this letter to André, Dujarié, or even the bishop. Moreau knows what he wants to do, and he wants it on his terms. There is no room in his scheme for a primary director who may be bringing old baggage with him into a new situation.

Is it to André's credit or discredit that he knuckled under? If he had engineered a break from a priest-director as Mother Marie Lecor had done, would the brothers have survived? They had scores of hard working men, some property, and the promise of a set of rules (yet to be written). Would these assets have been enough to float them under André? They had, however, grown up tightly enmeshed with a priest at their head, and when they had to rethink their organization, they quite naturally would think about revitalizing their community under a structure similar to the one that had brought them great growth in the years before the 1830 political unrest. They knew Moreau would not be Dujarié, and André was one of their first sacrifices to the new order. It is important, of course, that organizations get new blood from time to time in administrative posts: it probably was a good idea for Moreau to replace André after twenty years as novice master, since subsequent growth attests to the excellence of the novice masters who followed André. André did keep his position, however, for four years after the amalgamation.

As the brothers at Sainte-Croix saw Moreau's auxiliary priests beginning to infiltrate the teaching apostolate, they grew concerned that their assets would be swallowed up. Moreau summoned all the men together (fifty-one brothers, ten priests) and outlined the brothers' assets. Then he drew up the "Fundamental Pact" (March 1, 1837) which served as a stepping-stone to the eventual joining of the two societies, just as their two properties and schools adjoined in Sainte-Croix. Moreau really believed that if the brothers were to survive, they would eventually need priests to be responsible for "the direction and government of their society."[51] Here could be the source of André's fall from power: he was not a priest. Did Moreau really believe Dujarié could have held the brothers together for fifteen years without André's help? Probably not, but Moreau did believe that his priests should hold the positions of leadership over the lay brothers: it was one of his requirements before he would merge the two societies.

Moreau was a well educated man who had connections to ecclesiastics and government officials, but as we look back at history, we know that Mother Marie Lecor was not ordained and succeeded very well in governing the Providence Sisters. Why did Moreau believe that only priests could govern brothers? Moreover, why did the brothers let him proceed with his clerical imposition? Were they that demoralized by the defections of recent years, the lack of a working set of rules, and the sad state of their academic preparation for teaching careers? Was Moreau the only answer to their crisis? He certainly came with excellent credentials: assistant superior of the local seminary, proven educator, and founder of the Good Shepherd Sisters. He was a man of immense talent. But so was André Mottais who, apparently in the interests of saving his community, accepted Moreau's theory of clerical governance. If André had had some of Mother Marie Lecor's vinegar and fighting spirit, the history of the Brothers of St. Joseph might well have been much different than it came to be.

Ages often tell us much. When Madame du Roscoät arrived in Ruillé, she was forty. She died four years later. Perrine Lecor arrived at age twenty-eight, a hardened peasant woman. Softened somewhat by association with Madame du Roscoät and the du Roscoät family, she never lost her original toughness. André arrived at Ruillé at age twenty and lived alongside Dujarié for eighteen years, always deferential to the man who had nurtured him spiritually. André was only a year younger than Moreau, but no match for the priest's education, position, and tenacity. It is easy to see how André, accustomed for half his life to clerical rule, would naturally slide from under the authority of one priest to another. He knew no other pattern—except for the example of Mother Marie Lecor and the Providence Sisters, but the separation in 1831 surely left him with a distaste for the direction that the women so determinedly set out for themselves against his priest-mentor. Dujarié was a friend whom André possibly hoped to find replicated in Moreau, but one should never count on finding a spiritual clone, especially in a person one's own age. André might have been in a way a threat to Moreau's vision, and the brother had to be controlled if Moreau's vision was to be strengthened,[52] a vision that would be strengthened on the backs of the brothers. Moreau was, after all, only bringing to realization the paradigm of a mixed community that both Dujarié and André had dreamed about.

A curious assumption by some historians is that the Bothers of St. Joseph were incapable of governing themselves or did not want to govern themselves. Catta writes, "Like M. Dujarié, he [Moreau] was persuaded that the frail little tree had to be grafted on to a stronger trunk, which would be the Society of Priests which the Founder had thought of but which he had been unable to realize."[53] In other words, a "frail" little organization of some sixty teaching brothers had to be put under the control of a non-existent group of priests. The logic is bewildering. At the end of the same summer that Moreau assumed direction of dozens of seasoned brothers, he had attracted exactly two priests and two seminarians to his auxiliary band who were apparently already superior to the established group of brothers. Seminarians superior to veteran teachers? Clericalism at its extreme.

Furthermore, the brothers were kept in the dark about their future. When they assembled for the 1835 summer retreat, they had no idea what was going to happen to them. Finally, on the third day, in the presence of the bishop, in a well recorded ceremony in the chapel, Dujarié officially handed control of his community to Moreau. The three ministers at the altar, flanked by the three Jesuit priests who had preached the retreat, presided over the scene, and in the pews sat fifty-six grown men oblivious of what had been determined for them. They had, of course, suspected Moreau would be their new superior and may have hoped it would be Moreau, but did none of those present ever think to wonder if the brothers under André could have controlled their own destiny as successfully as the Sisters of Providence had controlled their own?

We know little about André's new life at Sainte-Croix. We do know that he was novice master up to 1840[54] and sat on the council with Brother Vincent, Brother Léopold, Father Marseul and Father Chappé.[55] One happy chore he was given was to travel back to Ruillé in October, 1836, to help Dujarié move to Sainte-Croix.[56] A little over a year later, Dujarié died (February 17, 1838), having been able to live his final year in the same home with André, who had been his stalwart religious helper for fifteen years in Ruillé. He was buried on the grounds at Sainte-Croix, then transferred in 1849 to the new community cemetery. In 1873 he was brought by the Sisters of Providence back to Ruillé and buried in the crypt of their motherhouse chapel. His old nemesis Mother Marie Lecor was still alive, having retired two years earlier (1871) after forty-three years heading the sisters. After the interment ceremony in Ruillé, she said, "Now I can die."[57] Even in death the priest was no match for the Breton nun.

André himself would not stay long at Sainte-Croix after Dujarié's death. In the fall of 1839, Moreau was asked to send missionaries to Algeria. In April, 1840, Moreau announced the names of the brothers to be sent: André, Alphonsus, and the novice Ignatius.[58] André was designated director of the houses in Africa, but in May an auxiliary priest was designated superior of the group: André would effectively not be in charge. In May another novice and another priest were added to the band. Meanwhile André, waiting at Lyons to embark, wrote a long letter to Brother Vincent Pieau, who had been chosen by Moreau to go on the new American mission. André tells Vincent to ask Moreau to write up the chronicles of the brothers, using himself (Vincent) as chief witness to the events. Vincent had come to Ruillé two years after André, had been one of the Brother Directors under Dujarié, and was a dear friend to André. André tells Vincent to give Moreau everything André had already written on the history of the brothers up to 1826. Then André adds a most interesting and important phrase: "tak[e] care to remove my name every time it appears, because I don't wish to be named anywhere."

> Having learned that you are destined to go to America with Father Sorin, I can't neglect the occasion to write to you to recommend to you something which seems interesting to me about the Congregation: to beg our honored Father [Moreau] to write up the chronicles of the Institute of the Brothers of St. Joseph before your departure. I don't know anyone more capable than you to give authentic witness about what has happened since our beginnings. Point out and give back to our worthy Father all the items relative to this work, which I implore him to undertake and finish for the next retreat. Give him what I myself wrote up to 1826, taking care to remove my name every time it appears, because I don't wish to be named anywhere. Someone can also remove the names of subjects who no longer remain and establishments which have ceased to exist, as one judges proper. You should see in your notes that I set out at the end of 1825 to visit all our establishments for the first time.[59]

What prompted this supreme act of abnegation? It is symptomatic of some who suffer humiliation in a cause to which they have devoted themselves generously to experience a sudden twinge of anger and frustration with which they wish to dis-associate themselves from the project. It is a way of saying, "You do not appreci-ate me, and therefore I do not want to be remembered or associated with you." The sentiment is a mixture both of admirable self-abnegation and not-so-admira-ble resentment born of frustration, but it is sometimes the only recourse for someone who has lost a battle: to be disassociated from any part of the humilia-tion. As André watched Moreau control the brothers, he may have felt some resentment at losing the premier role he had enjoyed under Dujarié, especially the increment of authority that gathered to him as Dujarié grew old and sick. When he had the chance to distance himself from Moreau by going to Africa, he would have felt relieved of the daily reminders of his own loss of power. Moreau, ever a wise judge of character, probably sensed in André a need for a change, and so the obedience to go to Algeria was a blessing for both men: for Moreau it removed a rival in the affections of the older brothers, and it gave André a dignified way to use his talents in a new venue, albeit still under obedience to a priest.

What stands out in this Lyons letter are the careful instructions André gives to set his affairs in order. It is almost as if he were writing his last will and testament. He asks Vincent to preserve carefully the notes on the financial separation from the Sisters of Providence. He notes how this event hurt Dujarié deeply. He wants the narrative of Dujarié's final illness preserved. Everything is to be attended to with the utmost care. André cautions, "I'm holding to this in my final wishes. Let it [the Dujarié narrative] be read to the Brothers at the retreat and let them have the liberty to speak their feelings and make their observations with total honesty, prudence, civility, and submissiveness."[60] It sounds like an order rather than a request. Underneath André's desire to preserve the memory of the father founder is a desire that the brothers honestly air their feelings about the transfer of authority.

He then turns his attention to his present state of mind, and remarks that at long last, away from the milieu he has known for twenty years, he is able to have a novitiate experience and become a new person. The former André Mottais is dead and the new André is emerging. He tells Vincent he has learned that the Algerian house the brothers were destined to occupy has been besieged by the Arabs. The man who knew only the calm beauty of Ruillé and Sainte-Croix is heading into hell. His farewell to Vincent, whom he had worked beside for so long, is touching: "Good-by then my very dear Brother Vincent. Good-by for eternity undoubtedly, because you are for America, we for Africa. Good-by—I embrace you with all my heart."[61] At last the man has time for himself, time to assess his own situation and feelings. Almost from the day he arrived at Ruillé, his concern had been for others. Now there is only himself. Even the three brothers with him will be the responsibility of the priest superior. André is free. But his purification is only beginning.

The three letters we have from André in Africa show us a person we had barely known up to this point. Finally, at age forty, freed from the cares of running the day-to-day operations of a community, he is free to look inside himself and reveal a character we previously had to reconstruct basically from events and duties. The Africa letters are the most important André wrote. Surely his letters to Bishop Bouvier were extremely important for the history of Holy Cross, but nothing is more valuable to the history of André Mottais the person than the letters from Africa. In one way, André's demotion was good for him because it afforded him at last the opportunity to make an extended retreat—just himself and his God. The three letters are, in this way, amazing.

The first letter, written from Moustapha on July 11, 1840, is directed to his parents. He tells them he arrived on May 27 and lives with orphans in a building adjacent to the seminary that his superior directs. One can only imagine the emotions that Jean and Jeanne Mottais would have felt on receiving the letter and sharing it with their children Jeanne and Joseph. (André's older brother Jean was already dead.) The crossing had not been easy: his five companions were all seasick. Since they had only four beds among them, André gave up his share of a bed and slept on deck "wrapped in a cloak among the soldiers."[62] They passed by Minorca and Majorca, stopped briefly at Mahon, before arriving at Algiers on a Tuesday evening. On going into the city, they met two sons of King Louis Philippe: the young men were returning to France after military duty. The sounds of war are everywhere. André calls the cannon shots that start the day at 4 AM and end the day at 8 PM "the sound of the Angelus in Africa."

André tells his parents that on first arriving, the brothers were placed by the bishop in a hospice where they had to help care for two hundred and fifty sick and mentally ill people, under the supervision of the Brothers of St. John of God. He comments on the various nationalities that have converged in Algiers, the language, patois, and jargon that dominate the streets. He comments on ceremonies that the bishop presides over and the prospects for evangelization in a war torn country. André has an eye for detail: native clothing (or lack thereof), sleeping habits, modes of transportation, local cuisine. He comments at great length on the crops and livestock—the Larchamp farmer coming back to life in him. Finally he mentions his own health: he is so weak he can hardly write. During a two week period he suffered terribly. Before the days of vaccinations and vitamins, one can only imagine the multiple germs and diseases that would meet a European coming to a dirty village where hygiene was primitive and food preparation less than sterile. Something from Africa would, in fact, eventually kill André Mottais.

The second letter from Africa is addressed to Father Moreau and dated August 1, 1840, several weeks after the letter to the Mottais family. We learn that after six weeks the brothers were given charge of an orphanage. To date there are only fourteen orphans, eight of whom board. Where the "six external" orphans slept is anyone's guess. Since the brothers cannot get authorization to open a school, Brother Louis is studying arithmetic, grammar, and history as he bides his time. The novice Ignatius is not a very good student, so the priest superior has put him in charge of the refectory and food purchases. Brother Alphonsus works as a carpenter. André takes care of the orphans from 10 to 11:45 each morning and from 4 PM until supper. Louis takes care of them at the other times. André sleeps in a dorm with the littlest ones, Louis in a dorm with the eldest. The orphans can stay until they reach the age of twenty. André's bed, we learn later, is a mattress on the floor.

In this letter André further elaborates on his health problems. He had earlier reported that bathing in the sea had made him ill, but now he attributes his sickness to hemorrhage, loss of appetite, and a weakness that has led to fainting. A local doctor prescribes "sitting baths," a procedure which suggests that André was suffering from anemia brought on by untreated hemorrhoids and loss of blood. He has a relapse every third day. He then turns to a particular account of the state of his soul and rejoices that the superior, Father Leboucher,[63] has relieved him of supervising the other brothers: "That makes me happy because I no longer have any responsibility on that matter, and anyway I already have too much to watch over myself."[64] He has overcome his preoccupation with death and is resigned to God's will. In spite of his health problems, he is determined to stay in Algeria for three reasons: he tells Moreau all who come are customarily sick for three to six months; the doctor has not advised him to leave; and many people suffer as he has until the end of September. Then he descends into the depths of self-loathing:

> I really want to end my career in this land of Africa that I cherish. If it rejects me from its breast, it is because I am more unworthy than the least of its inhabitants. Then please, my very reverent Father, have the kindness to send me to America, if you have the least task (temporarily or not, it doesn't matter) that I can fill. Otherwise if you call me back to France, I beg you on my knees, get into God's plans which are evidently to cure my folly and my pride, as well as to convince me of my lack of ability in everything and everywhere, because this God out of His goodness allows every job (like every country) to vomit me out as soon as it gets a taste of me. So I beg you, if you recall me to France, in the name of charity, give me the last and the lowest job in the Congregation. Dressed in a shirt if necessary rather than the religious habit which I now believe I am unworthy of, I will clean shoes, wash dishes, etc. I have but little time to repair my unworthy life. It is time for me to think about it.[65]

How could a grown man drop to such a poor self-image? He has been convinced that nothingness means saintliness, and he craves oblivion. He clearly does not want to return to France where God "allows every job like every country to vomit me out as soon as it gets a taste of me." Where did he get the idea that he is unworthy to wear a religious habit, he who was one of the first two to receive the habit of the Brothers of St. Joseph, and is good for nothing but to clean shoes and wash dishes? This is the dark night of the soul when all the good he had effected in twenty years seems erased by his being "vomited" first out of France and now out of Algeria. Thankfully, the sentiments passed away: two weeks later he adds two paragraphs that are joyous and upbeat. He looks forward to spring (coming at the end of September) when the planting is to begin. He will need vegetable seeds. Possibly a return to health brought him out of gloom or possibly the fear that the despair he expressed earlier would prompt Moreau to summon him back to France. The latter explanation is probably not true because, after all, he did not destroy the dark paragraph before mailing the letter to Moreau. Better to live and die meagerly in a foreign land. Anything but return to the work that had rejected him. So he changes his tone and ends the letter upbeat.

The third and final letter of André from Africa is dated December 1, 1841, fifteen months after the second letter. It is sent from Philippeville, where André had been sent to open a school. He expresses shock to learn (via Moreau, not anyone in Algeria) that Brother Louis, a fellow Algerian missionary, had drowned in the Mediterranean a month and a half earlier while swimming with the orphans. At Moreau's request, André assesses the suitability of each of the brothers, something André does reluctantly. He remarks that his hemorrhoids are worse than ever, and he is having difficulty with the parish priest who denies him classroom furniture, clothing, and even a salary. The water is putrid and teems with "little critters." He teaches six hours a day to varying numbers of the thirty-six students enrolled in various courses: computation, spelling, penmanship. He receives no salary while the public school teacher, who has only ten students, is paid by the government.[66] The classroom ceiling leaks dust from the pastor's bedroom above. There is no bathroom: André has to trek "into the mountains" while the parish priest has a bedpan that the maid empties at night. André takes Thursdays off, his only break because on Sunday he has to clean the church, teach catechism, perform baptisms, and wind the clock! For breakfast he has a piece of bread and some dried fruit or a lump of sugar. His afternoon meal is generally something cold or sometimes a cup of soup. All is not bleak, however. During the vacation break from July 15 to August 19, André visits Hippo to see the ruins of the ancient basilica. He remembers that St. Augustine sat nearby on the beach and meditated on the Trinity.

The bad situation in Algeria did not improve. The relation between one of the priests and the bishop soured, and the brothers were still living in terrible conditions. Moreau finally recalled all the men in June, 1842. It was surely Moreau's fault that he did not investigate conditions in Algeria thoroughly before sending men there. He did not visit or send a visitor before shipping André and the others off. One of the harshest criticisms he had for Dujarié and André was their indiscriminate scattering of personnel, yet when it came to his own missionary forays, he showed no better judgement than Dujarié or André. He sent Father Hautebourg to Algeria after the man spent three months in the novitiate, Father Leboucher after five months. It is true that these two men were already ordained and had years of seminary training behind them, but their community formation was as rudimentary as that of many of the men under André's care at Ruillé. Algeria was a disaster from the beginning. America at first, as we shall see, was almost as bad.

André returned to Sainte-Croix in broken health. At age forty-three, he was a man near death. Only two letters remain from his last year, written on May 25 and May 26. The first is a formal greeting on the occasion of the second colony's departure for America. It is a public letter of encouragement from the brothers at Le Mans to the brothers in America, signed by twenty-six men. The second letter is a private letter to Brother Vincent signed only by André. How fitting that the final thoughts which remain from him were sent to his comrade of so many years, reflecting a brotherhood that went back twenty-two years to the early days at Ruillé. He tells Vincent that the brothers are soon to go back to Algeria. As for André himself, Moreau has made him a member of all the councils at Sainte-Croix and given him the title "Assistant."[67] At Sainte-Croix, André reports, there are forty-six brothers and postulants, not counting another thirty men at the Solitude. André teaches bookkeeping, writing, and reading. He is convinced that the brothers have turned a corner under Moreau's direction, and that the union of brothers and priests is solid: "I cannot grow tired of thanking the Lord and praying that He will maintain forever the union of priests with the brothers."[68] He ends with the hope that he and Vincent will rest together in heaven.

André died at Sainte-Croix at 8 PM on Saturday, March 16, 1844. The chapel was draped in black linen, and the boarding school students, four of them carrying torches, processed with the body up the hill to the community cemetery. We do not know where he is buried today because all of the graves of the early Holy Cross brothers and priests were used for later burials. Thus fades the life of the second founder of Holy Cross without whom the survival of the brothers of St. Joseph may never have happened and without whom Holy Cross may never have coalesced. The *Chronicles* in noting his death make the point that on his return from Africa, he wanted to be kept in the background: "His conversations and example made him a perfect model of the religious life for everyone."[69] Espousing St. Joseph's primary virtue, humility, André thus effaced himself and has become a beacon at those times when history opens from time to time to reveal him for what he was: a selfless servant, a hard working minister, and amiable founder. History should never again underestimate his importance at Ruillé or at Sainte-Croix. Vanier, the first to name André the "second founder" of Holy Cross, summarizes André's contributions:

> Four directors had been established to head the Institute [at Ruillé]: but the last three are more assistants than equals. Brother André directs everything: he rules on everything and is the judge of last resort. He is responsible for formation of subjects; he is master of novices; he presides over all exercises including meals; he gives all permissions; he resolves all difficulties between religious; he harries the lukewarm; he encourages the zealous; he gives direction.[70]

These are the day-to-day necessities of running a community, and André carried them out well for fifteen years. If Dujarié was the heart of the organization, André was the head: without him, Dujarié's group would not have lasted as long as it did.

It is no easy task to convince an established religious community that it has three founders instead of two or one. Part of the problem may be iconographic: we have no idea what André Mottais looked like. We have no photo, no oil painting, no statue. Therefore we have nothing to help anchor an image of the man in our imagination. Moreau, Dujarié, Mary of the Seven Dolors—these people are fixed in our brain from graphic images. But what do we have for André? The mind works on image, and for André Mottais we can only fabricate. We do not even know if he was short or tall, fair haired or dark, brown eyed or blue eyed.

We cannot even stand at his grave because his remains lie somewhere with dozens of other remains in the Marianite cemetery in Le Mans. Where is anybody's guess. To be in that cemetery today among the neat rows of crosses for the Marianite Sisters is to confront the chaos of history. The graves of the early brothers were ignored after Father Moreau was hounded out of the Community, and his nephew, Father Charles Moreau, in retaliation for the treatment of his uncle, simply had the Marianite Sisters bury their dead over the early graves of the men of Holy Cross who had treated Basil Moreau so shabbily. One can point to a spot for Mother Mary and a spot for Charles Moreau, but André? Only his spirit remains, and it struggles from time to time to be revitalized in a religious here and there. Today on the back wall of the Marianites' portion of the cemetery is a large attractive panel naming and commemorating all the brothers and priests of Holy Cross who lie somewhere in the cemetery soil. André, who had no part in the vilification of Basil Moreau, is remembered in that plaque. He lies among the scattered.

By the time André returned to Le Mans in broken health (1842), Gatian had already been in America for a year, but everywhere the boy Gatian would have turned when he lived in Le Mans, he would have encountered André in the brothers who were formed by André, who were supervised in the schools by André, who were spiritually directed by André. Gatian, in fact, would have been more influenced by André than he would have been influenced by Dujarié. André was responsible for the practical day to day matters that stick most often in people's memories. It was stories bout André that would have enveloped the boy Gatian. The aura of Dujarié's holiness would have been, of course, important to the boy, but his formation was carried out by Moreau in the shadow of Brother André.

Part III:
Basil Moreau, The Third Founder:
"Respect and deference to all the priests without exception"

Of the three founders of Holy Cross, Basil Moreau had the most direct hand in forming Brother Gatian. Moreau was in charge when Gatian arrived at Le Mans in August, 1839. Dujarié had died a year and a half earlier, and André Mottais would leave in the middle of the following May for Algeria. By the time André returned from Africa, Gatian would be in America. But Dujarié's legacy would have been everywhere felt when the little thirteen-year-old boy arrived from Chéméré-le-roi ready to become a brother at Sainte-Croix. The spirit of the first two founders would have been infused into the men who formed the faculty at the novitiate, and the names Dujarié and André would have surfaced often in conversations. Gatian may even have read or heard read early letters sent by André from Algeria. But the spiritual tone for Gatian was set by Moreau who carefully shepherded all of the new young men who came to be either brothers or priests at Holy Cross. One of Moreau's strengths was his being tethered to his location, free to devote his primary energies to the development of the Holy Cross Congregation growing in Le Mans by the time Gatian arrived. Moreau's responsibilities at St. Vincent's seminary had evaporated in 1836, and his pastoral and financial responsibilities for the Good Shepherd monastery were gradually reduced.

Basil Anthony Mary Moreau was born on February 11, 1799, in the waning years of the Revolution, at Laigné-en-Belin, a village of a thousand people just south of Le Mans. In this same year, Napoleon entered Paris and suppressed the final remnants of the fanatics who had devastated not only the city but the entire country of France for a decade. The Paris mobs, which had instigated many atrocities, had finally met their match in a dictator who imposed on them the stability of the *ancien régime* without bringing back the sad inequalities of the former times. By the time Moreau was three years old, the Concordat brought out of hiding the non-juring clergy so religion could breathe free once more without submission to the government. Moreau's own baptism had been delayed in 1799 until a non-juring priest on his rounds could administer the sacrament. He was the ninth of fourteen children of Louis Moreau and Marie Pioger. Only one of the children (Victoire) was baptized by a juring priest. It is curious that the parish records give the name of each priest who performed the family baptisms, including the men who were in hiding for not having sworn the oath of allegiance. Thus the names of juring clergy and non-juring clergy appear interspersed in the same record book with no apparent effects on the safety of the "Catholic" priests. Historians have no explanation for this phenomenon, which, given the diligence of the Jacobins to ferret out non-constitutional clergy, is strange indeed. The two parish priests who were resident at Laigné-en-Belin in the early Revolution were arrested in 1791, the elder priest eventually dying in prison and the younger priest emigrating to Spain.[1] Basil Moreau's father was a wine merchant, and the building in which he stored his casks can still be seen today, just back of the family home. Above the cask storage room is a second floor room where the Moreau boys may have slept.[2] The family cultivated eighteen acres of land.

As a young boy Moreau was singled out by his pastor, Julien Le Provost, for classes in the rectory since the parish school, closed throughout the Revolution, was still not reopened. Proving himself to be a leader among the children, Moreau was selected to enter the high school at Château-Gontier which was serving as a kind of preparatory seminary. At age fifteen, in October, 1814, Moreau and his father walked to the school where he would study for two years before entering the major seminary in Le Mans. His theological studies in Le Mans lasted five years. In 1820, he was ordained subdeacon, and in 1821 deacon and then priest, a year and a half before he was canonically eligible by reason of age for the sacrament.

Rather than being assigned to a parish, Moreau was sent by his bishop for further training so that he might become a seminary professor and administrator. Thus Moreau spent a year with the Sulpicians in Paris (1821) and a year on the outskirts of Paris at Issy in a kind of intense spiritual retreat under the watchful eye of the saintly director Gabriel Mollevaut. In 1823, he was assigned to the faculty of the preparatory seminary of Tessé where he taught philosophy, and in 1825 he was appointed to the faculty of the major seminary, St. Vincent's in Le Mans, where he taught dogma and remained on the staff until 1836, eventually rising to the position of assistant director. It was these formative years that distinguish Moreau most from Dujarié and André Mottais. Dujarié had solid seminary training but no special training in the direction of young men and nothing resembling the intense year at Issy where Moreau underwent a kind of monastic novitiate. André Mottais had a fraction of either man's formal education and no rudiments of direction: his was a utilitarian crash course in basic subject matter and some pedagogical techniques from the Christian Brothers. Dujarié and André were both energetic and virtuous men, but neither was afforded the extended experiences that Moreau had as a director of seminarians. By the time

Urbain Monsimer was born in 1826, Moreau was already settled into a satisfying career as a seminary educator. He would grow steadily into a confident supervisor not afraid to undertake new religious tasks. In 1833, for example, he established a monastery for Good Shepherd nuns in Le Mans to help young girls.[3] In 1834 he founded a small band of auxiliary priests, and in 1835 he took over direction of the Brothers of St. Joseph. In these years little Urbain was still a child, but it would not be long before he would come under the direction of Basil Moreau.

Anyone who doubts Moreau's gifts has but to read the circular letters that he sent out over of period of thirty years (1835 to 1866). Moreau was a man of great virtue and great talents. He had a vigorous mind and high energy. To read his circular letters is to experience a man who knew how to write well. Mixed with the spiritual exhortations and matters of business are eulogies that read like vivid stories. His account of Dujarié's life and death is a little masterpiece. In his sixth letter (February 11, 1838), written on his thirty-ninth birthday, Moreau recounts the death of Brother Dositheus (François Leblanc), a man who had been a boarding student at Ruillé and entered the community in 1832. Dying in Le Mans at the age of twenty-one, Dositheus pronounced his first vows on the day he died. The details of his last days are touching evidence of Moreau's regard for the young man as well as his wish to share his grief with the brothers out in the parish schools. Moreau rapidly became a true father to his religious groups.

As Moreau struggled to balance his work with three communities, he gradually pulled away from the Good Shepherd monastery. He continued to raise funds for the sisters as late as 1852, but his primary energies came to be focused on the men gathering at Le Mans in the Sainte-Croix area. The auxiliary priests were actually the only foundation he started from scratch because the sisters more or less organized themselves as an outgrowth from the Good Shepherd house in Angers, and the brothers were carried over from Dujarié's foundation in Ruillé. By 1835 France had settled into the reign of Louis Philippe, the "citizen king," who would remain in power until the revolution of 1848. The longevity of his rule (eighteen years) gave the country a breathing space between two revolutions (1830 and 1848) so men like Moreau could count on stability in government officers when it came to getting official permissions for various enterprises.

Although Moreau dealt with multiple religious communities, his intense association with seminary training helped convince him that priesthood brought with its indelible sacerdotal mark a certain privileging within the church. Undoubtedly a case can be made that the many years of training required for ordination might make a candidate more fit for leadership roles than not, but one might also wonder why similarly rigorous training would not have been asked of brothers destined for teaching. The revolving door that took in a young man at age eighteen and spit him out a year or two later to teach in a rural school proclaims loud and clear that the operator of the door has little regard for the teacher and less regard for pupils. The Christian Brothers, even after the crying need for teachers arose in post-revolutionary France, always required careful preparation of their brother-teachers. Dujarié, André, and Moreau never did, and added to the hasty training that men would have received in Ruillé, Moreau added a caste system as he gradually amalgamated his brothers and his auxiliary priests into one unit, always intending that his priests would be superiors for the brothers because priestly training and grace of state rendered them superior to laymen. Had Moreau completed his vision for Holy Cross and united lay women (the Marianite Sisters of Holy Cross) under one administration, he would not have used priests as local superiors for the women, but he persisted in seeing his priests as leaders and his brothers as humble servants, a role too many of the brothers may have accepted in their gratitude for his having rescued them from dissolution in 1835. Indeed, once the brothers were secure at Le Mans and the novitiate transferred there, they thrived under Moreau's direction. By 1837, there were twenty-five novices at Sainte-Croix, and by 1838 there were one hundred "souls whom Providence had brought together."[4]

As soon as Moreau had consolidated his Community at Le Mans, requests began to arrive for brothers, the first request coming from the French government: in 1836 the Prefect of the Department of Sarthe requested brothers for the colonies of Martinique and Guadeloupe.[5] But Moreau was not yet ready to spare men for the missions. Then in the summer of 1839, Célestin de la Hailandière, Vicar General of the newly created American diocese of Vincennes, visited France, his homeland, to beg for money and missionaries. Sent by Simon Bruté, first bishop of Vincennes, Hailandière did not visit Moreau, but wrote to him from Paris. Again Moreau was not yet ready to fracture his little community, undoubtedly remembering all too well that Dujarié's zeal to fill requests for brothers was a detriment to the stability of the group. In the fall of that year, however, an urgent request from Bishop Dupuch of Algiers touched Moreau's mind and heart, and the following May the bishop got a promise of three brothers and a chaplain. Specifically the brothers were needed to take care of twenty-five orphans, "The children of poor colonists who died on the plains or were cut down by the yatagan of the Arabs."[6] Moreau's men, therefore, would not be ministering to the African natives but rather to the children of French settlers, and the brothers would be housed in a suburb of Algiers, not far from the diocesan seminary, St. Augustine's. Moreau must have been impressed by the value of this enterprise because in his eleventh circular letter (January 8, 1841) he tells the Community that there are now seven Holy Cross brothers and three priests in Algeria, running not only the orphanage but the seminary as well. A letter which Moreau proudly reprints from Father Mary-Victor Haudebourg, however, demonstrates apostolic motives that would be suspect today:

> You have doubtless learned with interest that, by order of Marshal Count Vallée, Governor of the French possessions in North Africa, the Grand Mosque of Belidah has been turned over to Catholic worship. On November 13th last, the Bishop of Algiers blessed it in the presence of the Marshal and his staff. The Cross not only surmounts the minaret of the finest Mosque of Belidah, but it has been raised still higher, so that it overshadows the Crescents of the other mosques which remain in the hands of the Mussulmen. Our brave soldiers, who are encamped at Ain-Thelezia (which means "lofty and beloved fountain") on one of the ridges of the Atlas amidst a covering of snow and hoar-frost, can gaze down on the Cross, the symbol of hope. On the other hand, the Arabs, who dislike the mountains and detest the very name of Christian, can see in this sacred sign the firm and irrevocable will of France "not to abandon this important place."[7]

One wonders how willingly the natives handed over their prime mosque, and one suspects that Father Haudebourg had as much of the soldier in him as he did the missionary. This sort of disdain evidenced for local people and their religion may have been typical of Christian zeal of the time, but we no longer feel comfortable with it, even when disguised as bringing a gift of civilization to the uncivilized.

In fact, the breach between Algeria and France had been smoldering for years, and it was, like so many conflicts, fundamentally economic. Trading partners for centuries, the two countries came to diplomatic crisis when French merchants were told by the French government not to pay their Algerian debts because Algeria had supported the revolutionary government during the Napoleonic wars.[8] The restored French monarchy was thus behind the debacle. In 1827 the irate Algiers bey (the highest ranking official in the country) struck the French consul with a fly swatter, vowing that no longer would French merchants enjoy the privileged trading they had had with Algeria. The French responded by blockading the country and then invading it in 1830. They stayed for over 130 years.

By 1847 the land was pretty much conquered although some fighting persisted until 1884. The conquest required one third of the French army, about 100,000 soldiers, to beat a native people into submission and make the land relatively safe for colonists. That the missionaries abetted the atrocities of the French government is, however, no more deplorable than the similar treatment of native peoples in America. When one civilization is intent on "civilizing" another, even religion cannot be kept out of the fray. Sadly religion is sometimes at the root of the catastrophe. France used Algeria as a dumping ground for its idle whom she called "colonists."[9] It was to these people that Moreau sent his first missionaries, and to a conquering army that had little interest in religion. Bishop Dupuch did the best he could to organize a sprawling territory first declared a diocese in 1837. He found four priests in the entire country (one near death) when he arrived and a colonial government more intent on thwarting him than helping him.[10]

On April 28, 1840, Moreau announced the names of the three brothers to go to Algeria (Alphonsus, Ignatius, and André), and the three, who were "radiant with joy at being chosen, immediately advanced to the altar to receive their obediences."[11] One wonders how "radiant" André would have been had he known what was waiting for him in Africa. Moreau came up with the phrase "radiant with joy." On May 3 Father Le Boucher was appointed superior over the brothers bound for Algeria. Why he was appointed is a puzzle. He had been in the Holy Cross community for less than a year. André had been with the community for nineteen years, yet he was put under the direction of a man who had not even completed a year of novitiate.[12] On May 17 Moreau changed his mind, named Father Victor Drouelle superior, and added more brothers. Drouelle had been with Holy Cross for a year and a half. Of the brothers, André was the only one to work at the Algerian seminary: he ran the study hall. Brother Louis (Victor Marchand) was in charge of the orphanage, a job he held less than a year and a half before he died while swimming in the Mediterranean with the orphans.[13] Brother Alphonsus, a carpenter (aged 42), and Brother Victor, a refectorian (aged 28), were two non-teaching brothers there. Brother Eulogius (aged 32) taught in a parish grade school, and Brothers Ignatius (aged 20) and Liguori (aged 21) studied to learn Arabic.

The missions in Algeria were dreadful places to work. The climate was intolerable, the food scarce, the housing miserable, and the brothers were forbidden to teach anything but catechism lest they take students away from the established schools. Brother André, the oldest of the nine missionaries, suffered greatly, but his letters from Africa, although full of details about his sicknesses, do not read as letters of complaint or despair. They are remarkable letters, but they never find their way into Moreau's circular letters.[14] One wonders why the correspondence and insights of so senior and respected a member of Holy Cross would be ignored in favor of letters written by neophytes. André's letters are full of homey details about crops and terrain, about food and daily schedules, about soldiers and native Africans. They lack the jingoistic bravado of Haudebourg's letters, and thus they probably would have served poorly in Moreau's circular letters designed to bolster pride in the new missions. One can only hope that André's letters made the rounds among the brothers. They are filled with details that make the man come alive even today 150 years after they were written. As noted in the previous chapter, they are totally unlike any of his early correspondence, letters written when he was in effect running the Brothers of St. Joseph. Those letters were business letters, almost stiff. The five Africa letters are the letters of a warm and real human being.

In some way André's being sent to Africa, away from the administrative jobs he had at Le Mans, was a blessing: it gave him time to look around and to look inside himself. He remarks how happy he is that he no longer has to admonish novices or supervise new teachers. For the first time in his religious life, he was free to observe without obligation to correct. The final years of his life were years of reflection, a spiritual luxury for a man used to being concerned about the welfare of others. Without the weight of an entire community on his shoulders, André could relax into himself.

We may never know why Moreau chose to shut André out of the inner workings of the new Holy Cross, but it undoubtedly had something to do with Moreau's belief that his priests would best be in control if the community were to succeed. After all, he founded them from scratch, Athena born from Zeus. He did not inherit them from another source. And, of course, they had the aura of ordination which, if it does not in fact bring with it talent *ex opere operato*, at least sports the tradition of privileged honor.

Gatian would have read at least one of André's letters, a letter dated May 25, 1843, written almost a year before André's death in Le Mans. The letter is addressed to "Brother Vincent and the other Brothers established in America." There is no mention of Sorin in the address. Conceived as a letter from the Le Mans brothers to their confreres in Indiana, the letter, signed by over thirty men, was actually written by André. The occasion is the departure of the second colony for America:

> The many youths that you instruct in truth and that you form in virtue will be a new generation in these faraway countries. Although in the midst of ice, snow, harsh winters, you will be the envy of the faithful. May we one day be judged worthy, if not participating in it, at least to be sent to soil where there is no lack of good to do and that Providence seems to give us to work on. A large part of Africa is just being considered for our Institute by a royal edict, so that we may establish schools there. Thus we hope that the many difficulties that our priests and brothers first encountered there will ever succeed in the

future, and that Our Lord, His very holy mother, and St. Joseph will return to raise up to their honor a small sanctuary in these burning countries.[15]

There is an exuberance here that borders on ecstasy. André sees in the viability of Notre Dame a clear indication that his moves to save the Brothers of St. Joseph have been blessed by a growing and widening community. It is Moreau's vision, of course, but André paved the way for Moreau. Without André, no Moreau. Reading André's last letter, Gatian would have sensed in the man a nobility and a spiritual joy that came from deep interior peace, sentiments that Gatian may have admired but enjoyed less and less himself as the years passed. Gatian's was a restless spirit, tinged by neurotic spasms that would bring the young man to more sorrow in Holy Cross than happiness, and ultimate disillusionment bordering on despair. André left a wonderful seed bed for Gatian to cultivate, but some people prefer their own methods of cultivation, no matter the cost to their happiness and acceptance.

André's final letter is dated one day after his general letter to all the brothers in America, and it contains a postscript dated May 28, 1843. The letter, addressed to Brother Vincent, clears up some facts about André. He had left Algeria on August 5, 1842, and, back in Le Mans, Moreau named him "Assistant" and "a member of all the councils."[16] The evident solicitude that Moreau tendered André should eradicate all suggestions that the priest neglected the founding brother, may have relegated him to Africa to get him out of Le Mans, and ignored his contributions to the founding of the Brothers of St. Joseph.[17] In his final letter André is full of sincere gratitude to Moreau for the very evident flourishing of the community:

> The boarding school at Our Lady of Holy Cross enjoys a great reputation. We have about forty-six brothers and postulants working, not counting those at the Solitude where there are about thirty under the direction of good Father Chappé…I believe that the Holy Spirit has brought about great progress in the Institute and that God truly blesses this work. I'm convinced moreover that the efforts undertaken so zealously by our Reverend Father Moreau will bring it much good. Assured by seeing all that, I cannot grow tired of thanking the Lord and praying that He will maintain forever the union of priests with the brothers.[18]

The letter suggests, of course, that André and probably other brothers had had misgivings about amalgamation with Moreau's little band of auxiliary priests, but presently the blessings of growth have shown that Moreau's vision and leadership are trustworthy. As we assess André today and regret his being underestimated by Holy Cross historians, we must admit that André himself would have wanted it no other way. Repeatedly reminded that he was inferior to clerics, he would not ask for himself any echelon in the annals of history. In fact, he preferred to be invisible. A man who requests a historian "to remove my name every time it appears because I don't wish to be named anywhere" has to have a heroic sense of his own insignificance in the greater picture of Holy Cross.[19] Sorin would never express such a sentiment, nor for that matter would Moreau, even in the depths of his final humiliations. If Gatian needed any example of abnegation, he would have found it in André. Unfortunately, Gatian was destined to be formed under Sorin's tutelage for nine years and not André's or Moreau's.

The subservience of the brothers to the priests was already well in place before Moreau linked the two societies together. His January, 1840, circular letter, which announces the planned linkage, outlines the form of government that the new community would have. A Major Council will be composed of the General Council of the brothers and the General Council of the auxiliary priests. Under the Council will be three elected superiors: one for the brothers, one for the priests, one for the sisters and boarders. It is evident from the letter, however, that the General Council for the brothers is composed of priests, not brothers, and thus the entire top administration of the proposed congregation would be top-heavy with priests. Moreau adds that the Council for the priests will have no say in the election of the brother-superior, but he adds that the priests who compose the Council for the brothers will elect the brother-director.[20] The highest ranking brother in the community is therefore elected by a Council of priests to whom he is answerable. There is no brother on either the Council for the brothers nor on the proposed Major Council which will be composed of the Council of Brothers and the Council of priests. This sad attitude which regards priesthood as a vocation higher than any ministry performed by laity persisted into the twentieth century. The Catta brothers, in their biography of Moreau, go so far as to assert that "the dignity of the priesthood [represents] Christ's truest expression of 'religion,'"[21] and their belief is reflected in what is essentially a clerical history of Holy Cross which often enough praises the work of priests but overlooks the work of brothers.[22]

It is easy, of course, to garner sympathy for the poor brothers who had to live and work under such a system of religious hierarchy, but what about the priests? When a man is told he is superior to other human beings, what does this do to his mental health? First of all, he has to assume a persona he probably did not have before, a persona based on a false assumption. Then he has to live up to

standards that are impossible to fulfill, and every time he fails, his shame is doubled. Over time, he may compensate for failure, or perceived failure, by rational-
ization. He may take out his frustration on his subjects. In all cases, someone is
going to suffer: Moreau beat his own body; Champeau became obsessed with his
apostolate in Paris; Sorin humiliated those who challenged his authority.[23] The
notion that a sacrament renders one human being superior to other people is at
the heart of sacramental theology, and it comes at a price to human nature, but
its sad effects are, of course, no less deleterious than those of a lawyer or doctor
who falls into the trap of believing his education and talents are of his own doing.
The very virtue that Moreau preached to the brothers, humility, was the very virtue that his auxiliary priests needed to maintain their religious stability because
humility is not subservience but rather the recognition that one is the instrument
of good deeds, not a creator of them.

In some ways the nascent community of Holy Cross ignored one of the basic
good principles of the Revolution: égalité. The *Declaration of the Rights of Man*,
approved by the National Assembly on August 26, 1789, almost half a century
before Moreau joined his brothers and priests in one community, insisted in its
first principle that "social distinctions may be founded only upon the general
good."[24] It is difficult to see how a church can prosper if it insists that some members are better than others. The sixth principle of the Declaration insists, "All citizens, being equal in the eyes of the law, are equally eligible to all
dignities…without distinction except that of their virtues and talents." One
could argue that a man approved for priesthood is approved only on the basis of
his demonstrated talents of leadership, but that explanation would not justify
Moreau's insistence that the brothers defer to all priests without exception. It
would seem that in post-Revolutionary France, the backlash of the persecuted
clergy was worked out in a return to a vestige of the old hierarchical idea that was
so anathema to the citizens of Paris: when they got the chance, the clergy took it
out on the laity (minus the guillotine) as surely but more slowly than the laity had
taken it out on the clergy with the various oaths of clerical subservience to the
government. These were conundra that whipped the soul of little Gatian: he was
formed under the eyes of believers in clerical superiority, but he found himself
deadended in a career that demanded of him what the Revolution had tossed
aside as illogical and debilitating. The brightest minds crack first under ideological distress. Gentler minds than Gatian's could ignore or work around clericalism: he faced it head on and lost the battle because the forces against him were
overwhelming. It is amazing what concessions a people can make when their
push toward progress has gone awry into something as terrible as the Reign of

Terror. Generations have paid for revolutionary excess by relapse into pockets of an entrenched and bureaucratic church unable to create a system of governance more workable than what the Middle Ages took centuries of feudal theory to construct for religion in Europe.

If Moreau's brothers were denied the egalitarian message of the *Declaration of the Rights of Man*, they missed as well the more strident calls from the *Declaration of the Rights of Women*. Written by Olympe de Gouges in 1791, it brought her derision and a trip to the guillotine in November, 1793, but hidden among its feminist tocsins on sexuality are some excellent points that the Brothers of St. Joseph should have heeded. She starts with a call to arms:

> Women, wake up; the tocsin of reason is being heard throughout the whole universe; discover your rights. The powerful empire of nature is no longer surrounded by prejudice, fanaticism, superstition, and lies. The flame of truth has dispersed all the clouds of folly and usurpation. Enslaved man has multiplied his strength and needs recourse to yours to break his chains. Having become free, he has become unjust to his companion. Oh, women, women! When will you cease to be blind? What advantage have you received from the Revolution? A more pronounced scorn, a more marked disdain.[25]

Substitute "brothers" for "women" in the passage and you get to the heart of the matter. De Gouges attacks the evil fomented by any group of people who exercise leverage on the basis of one principle: for her it is gender, for the Brothers of St. Joseph it was sacrament.

> If they [legislators] persist in their weakness in putting this *non sequitur* in contradiction to their principles, courageously oppose the force of reason to the empty pretensions of superiority; unite yourselves beneath the standards of philosophy; deploy all the energy of your character, and you will soon see these haughty men, not groveling at your feet as servile adorers, but proud to share with you the treasures of the Supreme Being. Regardless of what barriers confront you, it is in your power to free yourselves; you have only to want to.[26]

It would seem that the brothers in 1837 could have used this wake-up call to prevent Moreau from a disastrous assumption that took over a century to undo.[27]

If he chafed against his treatment as a secondary member of a religious community, Gatian himself never apparently questioned the privileging of a priestly class. Recognizing Sorin as a person of higher talent, authority, and position with God, Gatian never took the step to question the right of one human to assert privilege over another. He railed against Sorin, defied him in councils, but he always recognized that Sorin was by grace of state a better human being than he was, closer to God and chosen by God to be so. The most significant indication that he reverenced the priestly state was his own aspiring to be ordained, and thus he was torn between his attacks on Sorin and his desire to be another Sorin. How long could a person thus retain any degree of mental health? It is no wonder that Gatian eventually cracked and his brilliant mind shattered into pieces. With his French heritage, knowing how the Parisians had leveled a king and established a republic, he should have, but never apparently could work to topple the inequities of religious hierarchy. Born as the Community was in an egalitarian system of teaching brothers, each equal to all, there had to be a memory of this system remaining in those men who knew the group dynamics enjoyed under the guidance of Dujarié's four brother-directors. But Gatian, unfortunately, came to Holy Cross when Moreau had adapted Dujarié's vision to the system Moreau knew as a diocesan clergyman working at the Le Mans seminary. He was close to hierarchy in a way that Dujarié never was. Of course, the floundering of the Brothers of St. Joseph gave Moreau all the reason he needed to tighten the community under a hierarchical system that used a priestly caste to make it run smoothly, but those brothers who remained from Ruillé days would have remembered what the old priestless organization would have been like, and although they appreciated very much the new amalgamation of priests and brothers, they would not have forgotten that the old organization had a distinct merit of egalitarian energy. It is true that a priest (Dujarié) had been their head, but the daily business of the Brothers of St. Joseph was handled by the brothers' council of four and its de facto leader André Mottais. Then too in the individual parishes where the brothers worked, one or two together teaching elementary students, the supreme law of the local parish priest was to be obeyed, but each brother always knew that any decision by a parish priest could be abrogated by the Ruillé headquarters which could pull brothers back from a foundation at will, as often happened: witness, the dozens of little schools that were opened and closed in the seventeen years of the Brothers of St. Joseph.

There is no doubt that Moreau wanted the positions of power at Le Mans to be filled by his auxiliary priests. He said so at the 1837 convocation, summoned to allay the fears of some brothers that the auxiliary priests were financial parasites. Moreau outlined the brothers' assets and showed that there were no grounds for fear. He noted that his plan was to make the brothers dependent on his priests "to whom he wanted the direction and government of their societies to be entrusted, on the basis of a mutual agreement to be reached by the council members representing the two communities."[28] The result was the "Fundamental Pact" by which brothers and priests readied themselves for the eventual joining of the two societies. Moreau's own generosity with the income from two properties that were his personally may have helped allay in the minds of the brothers any suspicions that he was acting for his own benefit. Why they should accept, however, submission to the auxiliary priests is a mystery. They were probably tainted by the notion that as laity they were indeed secondary members of the church. Thus it was not only Moreau and his priests who adhered to this notion, and when Moreau named his first administration at Le Mans, all were priests: Cottereau chosen as assistant superior, de Marseul as director of studies, and Chappé as master of novices.[29] The years of religious discipline practiced by many brothers was accounted for little.

Moreau, however, was very careful to make sure the brothers as a group were not humiliated by any priest who was not an administrator. In his circular letter for September 1, 1841, he specifies the relationship between brothers and priests:

> I have not the slightest intention to subject the Brothers to the priests in such a way that any priest would have the right to give orders to any Brother, or that the Brothers would be obliged to obey all the priests indiscriminately. Even though the brothers owe respect and deference to all the priests without exception, because of their sacerdotal character, still the priests cannot give orders to the Brothers unless they have been elected to an office or employment to which this right is attached. In addition, both priests and Brothers shall always show themselves grateful for the least favors which they receive from one another.[30]

These remarks were important in preventing any single priest from becoming a self-appointed superior, but that priests deserve respect "because of their sacerdotal character" is an unfortunate addendum: by this line of logic, a layman would have to respect the basest of clergymen, including Bishop Talleyrand and countless sacerdotal rascals who did not deserve respect even though ordained. Fortunately, on the local level Moreau's auxiliary priests did not lord it over the brothers. In fact, when five priests took vows in August, 1841, after the ceremony they served a meal to the brothers.[31] Such was the lack of rank Moreau envisaged for his men, but too bad that he, and everyone else at the time, retained the belief that ordination, while not necessitating privilege, does intrinsically render a human more suitable to govern than a mere Christian.

Some of Moreau's preference for priests rather than brothers in positions of authority is understandable from the point of view of their respective educations.

If one looks at the career preparation of a man like Moreau, one sees beyond grade school (essentially André Mottais' level of education), many years in a preparatory seminary and more years in a major seminary where classes were small and the teachers well prepared (Dujarié's level of education). A brother like Gatian, on the other hand, after grade school got at most one year of classes before he was out teaching in a school, often running it himself. While advanced education does not guarantee leadership, it certainly sets up the atmosphere where leadership skills can be cultivated.

Moreau's mistake was to subordinate the Brothers of St. Joseph to his Auxiliary Priests. He was, of course, a man of his time, and nineteenth century Europe was still much impressed with hierarchy. Thus the pope at the top gave directives to cardinals and bishops who directed the clergy who instructed the laity. The French Revolution shook governmental hierarchy but failed to dislodge hierarchy from the Church, although the Gallican bishops tried hard to stem Rome's hegemony. Bouvier, the last of the Gallican bishops, became, however, a potentate in his own diocese, a local pope. When summoned to Rome, he died there, the pope visiting him on his deathbed as a gesture of reconciliation. Instead of accepting St. Paul's insight that there is no hierarchy of gifts, the Church continued to view priesthood as a higher calling than lay ministry, the pastor above the lector or the organist.[32]

Given the preeminence that clergy have enjoyed within the church, it is no wonder that a man of Gatian's aggressive talents would have yearned for the chance to be ordained into the ranks of the honored. As a teenager, he was enamored of Brother Vital, so naturally his first calling would have been to the brotherhood. After all, it afforded its members the chance to travel, to emigrate to exotic lands, while the workaday world of the diocesan clergy in little towns that Gatian knew would not have appealed to the adventure in Gatian's soul. Once he arrived at Le Mans, however, he would have been introduced to the other part of Holy Cross, the nascent group of auxiliary priests who could do all that the brothers did (teach, administer) but seemed to be getting all the plum positions and enjoyed the deference that came with inclusion in the privileged ranks of the ordained. Gatian could not switch novitiates once he got to Le Mans because the brothers forbade it (as we learn from a letter), but once he arrived in America and the first blush of geographical novelty died off, he naturally could have felt stirring within him once again the urge to climb the ecclesiastical ladder. As a brother he was deadended, fulfilling the roles of teacher at Notre Dame and supervisor in Brooklyn, but as a priest, advancement could have been possible: first priest-teacher at Notre Dame but someday perhaps religious superior replacing the eminent Sorin. These are not very worthy sentiments to characterize a religious calling, but all motivation is tainted, even in church circles. While Gatian may have been a prayerfully pious young man and a stickler for rules, he also was brash, temperamental, ambitious, and paranoid, hardly prime ingredients for candidacy to ordination.

As 1840 brought stability to the Le Mans community, numbers grew. In May, a few months before Urbain arrived, the head count was eighty-six men in thirty-nine houses. There were also forty-five novices. The fear of taking final vows had winnowed some brothers from the grain, but others were satisfied with the strengths that Moreau was bringing. The Fundamental Pact of 1837 had proved to be a presage that good would come from the amalgamation of brothers and priests at Holy Cross, and apostolates were moving in the direction that Moreau wanted them to move. One of his most notable character traits was an unabashed courage that took him into the face of government officials and even, on occasion, the local bishop. When it came to schools, Moreau knew what he wanted. When health officers, for example, put on hold for a year the opening of the new boarding school at Le Mans, Moreau simply opened the school and invited families and local doctors to see for themselves how healthy the facility actually was. By winning over an official here and an official there, he garnered enough friends in high places to secure the permissions he needed to open his school. Likewise, when the bishop voiced disapproval over Moreau's plans for a high school, Moreau offered to resign if he could not get the school. The bishop backed down. Moreau never blinked when he knew he was in for a fight, and some of this same tenacity he must have sensed in the thirteen year old Urbain Monsimer who came to him in 1839. Although Urbain's feistiness would never flower into marvelous projects like Moreau's, Urbain's same gritty stubbornness would make the young man, in Moreau's eyes, a perfect recruit for the hardships of life in America.

When Gatian shipped for Indiana, he would never see Moreau again, and by the time Moreau faced his ultimate set-backs, Gatian would be dead. Moreau, like Gatian, too saw his world crumble around him. In 1866, he was forced to resign as superior general, amid accusations of his mismanagement of funds, accusations from some clerical malcontents—without foundation but sufficient to bring about his disgrace. His college and motherhouse were lost, and he himself had to move across the street to a small house where two of his sisters (Victoire and Josephine Moreau) lived. As the auction of the school property took place, Moreau worried only about the creditors he had assured would be satisfied. They would not be satisfied, however, until one year after his death. In a small room nine feet by seven, he lived out his final years, sleeping in an armchair every night, his meals brought to him by the Marianite Sisters of Holy Cross who never lost faith in him. His principal detractors meanwhile, Holy Cross priests Champeau, Drouelle, and Sorin, saw to it that the liquidation of his dreams in Le Mans was finalized, including the sale of the two novitiate properties. In 1873, while on a mission to relieve a sick pastor in nearby Yvré-l'Evêque, Moreau collapsed and was taken back to Le Mans where he died on January 20, convinced that much of what he had built for Holy Cross was in ruins.

What exactly was Moreau's vision, the energy that attracted hundreds of young men and women to gather into his institutions? Father Dujarié's vision was parochial: he did not think beyond Ruillé-sur-Loir and northern France. On the other hand, Moreau, cosmopolitan as he was, looked as far away as Africa, America, and India to extend the goodness of his dreams. "Catholic," meaning "universal," was for him a reality. For him, the larger reach of religion and philosophy. For Dujarié, the simple confines of a single segment of France. Moreau was forced, however, to found two separate communities at the Le Mans suburb called Holy Cross: one community in which the Brothers of St. Joseph would be united with his band of auxiliary priests, and one community of religious sisters. In practice, however, he assigned members of both communities to the same mission apostolates: thus the 1849 foundation in New Orleans opened with sisters, brothers, and eventually a priest. The sisters cooked and cleaned at St. Mary's Orphanage; the brothers ran the dormitories and taught the orphans rudimentary academic skills. This division of labor was repeated in institution after institution, mirroring the paradigm of family. In New Orleans the orphanage thrived under the Holy Cross brothers, sisters, and priests. Thousands of homeless boys, the cast-offs of the city, were fathered and mothered into maturity. Moreau's dream blended the best of family, care, and love, into an institution for needy boys and redeemed a corner of frontier civilization.

As a model for his religious, Moreau chose the Holy Family, specifically dedicating his priests to Christ, his sisters to Mary, and his brothers to Joseph. He consecrated each group to representative hearts: the Salvatorists to the Sacred Heart, the Marianites to the Immaculate Heart of Mary, and the Josephites to the Heart of Joseph. From its earliest years, therefore, the two communities, men and women, were strongly aligned with the ideals of family, none of the branches subservient to any other branch, although Moreau did design the priests to assume the highest leadership roles in the men's society. But authority, as problematic as it can often be in the best of families, is the least interesting of Holy Cross family dynamics. The spiritual values that Moreau instilled at the core of his religious communities gave the two groups a firm base from which to exercise their goodness. A decided regard for each other and their charges marked the stability of their enterprises. Their day-to-day living was meant to be protected by an honest interchange at weekly chapters: grievances and joys could be aired and shared in a group setting. The communality of sincere interest in each other's well-being blossomed into healthy spiritual growth among themselves and the children entrusted by society to their care. Moreau's dream endured.

1

The Monsimers of Chémeré-le-roi and Saulges

Every history of the Holy Cross Congregation begins with the French Revolution, the single most important cause of the Congregation's genesis. Even though the political turmoil ended more or less officially in 1802 and the first roots of Holy Cross were not planted until 1820, the trauma of the Revolution endured long after Napoleon had brought the country to a kind of stability and had himself exited the stage. When we dig into the French Revolution, what do we find that influenced the structure and vision of the Holy Cross founders? More particularly, what do we find in the Revolution that explains things about Brother Gatian? He seems, after all, a minor player in a long and complicated history. He was not a founder of Holy Cross. Why should he of all people be examined for insights into the birth of Holy Cross? He was, of course, a product of his time and place: a farmer and a fine student. He became a successful teacher and a superb writer. He was entrusted with supervisory missions. His opinions were solicited. But his life ended in apparent failure, an itinerant outside of his chosen religious family, a sickly man dependent upon the generosity of his father and step-mother. There is tragedy in his life, cut off as he was at thirty-four, but there are moments of grandeur too in his life, and those reflect the energy of a man not afraid to confront authority and forge his own destiny.

Urbain Monsimer (Brother Gatian) was a man who knew what he wanted and pursued his dreams doggedly. Had the boy been born fifty years earlier, he would have been at the heart of the Revolution. Had he been in Paris, he would have been an energetic participant, surely beyond the mob, undoubtedly a member of a political debating club and close observer of the many assemblies that replaced and despoiled each other year after year. He had, after all, the intelligent tenacity of Mirabeau, the ascetic rigor of Maximilian Robespierre, and the fanatical rant of Jacques Roux.[1] Of the three, he seems closest to Robespierre, whom Sagan characterizes as "virtuous, narcissist, and paranoid."

> These three psychological attributes are brought together here because there seems to be an intimate, complex relationship among them. Virtue, an undoubted human good, is subject to particular perverse manifestations. There is a narcissism of virtue: I shine because I excel most other human beings in integrity and honesty. This superiority gives me the right—and the obligation—to judge harshly the mere mortals with whom I am forced to live. At its most complex stage of development, this perversion assumes a paranoid dimension, a grandiosity of moral critique: so far above the crowd do I soar, so far into the future extends my moral vision, that I inhabit a realm—like the heroes of old—midway between mortals and the gods.[2]

Most people associate Robespierre with only the Reign of Terror, of which he was, of course, an architect. People dismiss him as a bloody butcher, but the young man was a brilliant orator and a disciplined thinker. He lived in Paris in a modest room he rented from a middle class family. He was abstemious in his eating and drinking, expecting much of himself and much of others. He died grotesquely. Shot in the jaw, he lay all night with a paper bandage holding his jaw together. The next day when he was thrown on the guillotine bench, the executioner ripped off the bandage so as not to impede the work of the blade. Robespierre screamed like an animal until the machine silenced him.[3] But Urbain was not born in the Revolution, nor was he born in Paris, so his story begins before he does, in quiet parts of rural France.

During the reign of Charlemagne a custom began of naming new areas with prefixes like "val" or "mons" descriptive of a local terrain. Thus *circa* 840 the name "Monsimer" was created to designate part of the Charnie forest,[4] and by the end of the twelfth century, the patronymic "Monsimer" was well established. The name originally referred to a mill built near St. Denis d'Orgues,[5] and the name surfaces in history here and there. In 1380 a widow named Jeanne de Monsimer (widow of Jean de la Cour) was among the citizens of Poillé forced to quarter English soldiers on their way to Brittany during the Hundred Years War. The earliest Monsimer to live in Chéméré-le-roi itself was born *circa* 1568, came from St. Pierre-sur-Erve at age twenty-four, and died on February 14, 1646.[6]

A monk named Johan de Monsimer lived in Bellebauche, between Chéméré and Grez-en-Bouère, around 1600, at an abbey located near a forest that is still standing, but the abbey itself was replaced by a château, the farm of which was worked until recently by a Monsimer. The courtyard of the farm stands where the abbey's cemetery used to be.[7] In the seventeenth century some Monsimers settled in Laval and St. Malo, and in the late eighteenth century during the aftermath of the Revolution (1792), one Monsimer family left Chémérè-le-roi to settle at the Préau farm near Saulges. It was there that Urbain Jean Baptiste Monsimer (Brother Gatian) was born on April 3, 1826, at 7:35 AM, and it was there that he died thirty-four years later on July 29, 1860.[8]

Brother Gatian's grandfather, Urbain Monsimer, was born circa 1770, the son of René Monsimer and Jeanne Chamaret. He married Marie Lebreton, left Chémérè-le-roi, and settled at Préau near Saulges where he died at age seventy-one in 1841, nineteen years before his grandson Urbain's death. The grandfather had two sons: François, who died in 1834 at age 20, and Urbain (Brother Gatian's father) who was born on January 9, 1800, and married (at Saulges) Rose Julienne Joseph Reneaudeau on June 22, 1824. She was a laundress from Saulges. The two had five children, including twins who died at birth in 1825. Urbain came next (1826), followed by Francis Constant (June 26, 1828) and August (August 12, 1833). In 1836 the family left Préau and moved to La Teillerie, a farm near Chémérè-le-roi where Francis died on July 26, 1841, at age 13, two weeks before his brother Urbain left for America as Brother Gatian. One can only imagine how poignant it must have been for the family to lose one teenager to death and another to a foreign country within so short a time span. The sole child of this marriage thus remaining with the parents was August who was to live only to age twenty-two. Later as a corporal in the Crimean War, he fought with the infantry, but contracted typhus several months after the war ended (1855) and died in April, 1856.

The mother of these three unfortunate boys herself had died at La Teillerie on March 24, 1837, only thirty-six years old. At the time her sons would have been ten, eight, and three. We do not know what she died of. Although the extended Monsimer family would have afforded some mothering to the boys, the widower Monsimer did not wait much longer than a year to remarry. On June 26, 1838, in the Church of the Assumption in Chémérè-le-roi, he married Frances Viéron. She was twenty-eight, he thirty-eight, and the marriage was fruitful: Henry Clement was born in 1840, Isidore Adolph on May 9, 1841 (died at age 9), Henry Armand on June 15, 1842, Francis Louis on August 18, 1844, and Eugene Adrian on January 26, 1846. When the grandfather died in 1841, the Monsimer family left the farm near Chémérè-le-roi and moved back to the grandfather's farm at Préau near Saulges.

We know quite a bit about one of Urbain's half-brothers. Born at the Monsimer farm La Teillerie just one year after Urbain left for Le Mans, Henry Clement was moved with the family on November 1, 1841, to Préau. His parents lived there until they died in 1872 and 1880. Henry came to America sometime before 1858 and herded buffalo in Kansas and Wyoming, then cut wood in Montana, and finally prospected for gold in California. Urbain refers to him at the end of a letter (November 18, 1858) to Edward Sorin at Notre Dame. After Urbain left for France to die, Henry went to New Orleans: his 1866 passport attests to his being there. In 1875 he married Rosalie Marie Espitallier near Santa Barbara, California. After the birth of their second child, they moved to Santa Fe. Then after a short stay in Oklahoma, they returned to Santa Fe but then settled in Las Vegas where they bought a bakery. In 1896 Henry bought a ranch north of Red Bluff, California, but soon he returned to Las Vegas where he died in 1906.[9]

If we were to project ourselves backward in time to the section of northern France where Urbain was born, what size family would we find? In 1778 the average household would have had five persons living in it.[10] Each household tended to be simple; that is, it consisted of just the parents and the children. Very few households were "extended" with grandparents and maiden aunts. In 1817, the little village of Yvelines, for example, had seventy-seven simple family households and only four extended family households.[11] Thus when we envision what little Urbain's daily social atmosphere was like, we should see in our mind's eye only the boy, his parents, and siblings. Although the family did move from Chéméré-le-roi back to the grandparents' farm at Saulges (where Urbain was born), it was a move made after the death of the grandfather. In Urbain's day farmers made up a good third of the population. In the villages near Rouen, for example, there were 106 farmers, 121 rural craftsmen, and 103 day laborers.[12]

The farm day started early (at sunrise), and farmers left for the field after a hearty breakfast because they took only a snack (e.g., bread and cheese) along on their twelve hour work day. Returning home in the late afternoon, they were then ready for a good evening meal, generally barley or rye bread and soup. The kitchen usually served as the living room as well as the kitchen, and the bedroom never boasted a bed for each member of the family. Some Breton peasant families, including servants, slept in one bed, but more generally parents had a curtained bed to themselves.

By Urbain's day, women were delaying marriage until the age of twenty-four, and many enjoyed a good deal of freedom to socialize. They were not slaves of the hearth. One witness around 1830 noted of girls in Lower Brittany that they "run around day and night with young men, without there having resulted for a long time any noticeable licentiousness."[13] When the young women did settle down to marriage, they faced the prospects of having many children to insure some would survive into adulthood. In small towns infant mortality ran seventeen percent (175 out of 1000) in 1809.[14] Some of the deaths were attributed to wet-nursing, a practice that arose to help get a wife back to her marital sexual routine before the child was weaned at two years of age. Sexual intercourse was thought to contaminate a mother's milk, so surrogate feeding would allow a child to suckle (thus avoiding disease from polluted water) and the husband to exact the marriage "debt." Even churchmen approved of the system: "The wife should, if she can, put her child out to nurse, in order to provide for the frailty of her husband by paying the conjugal due, for fear that he may lapse into some sin against conjugal purity."[15] One churchman went so far as to declare that the death of an infant by separation from his nursing mother would be a lesser grief than having a husband commit adultery.

The farm where Urbain was born and died at Préau is today owned by Geneviève Duboscq, a woman who at age twelve was a heroine in World War II, helping her father save American paratroopers of the 82nd Airborne Division during a June, 1944, parachute drop into the swamps around her family's home on the railway line between Paris and Cherbourg. Her heroism is chronicled in *My Longest Night.* In 1994 Duboscq made a parachute jump herself with members of the 82nd Airborne into Normandy to help celebrate the fiftieth anniversary of the 1944 events. Although some of the buildings on her farm survive from Urbain's day (one barn has been converted into a kind of chapel), the house in which Urbain was born and died is gone. Only a slab of concrete remains to mark the spot. The Préau farm is quite remote from the access road. A long dusty road leads to the grassy driveway of the farm which sits quite isolated among its fields. The nineteenth century buildings which remain are constructed of field stone, meant to last, but none hold animals any longer. The Monsimer boys would have had a long hike from Préau to a school in Saulges, if there was one there—we know there was none run by the Brothers of St. Joseph. This may have been one reason why Urbain's father moved his family to La Teillerie near Chémérè-le-roi although more probably the growing family may have needed a place of its own.

Saulges is a tourist attraction because of the local caves, and thus it has a steady income that other towns, like Gennes, do not enjoy. One of the caves, La Grotte de l'Erve, a sepulchral cave with human bones, was discovered in 1816, shortly before Urbain was born. He undoubtedly visited the caves since local children were convinced that a witch lived there. Notre Dame, the parish church at Saulges, dates from the twelfth century and faces a square of municipal buildings, all newly refurbished. The church is a gem, sparkling clean and bright. The impressive façade holds a plaque to the right of the main entrance: "To the memory of the blessed Julian Moule, priest at Saulges from 1765 to 1792, martyred at Laval January 21, 1794," a victim of the Revolution.[16] Priests who refused to take the oath of allegiance to the new government were summarily executed, even in the hinterlands far from Paris. The founder of the Brothers of St. Joseph, James Dujarié, hid for the first four years of his priesthood, farm to farm, barn to barn, ministering by night in fear of his life, until the political climate changed. France, so often dubbed "the eldest daughter of the Church," has had a checkered history of both support for and persecution of its clergy and religious. Even as recent as 1902 all religious were expelled from the country. Outsiders find such events difficult to comprehend. The church at Saulges until 1848 had only a romanesque nave with small windows, but two chapels were added in 1848. The building is Merovingian and was encircled by a cemetery until 1784.

As one enters the church of St. Peter in Saulges, one is struck by the evident care taken to preserve this ancient building. The pure white walls and ceiling reflect the light let in by windows with foot-thick sills. A beautifully ornate wooden pulpit graces the left wall and next to it a statue of Our Lady of Proulx, with her waist-length black hair and dark blue gown shimmering with gold stars. The stained glass windows on each side are simple with blue and red figures, but the back window depicts a rich crucifixion scene. There are wonderful medieval treasures in the church. A wooden bas relief, donated in the early fifteenth century by the Seigneur de Valtrot, contains a crucifixion tableau with assorted saints. Nearby, a statue dating to 1401 shows God the Father seated, supporting with His hands His crucified Son. The Holy Spirit as a dove floats above the Son and seems part of the Father's beard but is actually emanating from the Father's mouth. The message is powerful here, reinforcing as it does the Father's acceptance of the Son's sacrifice. It is a truly imaginative piece of art. There is also in the church a bound St. Sebastian, waiting for the arrows to fly, a statue similar to those of the saint found in most village churches in this part of France. The pious fascination with the saint goes beyond the medieval and Renaissance excuse to get the male torso public. It is a ghoulish reminder of what happens to men who do not toe the political line: they get martyred, go to heaven, and are honored in churches forever.

As wonderful as all these works of art are, the pièce de résistance is the main altar, a powerful work towering with its reredos twenty-five feet to the ceiling. It was made by Langlois in 1692. Painted white with black columns highlighted in gold, the piece is a study in itself. The main panel depicts the Virgin Mary, her foot on a crescent moon, being assumed into heaven, crowned by cherubim. Her empty tomb gapes below. Two carved statues painted in brilliant colors flank the painting. To the left is St. Paul, and to the right, sporting a strangely inappropriate Bourbon goatee, is St. Louis. This is not a church of simple beauty: it is a lavish feast and must have had as great an impact on parishioners in Urbain's day as it does today. He would, after all, have walked among people who knew the martyred Curé Moule, and Urbain's bright eyes would have thrilled to the superb craftsmanship of the church's art pieces. Facing the church is a tenth century church (dedicated to St. Peter) to which locale people bring their animals to be blessed. Faith has always been strong in the area. Near Saulges is St. Cénéré's oratory (dating to the seventh century) with a special fountain from which people still drink the curative water.

The other farm, La Teillerie, near Chéméré-le-roi, is also very beautiful. Many of the buildings from Urbain's days remain standing in fine shape and are still in use: the cow barn, the pig barn, and the main house show little wear for the century and a half between us and him. They are picturesque structures, removed from the paved road by a dirt road some hundred yards long. The well cultivated fields stretch far into the distance beyond the dirt road. The buildings are constructed of field stone and the sloping rooves are tiled with grey slate. The rustic doors to the barns are wooden, and everywhere there are flower beds full of color in the summer. The farm house itself is to the left of the short driveway off the dirt road, and its far end is the oldest section, probably the only part of the house that dates to Urbain's youthful days there. The house is two stories high. For the two decades that the family worked the La Teillerie farm, they worshipped and schooled the boys in Chéméré-le-roi.

The Brothers of St. Joseph first established a school in Chéméré-le-roi in 1833 and would remain there until 1860. In the years that Urbain attended the school, he would have come under the tutelage of Brother Vital (August Lebreton) who was born in 1808 and entered the Brothers' Community in 1825 at age sixteen. He lived a long life in the Community, weathering the storms of 1830, the transfer of the novitiate in 1835, and the loss of the motherhouse property in 1869. He died at Angers in 1886 at age seventy-seven. Arriving at Chéméré-le-roi in 1836 from just having founded a school at Montourtier the previous year, he would have had under his wing the very bright, very energetic little Urbain Monsimer, who at age nine would have rapidly fallen under the academic spell of the capable Brother Vital.

Those happy idyllic days at La Tellerie and in the school at Chéméré-le-roi would instill in little Urbain a thirst for religion that could be slaked only by his joining a religious group of men. There he would find the challenge his young soul longed for, and there he would be enriched by the spiritual maturity of three men who would shape his destiny: Jacques Dujarié, André Mottais, and Basil Moreau. The first of these men was already dead by the time Urbain left home to join the Brothers of St. Joseph, but Dujarié's spirit endured in the group he had founded in the previous generation. André Mottais would spend about a year watching Urbain's first growth at Le Mans, but André too had exerted such a compelling influence on the spirituality of the brothers that he should not be overlooked as an important influence on Gatian. The third man, Moreau, has received the most scrutiny of the three founders, and it was he who would see in little Urbain the potential for great good. Would that Urbain had spent a lifetime in Moreau's care: this biography would have a totally different ending. The three founders of Holy Cross are so inextricably wound into the history of their Community, none of them should be ignored for the influence each had on the little thirteen-year-old Urbain who presented himself at Le Mans one August day in 1839.

2

Urbain Comes to Holy Cross

When Basil Moreau assumed control of the Brothers of St. Joseph on August 31, 1835, at the end of the Community's annual retreat, he had already made up his mind to transfer the brothers' novitiate from Ruillé to Le Mans.[1] The relocation of the novitiate program was a good idea for several reasons, one being the association that Ruillé had with the all too obvious disintegration of the brothers, and another being the advantages that training in a large city would bring to the novices. Moreau never had any intention of himself moving to Ruillé when negotiations were underway to have him replace Father Dujarié, nor would he have had opposition from the brothers still working in and around Ruillé. As early as 1832 when he preached a retreat to the brothers in Ruillé, he had won their confidence as a spiritual leader. Any decision he would make on the location of the novitiate would have met with sincere approval. He was, after all, their savior, and established as he was in Le Mans, bringing the brothers north was a very good idea. He was assistant rector of the major seminary in Le Mans and taught Scripture there, having among his duties the spiritual direction of the seminarians. He also maintained a close relationship with the Good Shepherd Sisters, the Le Mans Community which he had founded in May, 1833, and he still remained in charge of their financial affairs and fund raising.[2] With his contacts among the clergy and important people of the La Mayenne district, Moreau would have made a mistake in taking himself to Ruillé instead of bringing Ruillé, as it were, to him. It was a matter of the mountain moving to Mohammed, and there is no indication in any extant correspondence that any of the brothers objected to the relocation of their motherhouse. Eventually even Father Dujarié would be brought to Le Mans where he lived out his final days among the brothers he had founded and loved so well.

The importance of a novitiate for a religious community is not to be underestimated. It is there where good willed recruits are introduced to the rudiments of a spiritual life that is supposed to sustain them throughout a life of prayer and

63

active apostolate. For years Holy Cross novices in the twentieth century heard an injunction from the writings of Father Moreau at the end of their noon meal: "Let the novices never forget that what they are in the novitiate that they will remain for the rest of their lives." In many religious communities so important has the novitiate experience been considered that the canonical novitiate year is often followed by another year in which the novices are slowly integrated into mainstream community life. In addition, most religious groups preface the novitiate with a period of candidacy that can extend up to two years or more. Thereafter, a post-novitiate study period can add several more years on to formation. It is not uncommon for a recruit to spend six or more years in training before beginning full time work in an apostolate. If we contrast this training with the training that Father Dujarié was able to give his Brothers of St. Joseph, we can understand all the better exactly why the little community had such a difficult time staying together in the first fifteen years of its existence. Brothers were often sent out to teach with as little as four months of novitiate, a situation that the brothers themselves in 1835 acknowledged had contributed to their disintegration.[3]

Thus when Moreau announced his intention to move the novitiate to Le Mans, the brothers could have sensed a strengthening of the training process because they trusted him: Moreau himself had studied with an established religious community (the Sulpicians), had already founded an order with a solid novitiate base (the Good Shepherd Sisters), and lived in the major seminary where he was accustomed to a daily schedule of prayer and religious exercises. Leaving their home in Ruillé and their beloved founder was poignant for the brothers, but their common sense saw that the move north might represent their only chance at survival as a community. To expect the cosmopolitan Moreau to relocate to the country village of Ruillé would have been less than a good solution since Moreau's contacts in Le Mans and his proximity to the bishop would mean in the coming years the difference between success and continued failure for the Brothers of St. Joseph. Had the Community stayed rooted in Ruillé, Moreau's leadership and talent for organization would surely have changed the Community there, but its transformation into the modern Community of Holy Cross would have been next to impossible outside of Le Mans. One wonders what might have happened if an earlier plan by Dujarié had been brought to fulfillment: in 1827 Father Dujarié had agreed with Father Gabriel Deshayes to amalgamate the Brothers of St. Joseph with two congregations that Deshayes had founded. Nothing came of the agreement, but the proposed merger, coming only seven years after Dujarié's first recruits arrived at Ruillé shows just how precarious his administrative grip was early on.

The moving of the novitiate from Ruillé to Le Mans was an extremely important step in Moreau's plans to subjugate the brothers to priestly direction. There is no doubt that he considered the brothers incapable of directing themselves, and the sad truth is that they had come to the same conclusion themselves. Regardless of the fact that the primary blame for their gradual disintegration in Ruillé was the fault of an aging priest, the brothers accepted their demise as self-induced. The lure of a cosmopolitan leader like Moreau was their last life line of hope, and they clutched at him like drowning survivors of a shipwreck. He had important connections in Le Mans. He was a bright teacher. He was an established administrator at a major seminary. He was the founder of a thriving community of nuns. The sacrifice of hegemony was a small price to pay, or so the Brothers of St. Joseph thought, for their salvation. They bowed themselves into a hierarchical system of government that would last for a hundred years, until the brothers after World War II decided that they had endured enough second-class citizenship. Moreau's vision of leadership was very much like the vision of the Southern United States toward leadership in the early nineteenth century: it takes an elite class with leisure afforded by a working class to create a few strong leaders like Robert E. Lee. Dujarié's vision was more like that of the Northern United States: equality among the ranks eventually produces leaders like U.S. Grant. The democratic process is messy, but it does win wars. The elitist method produces a few outstanding leaders, but it relies for its effectiveness on a willing base of indentured servants. What Moreau asked the Ruillé brothers to do was to empty themselves of any hope for total self government. They could aspire, of course, to principalships in grade schools, but they could never rise to the top slot in the Community—that position was reserved for a priest-director.

This was the situation in place when Urbain Monsimer arrived at Le Mans. Leadership takes time and training. Dujarié could offer neither to his recruits. As soon as they had had a few months of novitiate at Ruillé, they were whisked off into the grade schools. It was a catch-as-catch-can training that paralleled Dujarié's own experiences: in the horrors of the Revolution, education was a luxury item modified by the insurrectionists. Although Moreau was ready to make the novitiate base for the brothers more solid than it had been in Ruillé, he was not interested in using the brothers for positions of the highest authority. Certainly there were brothers on his local Council, but every colony he sent out to a foreign country was placed under the direction of a priest, in effect creating new cells based on the motherhouse model of priests-in-charge and brother workers.

The prime sacrifice to his model was Brother André Mottais who had served as novice master and director of the schools for fifteen years while the brothers were headquartered at Ruillé. With the move to Le Mans, André was gradually relieved of his responsibilities: Moreau sent him to Algeria (under the direction of Father Drouelle) to teach in wretched conditions. We should recognize that there is no evidence of any rancor in Moreau's treatment of André, no more so than antebellum Alabama whites had hatred for their slaves, but André's treatment rested on a firm belief in his own inadequacies as a leader, a belief held by both Moreau and André. After all, André was unable to keep the brothers afloat in Ruillé. No matter that Dujarié was ultimately the cause of the failure: André was a man in his prime who should have saved the Brothers of St. Joseph. That was the received opinion. He felt himself incapable, and he accepted his demotion at Le Mans.

The property to which Urbain Monsimer would have presented himself in the summer of 1840 was located in a Le Mans suburb called Sainte-Croix ("Holy Cross"). Its original church, founded by St. Bernard circa 600, was torn down in 1795 and the parishioners worshiped at Notre Dame de la Couture, within easy walking distance. The property Moreau used for the novitiate had been given to him in 1832 by Canon de Lisle: seven acres with a large house and a small caretaker's house. In the main house, a dining room and a study hall were created on the first floor, Everyone slept in two dormitories in the attic. The situation was not unlike what Dujarié's sisters had known at La Petite Providence at the beginning of the century and what the brothers had experienced at Father Dujarié's parish in the early 1820's where they shared, however, the accommodations with rats who often stole and hid the young men's brushes and combs during the night. The transplanted 1835 Community at Le Mans numbered ten brothers and nine novices, all housed at Sainte-Croix. Scattered in twenty-five parishes outside of Le Mans were fifty other brothers.[4] It was not an inauspicious beginning for a Community that would peak with over fifteen hundred brothers a century later.

What Urbain Monsimer found in the Le Mans novitiate was a tight regime quite different from that afforded recruits to the Brothers of St. Joseph a decade earlier. His academic preparation would have included classes in "arithmetic, grammar, geography, sacred and profane history, linear drawing, measuring, architecture, and singing, not to mention bookkeeping and a course of instructions on Christian doctrine and the religious life."[5] Such tutelage was geared to prepare him to teach the basics in country elementary schools where often a brother would be the only teacher or sometimes one of two brother teachers.

Whatever he did not learn in the novitiate, Urbain would have to learn on the job or in the summer months when schools were closed for two months. Urbain had in his novitiate year, however, some of the finest teachers that the Brothers of St. Joseph boasted.

Father Dujarié, good-hearted as he was, knew little about the principles of a vowed religious vocation. His was a practical goal: bring young men of virtue to Ruillé for a blitz introduction to the life style, during which time he could determine their suitability, and send them as quickly as possible out into the harvest. He relied on Brother André to guide the recruits in their daily studies and to supervise the young teachers out in the various parish schools. André was the lynch pin that kept the Community together in its darkest days, particularly after the Revolution of 1830 and in Dujarié's waning years when the old priest no longer had the energy to rally the troops. André, as primary director of four Brother directors of the Ruillé institute, suggested to Bishop Bouvier that Basil Moreau was the best choice to replace the ailing Dujarié.[6] Although Moreau's modern biographer is probably right in this regard, there is actually no evidence in any of André's 1834 or 1835 letters to Bouvier to substantiate the Cattas' claim. The private talks that André had with Moreau, according to André's letters, concerned André's idea of a three-fold community of brothers, priests, and lay men, an idea that André mulled over for six years before he broached it to either Moreau or Bouvier.[7] But be that as it may, it is immaterial to determine who first suggested to Bouvier that Moreau be Dujarié's successor because Moreau had been close to the brothers since 1832, and he was the obvious choice to take over direction of the Brothers of St. Joseph. André's private session with Moreau would have been a natural outgrowth of André's position as primary director and Dujarié's right hand man. The brother and the seminary professor undoubtedly discussed the latter's suitability for the position just prior to André's letter to Bouvier (November 14, 1834) in which he tells the bishop of his private discussion with Moreau about the three-fold community he envisioned. André, in fact, tells the bishop that Moreau himself advised André to tell the bishop of their conversation: "he directed me at once to explain the affair to your Eminence."[8] Since Moreau had recently organized a small band of auxiliary priests in Le Mans to preach retreats and help out in parishes, he would naturally be interested in amalgamating his priests with an extant group of brothers, among whom were some highly qualified veteran teachers. But nowhere does André tell the bishop that Moreau is the only man to replace Dujarié. This is the influential brother who would have a direct hand in forming little Urbain Monsimer.

Gatian arrived at Ste. Croix in August, 1839, at age thirteen and began his novitiate training on August 23, 1840, in a group of seventeen young men ranging in age from thirteen to thirty-four. The oldest, Brother Flavian (Jacques Leroy) was born in Clinchamp. He left the Community in 1845. The next oldest, Brother Alexandre (Victor-Jacques Tul), was eight years younger than Flavian. Born at Epineux le Séguin, he had come to the Le Mans Community in 1838 not knowing how to write. He left after four months of his novitiate training, but returned the following year and remained until he left again twenty-eight years later at age 54, in the same year (1869) that the motherhouse in Le Mans was sold to pay off debts and Father Moreau had to abandon many of the properties he had developed over the years, including the Solitude and the school he had established at the motherhouse.

Brother Lawrence (John Ménage) and Brother Pascal (Leonard-Aimé Desprez) were both twenty-five years old when they began their novitiate with Gatian, and both had a long and interesting life in Holy Cross. Lawrence was born in Brécé and arrived at Le Mans just one month before he began his novitiate. He took vows eleven months later and left the following month (August 8, 1841) for America with Gatian. A farmer and businessman, he was the financial manager of Notre Dame and was sorely missed when he died in 1873 at Notre Dame at age fifty-eight. Brother Pascal, born in Courtamer, was professed in 1846 and two years later went to Canada in the second group of missionaries sent to that country. He served as Master of Novices there, then entered the seminary in 1853 and was ordained the following year in Montreal. He left the Community in 1868 and died in 1882 at age sixty-seven while serving as chaplain to the Carmelite Sisters in Le Mans.

Brother François de Paul (Pierre Desgages) a twenty-two year old in the August novitiate class, was born in St. Brice. He had entered the Le Mans Community in August the year before but had left within three months of starting his novitiate. Returning in 1843, he took the name Brother Bartholomew, but he left again in 1846. One nineteen year old was in the group: Brother Ernest (Gabriel Désiré Fléchais), born in Marigné-Peûton. He left in 1851, returned three weeks later, only to leave again in 1854 at age thirty. Four eighteen year old men represent the largest age subgroup in Gatian's novitiate class. Brother Jean (Jean Baptist Hilaire Diard) was born in Château-Gontier. He lasted only a year and a half in the Community. Brother Gerasimus (Jean Cholot), born in Courgerie, lasted an even shorter period, leaving in February of 1841. Brother Felix (François Damourette), born in St. Denis de Gastines, remained about ten months. Brother Francis of Assisi (Jean René Lelièvre), born in Conlie, was dismissed in

1848. The sole seventeen-year-old, Brother Henri (Pierre Cornué), born in Bouère, left the month his novitiate started. He returned the following July, but left again within the month. Of the three sixteen-year-old men, Brother Thomas Aquinas (François-Henri Fleury), born in Coignières, lasted the longest before leaving in 1854. The other two, Brother Cyprian (Pascal Salmon), born in Méral, remained two years, and Brother Marie (Joseph Thureau), born in Douillet, stayed only two months.

The two youngsters of this class, Brother Anselm (Pierre Marie Joseph Caillot), aged fifteen, and Brother Gatian (Urbain Monsimer), aged 14, were assigned by Moreau as partners for the first colony to be sent to America. There will be much to say about Anselm later, but some facts are in order here. Anselm was the youngest of four children born to a weaver, Pierre Caillot, who had married Jacquine Chartier in Gennes on July 28, 1818. Perrine, the oldest child, was born in 1819. A boy, Constant, followed in 1822, and a girl, Felicity, in 1823.[9] Anselm (Pierre) was born March 19, 1825, and in Gennes attended the little school that the Brothers of St. Joseph ran. He would have enjoyed three years in the school, long enough time to be influenced sufficiently to want to devote his life to the teaching Community. The novelty of having a single lay brother in town, dedicated solely to the education of the town's youth, must have had a kind of fascinating magnetism for many of the boys at the school. He may have represented for them, aside from the devotional attraction, a way out of their sleepy little town. For boys who had only heard of the disturbing fever of big city revolutions that the previous generation would have encountered, a ticket to adventure showed its face every time the brother teacher entered the classroom at Gennes. Little Pierre Caillot would not be disappointed at the level of his future adventures: on the high seas by age sixteen, in a foreign land among "Indians" before he was seventeen, running a school for forty boys all by himself by age eighteen. Many of his classmates at Gennes, on the other hand, would never live beyond the department boundaries. Young Anselm (Pierre), beginning his novitiate on the same day as Gatian, would share with the intrepid young man from Chéméré-le-roi a similar missionary dream within one year's time, selected by the founder to be among the first seven Holy Cross men bound for America. It was an adventure guaranteed to warm the hearts of teenage boys.

In Gennes the Caillot family may have lived in a small house across the street from the church as that house seems to have the only windows that would open onto the street, windows that a weaver would have found helpful to his trade.[10] Gennes is not much bigger today than it was in Anselm's day. It is dominated by the village church which is in remarkably fine condition. The baptismal font at the rear of the church is carved from stone and stands on a black stone pedestal. Anselm would have been baptized in this font. Facing the front altar, one can still see today a wooden pulpit appended to the left wall, above the first ranks of pews. Two side altars flank the main altar, and above, carved on the arch, are the words "Mais priez mes enfants Dieu vous exaucera en peu de temps. Mon fils se laisse toucher." And above this inscription, quite near the rafters, is a statue of Our Lady of Proulx. A side chapel contains a recent statue of St. Therese, the Little Flower. A rugged statue of St. John the Baptist, very old, in another corner attests to earlier, stronger tastes in religious icons. The church, constructed of rough hewn field stones, seats about one hundred.

The only other member of this rather large novitiate class was Brother Emile (François Noury) who was born in Le Mans, but left the following May, perhaps daunted by the prospect of having to wait for five years until he would be old enough for vows. He did return to the Community in August of 1845, but he remained barely a month. Of the entire August, 1840, novitiate class, only Lawrence and Anselm died within the Community. Both of them were among the first six brothers that Moreau sent to the Indiana territories, and both died there, Lawrence in northern Indiana, Anselm tragically at age twenty in southern Indiana. Although low rates of perseverance like this one for Gatian's novitiate class may seem debilitating to a religious community, most communities (especially in earlier days when screening of recruits was sometimes perfunctory) recognize that one of their contributions to the church is affording youth an in-depth taste of religious life for some months or years. As a result of their sincere good will to experience a communal life style, these young people return to the world where they often become stalwart members of a parish, the richer for their having emptied themselves into a consecrated life style for some period of time. Their introduction to the rudiments of meditation enriches their prayer lives, and their brush with vowed poverty and celibacy makes them the stronger when they enter parish life, marry, and raise children. Some of the finest parish leaders are men and women who sampled a vowed religious life to determine whether or not it was suited to their talents. Were we to follow the fifteen members of Gatian's novitiate group, we would undoubtedly discover many of those who left Holy Cross went on to become contributing members in the parishes back home in the little French villages from which they had come with youthful hearts to Le Mans.

In addition to the seventeen men that formed Gatian's novitiate class of August, 1840, there were others that Gatian would have lived with during his year at Le Mans. Three men had begun their training the previous autumn, and the following autumn three others joined the house. Six more arrived in February, seven in March, and nine in June. Thus Gatian would have interacted with forty-four young men in the course of that one year. Of course, the demographics were constantly shifting as men came and left so that at any one time there were never more than twenty or so in residence. Some boys came and stayed only a few weeks or months. Thus two men were given the religious name "Mary" during that year: one who began the novitiate with Gatian in August but left in October, the other who arrived in September but did not assume the name "Mary" until he began his novitiate training the following February. The latter would join Gatian in the colony for America, eventually changing his name to Francis Xavier. He lived at Notre Dame until 1896, outlasting all the other members of that first missionary band, outliving Gatian by thirty-six years. It was common practice from the earliest years of the brothers to recycle the names given to novices. Thus the first Brother Mary to live with Gatian in the Community was actually the fifth to have been given the name, and the Brother Mary that Gatian lived with at Notre Dame was the sixth so named.

Gatian, in a letter dated ten years after his entrance at Ste. Croix, names Silvin-Auguste de Marseul as his first teacher. This priest was ordained in 1835, joined Moreau's auxiliary priests in 1836 but left six years later. He did return to Holy Cross in 1857 but stayed only until 1868. Gatian also took some classes from Brother Euloge (Antoine Boisard), a fellow novice who was thirty at the time and already a teacher. He went to Algeria in September, 1840, with the second colony, but he left Holy Cross in August, 1840. Gatian's math teacher was Brother Hilarion, who had come to Ste. Croix at age twenty, a few years before Gatian, and would die at age thirty-two in Algeria after teaching there for five years. Gatian does not mention having Brother André Mottais as a teacher, nor Brother Vincent, even though both of these religious veterans were living in Le Mans at the time. For his manual labor duties, the thirteen-year-old Gatian worked as a cook the first month of his arrival. He served as a subordinate prefect in the study hall under Brother Chrysostom and in the boarding students' dormitory under Brother Hilaire. He also prefected the grade school children's outdoor recreation and laid bricks for Brother John of the Cross.[11]

Young Brother Gatian soon impressed the men who formed him in the religious life. His devotion at prayer, his bright, quick mind, and his attentive adherence to rules made him stand out as a natural for the Brothers of St. Joseph. Moreover, when Moreau started to mull over candidates for an American foundation, Gatian would have been among his most proximate prizes. One summer before Urbain came to Le Mans, Célestin de la Hailandière, bishop of Vincennes, Indiana, had arrived at Sainte-Croix to beg for missionary brothers. Having already secured for the American frontier several Sisters of Providence from Ruillé, he would naturally have followed the trail from that little town to the new home of the brothers. Hailandière was a man zealous for his work on the frontier, but he ultimately proved himself totally incapable of handling his position: "his haughtiness, his savage sarcasm, his unreasonable demands upon and almost hysterical suspicion of those who dealt with him daily, persisted in all their vigor."[12] Yet his own deprivations were evident. When Mother Theodore Guerin first saw the "cathedral" in Vincennes in 1940, she was shocked:

> Our barn at Soulaines is better kept and more comfortable. On beholding such poverty I wept so bitterly that it was impossible for me to examine the church that day. The next day I looked at it more calmly. It is a brick building with large, uncurtained windows, the panes of which are nearly all broken. At the gable end there is a sort of unfinished steeple, resembling a large chimney in ruins. The interior corresponds perfectly to the exterior…The episcopal seat, an old red armchair which a peasant would not wish in his house: in fact, I never saw anything so poor as this church at Vincennes.[13]

One can understand some of Hailandière's sharpness with those who made demands on his charity when the man had not much cheer in his own physical surroundings.

Hailandière had been recruited for the Indiana territories by William Gabriel Bruté, first bishop of Vincennes. In June of 1836, both Hailandière and Maurice de St. Palais[14] shipped with Bruté out of Le Havre as part of his recruited entourage, a group of twenty priests and seminarians Bruté had successfully convinced to join him in his American diocese. As anti-Catholic sentiment swelled in some parts of the United States, the frontier became a safe haven for the newly persecuted. Father Joseph Kundek, who came to southern Indiana in 1838, wrote of the rich possibilities that the area offered Catholics:

> I believe that [Catholic] settlements are the most apt means to safeguard and to spread our holy religion in America, because in this manner the members of the same faith unite as it were into one family, live together, mutually share their religious sentiments and impressions, as one body attend the divine service, receive from their pastor all the comforts of religion as they desire, have the opportunity of having the necessary instructions imparted to their children in school, mutually support one another in commerce and occupations, and thus form a society that meets all their interests. Such colonies and settlements are, according to my conviction, the best means to protect the Catholic immigrants against the loss of their faith, to safeguard them against the

inducements and seductions of our adversaries, and to enable them to preserve incorrupt the sacred treasures of religion and to transmit it to their children.[15]

The diocese of Vincennes was formed in 1834, and although Bruté led the fledgling diocese for only five years, his visits to France resulted in bringing many strong clerics to Indiana, including Hailandière, Benjamin Petit, St. Palais, and Michael Shawe. The last was actually British but was a student at St. Sulpice when Bruté visited Paris.

When he was consecrated bishop, Bruté found the only priest officially under him at Christmas, 1834, was Simon Lalumiere, who had been raised in Vincennes and worked the missions in the adjacent Daviess County. Four other priests were on loan from other dioceses, including Stephen Badin and Louis Deseille at work in the northern fringes of the diocese. During his first month as bishop, a single communicant was ministered to in Vincennes.[16] But within six months, communions had jumped to sixty. Bruté's income for the first year was three hundred dollars, mostly in the form of grain and vegetables. When he visited the total diocese his first year on horseback, he found but 25,000 Catholics among 400,000 inhabitants. Four years later he guessed the number of Catholics had doubled.[17] The diocese included all of Indiana and a third of Illinois. In 1843 Chicago and all of Illinois was taken from the Vincennes diocese, and by 1850 Indiana Catholics numbered 50,000. In 1834 there were but two priests for the entire territory, but with aggressive recruiting in France, Bruté and his followers increased the number to twenty-two by 1838, thirty-five by 1849, and one hundred and twenty-seven by the time of Bishop St. Palais' death in 1877. Hailandière was recruiting in France when he learned of Bruté's death in 1839. Not only was Hailandière a convincing recruiter, he was also eloquent enough to bring back to America large sums of money.[18]

Hailandière, a lawyer by profession before he was ordained and emigrated to America, was a shrewd and manipulative prelate. His intense zeal in shaping up the Vincennes diocese, which covered an area equal to a quarter of France, led him to cajole and make promises he later finessed. He could, however, be apologetic when he knew it would get him somewhere. In a November 30, 1840, letter to Moreau he writes:

> I have just received (on my return from a long journey on horseback) the delightful letter which you wrote to me on October 2. It filled me with great pleasure; it renewed my hopes. I was in need of it, I assure you. For this foundation so longed for is one which holds within it a kind of blessing which in the future can have immense possibilities. I no longer thought that you wished

to found it for us, as you formerly did. Because of this misunderstanding it is possible that my last letter was written in a way that it offended you and that some expressions were not written as they should have been. If that is so, please accept my apologies and believe that my esteem and respect for you are ever the same and that I shall never forget the holy and hospitable manner in which you welcomed me.[19]

Here is a man anxious to get recruits, and he wants more of them than he originally envisioned:

For your foundation the most important thing is to have some solidly pious Brothers and as large a number of them as possible. The younger men will bemore useful for teaching as they will learn English more quickly. The older men are indispensable in order to maintain the religious spirit.[20]

Hailandière's suggestion that younger men could learn a new language faster than older men was already something Moreau was aware of: in the Algeria mission two young brothers were sent expressly to learn Arabic, and at Le Mans Gatian had already shown an aptitude for language. As Hailandière weaves his web, he is not above decorating the invitation with details that seem too good to be true, as indeed they proved to be:

My plan, unless I am better advised, is to place your Brothers about 25 miles from here and 5 miles from a little city where we have a church and a priest. This would be in the middle of the country and almost on the main highway. There we also have a church, a priest; most of the farmers in the neighborhood are Catholics. There would be perhaps some hope of recruiting from among them. Moreover, we have in that vicinity 160 acres of land which have been given for a school, and which, if they were cultivated could furnish a means of subsistence for the Brothers. They have enough buildings already there. Later on, better living quarters will be possible. A novice who speaks French well and already (a little) English will offer his dowry of 6700 francs. I am going to give this project all my energy in order to procure some other young people. One of those on whom I was counting positively refuses. At Vincennes the schoolhouse is built. I have also built two rooms for two Brothers. They will be, on arriving here, much better off than any of us were [on arrival]. Our progress this year has been great. At this time we have under construction several churches, seven of which are of brick and stone. This will certainly be the work of Providence; because my priests do not know how to pay either for what there is to be done or for half of what has been done. Nevertheless, we live in hope.[21]

The designated area included St. Peter's Church where the living quarters were anything but fit for living. When Mother Theodore Guerin saw the brothers a year after they had left St. Peter's for Notre Dame, she could not believe anyone could survive a winter in what the men lived in: her own sisters had deserted the place in 1840. The promising novice that Hailandière boasts of would turn out to be Charles Rother, a strange and impulsive man with creative but bizarre ideas for raising money. The only admission to be taken at face value in Hailandière's letter is the closing remark about lack of funds in the diocese. This segment of the letter should have been a danger signal to Moreau. Moreau, to his credit, was not hasty, however, in sending the brothers to America. Brother Vincent knew over a year before they embarked that he would be in the American colony. Brother André Mottais in a May, 1840, letter to Vincent tells us as much: "Having learned that you are destined to go to America."[22]

Moreau could promise Hailandière nothing at the time because of the commitment to Algeria, but within a year, after a second appeal from Hailandière, who was back at Vincennes, Moreau was ready to acquiesce. A few months before Gatian arrived at Le Mans, Moreau wrote Hailandière to tell him that the bishop would be sent two teachers. Then Hailandière wanted more. So Moreau increased the colony not only to three teachers, but added a farmer, a tailor, and a carpenter.[23] The oldest of the group was Vincent who, at forty-four, was the only one certified as a teacher. He was chosen because he could train the two novices (Gatian and Anselm) sent with the group, and he could train new recruits in Indiana. Bother Joachim (aged thirty-two) was a tailor, Edward Sorin (aged twenty-eight), the chaplain-superior, Brother Lawrence (aged twenty-six), a farmer, Brother Francis Xavier (aged twenty-one) a carpenter, Brother Anselm (aged sixteen), and Brother Gatian (aged fifteen). The two youngest were chosen for the mission because, of course, they had shown promise of learning English quickly. Indeed both did learn the language within two years, and Gatian developed an especially fine sense of English vocabulary and style.

It would be difficult to overestimate the significance that the eldest emigrant played in Gatian's religious development. Brother Vincent, patriarch of the Holy Cross Congregation in America, was born John Pieau on February 15, 1797, in Courbeveille, France. The town, located ten miles southwest of Laval in the province of Mayenne, is one of a number of small towns that contributed its young men to a resurgence of religious life after the atrocities of the French Revolution and rampant anti-clericalism had died down. Though volatile sentiments against church workers had never been as strong in the Laval area as they were in Paris, there was enough hostility even in the outlying provinces for clergy to hide during the notorious Reign of Terror. How the French Revolution affected the young boy named John Pieau in particular we have no way of knowing. He was born near the waning of its worst violence so his own schooling was not nearly as troubled as was that of Father Dujarié. Vincent was orphaned early. In 1822, at the age of 26 John Pieau travelled to Ruillé to join Dujarié's young band of brothers, organized a little over two years earlier. When he arrived, he would not have lived at the Grand Saint-Joseph because it would not be purchased until 1824. He would have lived in the rectory, sleeping in either the rat-infested attic with other brothers, or in the laundry room, barn, or stable where young men had to bunk because of the numbers arriving to join the group. Dujarié housed twenty-five to thirty recruits in the early years at any one time. How spacious the Grand Saint-Joseph must have seemed later to the brothers—it had a large refectory, classrooms, and ample sleeping quarters. The property also boasted a garden, a pond, and a small brook.

When John Pieau joined the brothers on October 9, 1822, the group numbered sixteen, including himself. Three of the four who joined in 1820 persevered; all six persevered from 1821, and the six who joined in 1822 before John Pieau arrived also persevered in the community. Few of them, of course, would have been on hand in the fall when John Pieau arrived since the school year would have begun already. We do not know either when Vincent would have gone out on his first teaching assignment. He began his novitiate training on August 17, 1823, and he was awarded his teaching diploma on November 2 of the same year, so he probably began teaching while he was still a novice. Religious rules were fluid at the time, and a young man's training was often expendable—to fill a need. At first the Brothers of Saint Joseph took no vows of poverty, chastity, and obedience. They made only a yearly "promise" of obedience to Dujarié. Thus without the canonical force of the evangelical counsels, it is a wonder that any members of the early group endured.

During the next seven years, Vincent rose to a position of respect and authority among the Brothers of Saint Joseph. During the tumultuous days of the 1830 Revolution, when Urbain Monsimer was but four years old, Vincent weathered with André and Dujarié the rocky economic times that threatened the existence of the frail community. During these years, after a decade of struggling for legal recognition of his little group of brothers, Dujarié faced harassment from local officials over his ability to hold religious property in his own name. By careful maneuvering in October of 1834, he ceded ownership of the motherhouse to Brother Vincent and Brother Baptiste (Jean Verger).[24] It is significant of the great faith that Dujarié had in Vincent that Vincent was chosen for this ruse, he and

Baptiste being styled on the document "two men of confidence...who agreed to dedicate themselves to the teaching of youth," as if Vincent had not already been so dedicated for a dozen years and as if Dujarié himself were not devoted to the same apostolate. Significant of the regard in which he was held in those early years, the following accolade was afforded Vincent in a letter to him by André Mottais: "I don't know anyone more capable than you to give authentic witness about what has happened since our beginning."[25] Vincent's position among the Brothers of Saint Joseph should be recognized for what it was: he is repeatedly named as one of the three "Brother Directors" resident at Ruillé, guiding the community as Dujarié's health worsened. His living at Ruillé (while most of the brothers were farmed out to pastors in small towns) indicates just how much Dujarié relied on Vincent's local presence. It was an earned respect that Vincent enjoyed throughout his religious life.

At the August retreat in 1835, held in Ruillé for the brothers, Brother André, along with Brother Vincent, Brother Leonard, and Father Dujarié, discussed with Moreau the details for transferring the superiorship. On the last day of the retreat, August 31, all the brothers gathered in the chapel at the Grand Saint-Joseph and waited. Dujarié laboriously struggled to reach the altar and address the bishop, formally asking Bouvier to entrust the brothers to Moreau's care. Brother Vincent must have been swept up in the emotion of the moment as he witnessed the man he had worked alongside for over a dozen years give up his role to a younger, more energetic priest. Within weeks, the novitiate would move to Le Mans, but Vincent would be left behind in Ruillé to continue running the boarding school at the Grand Saint-Joseph. The school dwindled to half a dozen students, so by August, 1836, the property was sold, and Vincent moved to Le Mans where he assumed direction of the new boarding school to open in November. Of the fifteen men who entered the Brothers of Saint Joseph previous to Vincent, only five were professed when the group came under the care of Basil Moreau. Some of the early brothers took years longer before they professed: Etienne Gauffre, the fourth man to answer Dujarié's original call, did not profess final vows until 1842, some twenty-two years after he joined the Brothers of St. Joseph. Brother Gatian himself had a checkered pattern of annually vowed commitments.

From 1823 until 1841, Brother Vincent taught in Ruillé and Le Mans, steadily building a reputation for being a highly effective educator, a reputation that stayed with him throughout his almost seventy years as a religious brother. We can surmise that he was content with the move of headquarters from Ruillé to Le Mans and that he was elated at growth under the firm direction of Basil

Moreau. Since the two men were almost the same age, Vincent two years older than Moreau, we can understand the warmth and respect the two shared for each other, evidenced on every page of the letters extant from Vincent to Moreau. Unfortunately we have no letters remaining from Moreau to Vincent. In fact, we have little correspondence at all sent to brothers by their superiors in the nineteenth century. Apparently it was considered of no consequence and destroyed by the brothers right after it was read or by superiors when worldly possessions were disposed of after death. History is the poorer for the loss. Whether the destruction was effected as a way of jettisoning unnecessary baggage for men who moved from location to location, often yearly, or whether the destruction was a result of some haste in disposing of the personal effects of the defunct, the letters are gone. Brothers were trained to live simply and save nothing they did not need for their apostolic work. Superiors like Moreau, on the other hand, had a sense of history and were rooted in one location, both factors that encouraged the retention of correspondence. Moreover, as administrators they may have needed a paper trail to prove motivation after the fact. Thus we have a rich lode of Vincent's letters written both to Moreau and Vincent's superior in Indiana, Edward Sorin, but none in the other direction. Likewise for Gatian: we have a mother lode of letters he wrote, but not a single letter written to him, except a few by parents of Notre Dame students concerning their sons' tuition.

One sad duty that Brother Vincent was called upon to share was to watch at the bedside of the dying Dujarié, who had been brought from Ruillé to Le Mans by Moreau so that the old priest could live out his final years among the brothers. As Dujarié lay dying on February 17, 1838, Moreau kept only three brothers in the room: Vincent, André, and Antonin.[26] They whispered encouragement to Dujarié and witnessed his final breaths a little past noon. For Vincent the death would have meant the loss of his first religious superior, the man who saw in Vincent promising virtue and the talents of a valuable educator.

When it came time to select a superior to guide Gatian and his companions to America, Moreau acted in the way he had promised to form his community: although Brother Vincent was almost a generation older than Sorin, Vincent was not entrusted by Moreau with the primary leadership position for the missionary group. That job was given to the twenty-eight year old Sorin. The young priest was talented, but his preeminence in the group of seven can be understood today only in the light of Moreau's concept of authority for the new Holy Cross Community. When Moreau was considering the offer from Dujarié to assume direction of his Brothers of St. Joseph, one of Moreau's stipulations, as we have seen, was that his new group of priests would be given the roles of religious superior over houses of brothers. There was reluctance on the part of Moreau to allow brothers, who as a group had proven to be less than cohesive in the religious life, to be settled in positions of authority, but Moreau's thinking was based in part on the pious fallacy that a calling to ordination is greater than a calling to vowed religious life. Thus Brother Vincent at forty-four, with twenty years of religious communal living behind him, was entrusted to the rule of a man with some three years experience in religious life. That Vincent accepted such an arrangement is testament to his supreme sense of humility, and, of course, Moreau's perception of leadership qualities in Sorin. Gatian, at the same time, accepted all with a fourteen year old's trust in adults, probably with a grain of salt.

Throughout his life Vincent never sought promotion or a position of authority, content to serve where he was needed in whatever capacity he was asked to work. A master teacher, he was not above kitchen tasks. At St. Peter's in Indiana he did laundry and baked bread which he pronounced "not bad" with his customary understatement in matters relating to his own talents. In the notes for the Council of Administration for Notre Dame, items for 1844 show that Brother Vincent was to "attend to sugar making."[27] What he used as a base for sugar is not indicated. Perhaps it was maple sap or sorghum. Vincent's duties over the years were multiple. Another council entry for 1844 indicates he was to care for the sick "in the new infirmary." In other entries he was to teach writing and catechism. In 1846 he was both steward and cook. In 1847 he was to go by train with Brother Stephen to solicit money for Notre Dame. In the same year he was Master of Studies and "overseer" (probably a prefect), Assistant Superior and "Singer," with no outline of his vocal duties. He clearly was a factotum who could be used to fill any vacancy that arose at Notre Dame. In this regard, Gatian learned from him how to wear many different hats in the Community.

The second oldest brother bound for America was Brother Joachim (William Michael André) who was born June 9, 1809, at St. Martin de Connée. A tailor by trade, he came to Le Mans on March 5, 1841, became a novice June 10 and was professed little over a month later on July 25. This was rather rapid religious formation. Even though the man was 32, he and Holy Cross deserved more time to look at each other before profession of vows. Less than a month later he was off to America. Obviously Moreau was impressed with the promise that this man held for the colony. Sadly, however, Joachim died on April 13, 1844, before many years passed in America:

> He was a professional tailor by trade. During the stay the Brothers made at St. Peter's, that is from October 1841 to February of 1843, he fulfilled the func-

tion of cook. But five or six months previous to their removal to Notre Dame du Lac, he was taken with consumption [tuberculosis]: no sooner had he arrived in this northern country than the symptoms of his fatal disease became more and more alarming. During his long illness, although born with a rather quick temper, he seemed constantly resigned to the will of God and greatly edified, not only the Community, but also the Catholics that visited him. Finally, after receiving the sacraments of the church, toward the evening of the 13th of April, 1844, in his 36th year, he breathed his soul without agony into the bosom of his Creator. His aspect after death was remarkably calm and free from all signs of pain or suffering.[28]

We never learn the quality of Joachim's cuisine: sometimes the shifting of skills is less than successful and in Joachim's case not only might the cook have been frustrated but the diners might have been less than complimentary, especially a diner prone to be outspoken like young Gatian. However, Joachim was a remarkable man in his own quiet way: it takes courage to emigrate under any circumstances, and with barely a few months' notice, he was nothing less than heroic in his sacrifice.

The third brother in the American colony, Brother Lawrence (John Ménage), was born March 12, 1815, at Brécé. Having come to Le Mans in July, 1840, he was professed as a religious July 25, 1841, a few weeks before the group shipped out from Le Havre. A farmer (like Gatian), Lawrence was also good at business and became Notre Dame's trustworthy manager. In 1850 Sorin sent him, however, with Gatian to look for gold in California. He returned to Notre Dame with little more than stories, and without two of the brothers sent along with him. He died at Notre Dame April 4, 1873, thirteen years after Urbain Monsimer's death, and was eulogized by Sorin in a circular letter dated April 5:

> Bro. Laurence carries with him the deep and unfeigned sentiments of esteem and respect, not alone of his entire Congregation, but of all with whom he came in contact, either as a Religious, or as Agent or Steward of the Institution. For more than thirty years spent here he was always, as everyone knows, foremost among those who sought honestly and earnestly to promote the interests of the Community; and if any one is to be named as having contributed more than others by earnest and persevering efforts of mind and body, to the development and prosperity of Notre Dame, if I did not do it here, the public voice would declare it, and name Bro. Laurence. No Religious in our family ever possessed and retained more constantly the confidence of his Superiors and of the Community at large.
>
> Uneducated and unpolished, and with all the appearance of a common man, he was undoubtedly possessed of an uncommon mind, of which he fre-

quently gave evidence in the weekly Councils of administration, and even in the General Chapters of the Congregation to which he was three times deputed, and where his voice was always listened to with marked attention.

Brother Laurence never separated in his mind the success of the Congregation from its strict adherence to the Rules. Hence his own regularity in attending all the exercises, unless duty prevented; and when I saw him last night die so quietly, at the very hour the Rule calls us all to rest, I could not help recognizing in the incident a special favor from our Blessed Mother, closing his last day on earth at the regular hour he had so many times closed his labors in obedience to God's holy will.

In the death of Brother Laurence we sustain a serious loss which none can realize better than myself, however much his memory may be held in gratitude and love among those who knew him best, or whom he assisted most by advice and example, or in pecuniary transactions. It was myself who brought him to the Community, thirty-three years ago; and although I have seen, more than many other men of my age, Religious of undoubted fidelity, of great zeal and devotedness, I can remember none whom I would place above our dear departed one on these various points.[29]

This encomium is remarkable for its sincere expressions of sorrow, but it is also remarkable for its hyperbole. As for Sorin's repeated insistence that he can "remember none whom I would place above our dear departed one" for fidelity, zeal and devotedness, one wonders what Brother Vincent must have felt in reading these lines, Brother Vincent who had given twenty more years to the works of the Community than had Lawrence. Surely Sorin can be somewhat excused for exaggerating the goodness of the deceased Lawrence because exaggeration is expected in eulogies, but hyperbole has its limits, and one of them is good taste. One gets the impression that Sorin is using the occasion to lecture his flock to knuckle under as Lawrence had: obedience was one of Lawrence's principal virtues. Gatian remarks in a letter that Lawrence always sided with Sorin in Council votes so Lawrence was a company man, and Sorin appreciated the support.

The fourth Brother to emigrate in 1841, Brother Marie (René Patoy), eventually changed his name to Brother Francis Xavier in September, 1848, seven years after emigration. Born July 27, 1820, at Clermont, he came to Le Mans in September 1840, became a novice in February of the following year, and was professed July 25, just weeks before leaving the country with the American colony. A master carpenter, he was also a good interior decorator.[30] For over fifty years at Notre Dame he would serve as the undertaker for both the university and the surrounding area. He lived longer than any of the other members of the original colony. When he died on November 12, 1896, a young novice who had arrived at Notre Dame only two days earlier was told to help dig Francis Xavier's grave: this was Brother Bernard Gervais who lived himself in Holy Cross sixty-seven years serving as superior of various houses, as a General Assistant, and as keeper of the very helpful General Matricule.

The first colony to America, like the first colony to Algeria, had two teenagers in tow, too young yet to be professed: Anselm and Gatian.[31] Moreau knew too, as in the Algerian colony, the need for any young brother to have comradeship. Thus, as Ignatius and Liguori could support each other in Algeria, Anselm and Gatian could in America. Once the decision had been made for Gatian, all he could do was inform his parents back in Cheméré-le-roi that their boy was off on a religious adventure. He may have visited them with the news, but it is more likely that he simply sent them a letter. They may have visited Le Mans to wish their boy well, but as it was harvest time, it is more likely that the Monsimers would have renewed their acceptance of God's will and thought about their son from leagues away. With the blessing of his parents, Gatian would have left in the boat from Le Havre knowing he might never see his family again: not only would the ocean voyage be precarious, but life on the American frontier would not be easy for a boy raised in the comforts of a closely knit farming family.

3

Arrival in America: Under Vincent's Eye

Once Gatian had been selected for the American settlement, it was only a matter of waiting for the journey to materialize. He was undoubtedly the envy of many of his novitiate classmates who were passed over in the selection process. Once the names of the seven colonists had been made public, the group of men would have started the bonding needed to sustain them on the longest journey any of them had ever made and that, indeed, several of them would ever make. Moreau, despairing of money from Bishop Hailandière to finance the voyage, turned to his lay associates of St. Joseph: a lottery brought in enough money to get the travellers north to their seaport, across the ocean, and then overland from New York City to Vincennes. Then an eighth member was added to the group by the Sisters of Providence who wanted to send a young protégée of their Mother Theodore Guerin to a new foundation just north of Vincennes: Sister St. Francis Xavier proved to be a fine travelling companion. She had for some time wanted to work in America, and the chance to travel with some of Dujarié's Brothers of St. Joseph presented her with an ideal opportunity, given the lack of her own sisters for the expedition. She affords us perspective on the trans-Atlantic voyage of the Holy Cross colony.

Sister St. Francis Xavier was born Irma le Fer de la Motte at Saint Servan in Brittany, April 15, 1816, the fourth of twelve children. Highly spirited, she loved audacious risks even at a young age. When her nurse told her not to spend so much time in front of a mirror lest the devil appear there, she spent hours one day gazing into the mirror waiting for Satan, much to the horror of her sister Pepa who begged her to stop. This taste for danger she probably inherited from her maternal grandfather, a Picardy captain loyal to the king and shot by the revolutionaries in 1793. His one child, Irma's mother, was raised by his widow after she had spent ten months in jail for having been married to a royalist. This woman, Madame de Ginguené, later lived at Tours-à-Chaux where she devoted herself to the poor who had been devastated by the Revolution's destruction of the ecclesiastical system of charitable institutions. Eventually settling at Saint Servan, this woman lived to see four Providence Sisters arrive to care for the poor. Irma's paternal grandmother had almost as sad a life as Irma's maternal grandmother. Born in Spain, she weathered the Reign of Terror in France while widowed with five young children. The revolutionaries stripped her farm, but she lived into old age without bitterness.

Irma's schooling was scant. What little she learned as a child she learned from an elderly woman who ran an informal school and from an English woman who lived in town. Hardships followed Irma and her family in 1830 when a new government took away the father's position because he refused to take the oath of allegiance. Irma assumed the tutelage of the younger children in the house, a task she took to with relish, although she proved to lack the gift of disciplining those who needed such attention. But the drudgery of her responsibilities was more than compensated for by the beauty of her surroundings. The family home sat on a hill overlooking the English Channel, and the surrounding countryside was full of rural charms for anyone who liked to walk.

As a teenager, Irma enjoyed the close friendship of a young girl named Angelina Payan. The two had as close an emotional bond as typifies young women drawn together by straitened circumstances. Although they visited daily, they kept up a vigorous correspondence, many of the fervent letters still extant. Unfortunately, Angelina contracted tuberculosis at age eighteen and was taken to Rennes to recuperate. She died six months later. It is not difficult to imagine the effect this experience would have had on the nineteen year old Irma. Two years later she was still pained by the loss and wrote with strong emotion about her dead friend. She took a turn away from the usual pursuits of young women her age: she had no interest in marriage and thought increasingly of devoting herself to educating children.

Beginning her Providence novitiate at Ruillé in 1839 with some trepidation because she feared the director Mother Marie Lecor (Dujarié's nemesis), she soon acclimated herself to both the grandeur of the motherhouse and the simplicity of the novitiate. She had intended to begin her novitiate in France and complete it in America under Mother Theodore Guerin, but her weakened health prompted Mother Marie to keep her out of the first Providence colony that left for American in July, 1840. When Irma told Mother Marie that she wanted to emigrate even if it meant she would be a martyr in America, Mother Marie replied, "And what shall I be? The executioner?"[1]

After her investiture with the Providence habit in December, 1840, Francis Xavier was sent to Brest since her superiors discouraged any thought of her going to America. Her letters continued to flow to her mother and sisters in St. Servan, and some of them are particularly insightful on matters political:

> The Lenten preacher treated of very lofty subjects...At times I seemed to hear Bossuet preaching his thoughts in the language of the nineteenth century. The speaker openly attacked the Fourierists, a sect which prevails in Brest and which is impregnated with the principles of Fourier. Abbé Cuzon, chaplain of the college, a very learned priest and somewhat like Abbé Cardonnet, has told us of these people. Let us pray, dear sister, that the Catholic faith may not be impaired in France.[2]

The facility with which Irma could handle political principles is rather impressive. After a further request from Bishop Hailandière specifically for Francis Xavier, the Sisters of Providence left the decision up to her. She went to Le Mans to confer with Bishop Bouvier, and with his encouragement she decided to emigrate. In a July 11, 1841, letter to her parents, she makes the first mention of the brothers bound for Vincennes:

> I cannot tell you exactly when Abbé Moreau's Brothers will leave Havre for New York. Be kind enough to write to Rennes, which is the center of deliberation. It is impossible for them to go before the 24th instant. They will inform me of the date from Le Mans.[3]

Later that month Francis Xavier took her first vows, and on August 7, 1841, she arrived at Le Havre to await embarkation.

When the eight set out from Le Havre on August 8, 1841, aboard the *Iowa*, five Sisters of the Sacred Heart also on board were delighted to have the ministry of a chaplain available. All travelled steerage, even Sorin who declined a cabin offered to him. The sea in the English Channel proved rough, requiring eight days to maneuver. Everyone got seasick quickly, except Vincent who took care of the others until he too fell under the sickness. Once on the open sea, they all recovered and enjoyed a privilege given them by the Episcopalian captain of going above their steerage quarters to a little room on the cabin deck where they assembled for religious exercises. The room was also used for the baptism of a two year old girl who was deathly ill. Her Protestant father gave in to the pleas of the sisters to have the girl christened, an odd decision since the child was probably already baptized. She died two days later and Sorin presided over her burial at sea, an event he narrates in his *Chronicles*.

After a month on board, Sister Francis Xavier wrote to her sister Cecile some details about the passage:

> Sea-sickness reduced me to the state of an infant in swaddling clothes; this is the unvarnished truth. I could not help myself in any way, and was cared for by the good Ladies of the Sacred Heart and our American negress, Rebecca...I preach English sermons to her; you can imagine how eloquent they are. I am taking English lessons from one of the passengers, Mr. Carls, who has a daughter of twenty-three on whom I am exercising my zeal...I have to limit my outward zeal...for a troop of actors and actresses make up the rest of the passengers, and as Madame Bathilde does not think it proper for us to associate with them, she does not allow me to give them little sermons.[4]

These are the comments of a witty and fearless young woman. In a letter to her younger brother Louis, also written on board, she gives details about the boat:

> Our packet is one hundred and fifty feet long...The doors of our rooms are of citron and mahogany, the locks of silver...You would see on board some beautiful birds that the passengers are taking with them; also a large cow, some sheep, pigs, ducks, chickens, and rabbits, which serve us for food. You would enjoy yourself climbing up the masts, but you would also see some little boys of your own age in the steerage, carrying water, cooking, and obeying their parents promptly.[5]

The details are precious, and it is not hard to imagine how life on the vessel would never be boring for such a high spirited young woman as Sister St. Francis Xavier. We can imagine that her youth and brisk intelligence found a match with Brother Gatian. The two could have had lively conversations about French politics and the new religious communities they had joined. On September 13 the Iowa pulled into New York harbor where Sorin kissed the ground. In his *Chronicles* he rhapsodizes on the act, his humility, and the wonderful sacrifices he had made coming to America.[6]

Sister Francis Xavier left her French companions at this point, and by October she faced her month long trip of nine hundred miles to St. Mary-of-the-Woods. On November 17, she settled into her new home in Indiana where she would work for fourteen years before her death there. This brave nun is often overlooked in the history of Holy Cross, but she became a very important figure as novice mistress in Indiana and Mother Theodore Guerin's right hand helper. She

was loyal to Mother Theodore even in the face of malice. While Mother Theodore was in France to talk to her superiors at Ruillé, Bishop Hailandière called
the six professed sisters at St. Mary-of-the-Woods into Mother Theodore's room
and told them to elect a new Superior General. All six votes went for Mother
Theodore. Irma died on January 31, 1856, a few months before Mother Theodore, and was replaced as novice mistress by her own sister Elvire (Sister Mary
Joseph). In 1907 the two sisters were reburied in the motherhouse crypt, one on
either side of Mother Theodore.

After staying in New York for three days with a family named Byerly, Brother
Gatian and the others began their trek west with three hundred dollars Hailandière had sent to them. The trip would take twenty-five days, almost as long as
the Atlantic passage. From Albany to Buffalo, they travelled via the Erie Canal,
and in Buffalo Brother Vincent went with Sorin to see Niagara Falls, which they
reached by train.[7] From Buffalo to Toledo the group travelled by steamboat.
Eventually they reached Fort Wayne and, two days later, Logansport, Indiana.
Unfortunately, as they passed by Terre Haute, they were unable to stop to visit
the Sisters of Providence from Ruillé. They finally arrived at Vincennes on October 8, the second Sunday of the month, at sunrise.

Vincennes, located almost equally distant from St. Louis to the West and Cincinnati to the east, sits on the Wabash River about 120 miles above that point
where that river joins the Ohio River. Although by 1900 it could boast a population of 12,000 people, when Gatian arrived in 1841, the town had but 3000.
Dating from a French settlement in 1702, the town went through various names
until its present name was chosen to honor Francis Morgan de Vincennes, a
Canadian officer who was captured by the Chickasaw Indians and burned at the
stake after he refused to stop his attention to those wounded in the 1836 Chickasaw skirmish.[8] Thus the naming of the town occurred barely five years before
Gatian and the other Holy Cross missionaries arrived. Traces of the great chief
Tecumseh had all but disappeared from the area by the time Holy Cross arrived.
The Shawnee leader, known as "The Prophet," had visited the Wabash area often
in his boyhood.[9] The See of Vincennes itself was erected only in 1834, and when
its first bishop died in June, 1839, he was succeeded by Célestin René Laurent
Guynemer de la Hailandière, a French aristocrat ill suited for running any diocese, much less one on the frontier. The first St. Francis Xavier Church, built in
1702 by Indian converts, was constructed of timbers secured by adobe.[10] It had
no windows. A replacement church was built in 1785, and a third (of brick) in
1830.

When Sorin saw Vincennes for the first time, he proclaimed it "another Jerusalem,"[11] but after twenty-five days of traveling from New York, anything would have seemed a heavenly city, as long as it afforded the weary a place to settle down and settle in. At 9 AM they went into the cathedral in time for the bishop's High Mass. After the little band said the *Te Deum* antiphonally, they went with the bishop to the seminary (where the bishop lived) for a meal, and all stayed there overnight. The next day the bishop saddled his own horse for Sorin and took him ten miles away to see a piece of property on the Wabash River. Although the tract was large (160 arpents), Sorin did not like the place. By nightfall they were back in Vincennes. The next day, Sorin rode east to see property at St. Peter's, his companion the priest who was leaving the parish. The farm and church being proposed as a settlement for the Holy Cross Brothers was near the town of Washington and was also comprised of 160 arpents, 60 of them under cultivation. Sorin liked St. Peter's, in spite of the fact that the buildings were old and in disrepair. Having been constructed for the Sisters of Nazareth, they were used only a year before the sisters left. It was, it turns out, Hailandière's preferred choice all along for the Holy Cross settlement.

The property had a little church, two log cabins (one a kitchen, the other a school), and a single cabin for the six brothers and the candidate Charles Rother they found waiting to join them. Sorin lived in a room off the church. The living quarters for the brothers must have been poor indeed as Mother Guerin later wrote of it, "Had I been there I should not have had the courage to allow them to pass the winter in such a house. I cannot conceive how the good Brothers could have lived there for a year."[12] The first log church was built at Black Oak Ridge, twenty-seven miles east of Vincennes, by Anthony Blanc soon after the first settlers arrived in 1816. A large log church was erected in 1823 and a frame one in 1827. The fourth church, made of brick, was the one that Gatian and his companions found when they arrived in 1841. Once the Community left for the north, the church came under the care of Father Ducondray. Then in 1847 Father Bartholomew Piers abandoned the location in favor of a site one half mile east of Black Oak Ridge, more convenient to the town of Montgomery.[13] There the fifth church was erected and still stands today.

On October 13 Gatian and the others moved out to St. Peter's, singing a second Te Deum in the chapel when they arrived. What Gatian's response was to the ramshackle accommodations we do not know, but we can suspect that his quick eye would have sized up the situation quickly and he may very well have offered some sharp opinions on the place. Sorin, at any rate, had no intention of fixing up the buildings to any great extent because he told Moreau that the group might be elsewhere by the following spring.

Within two days a religious decorum was put in place with a local council formed and obediences assigned. The group of seven colonists was enhanced by five young boys, former pupils of the St. Peter's pastor. Rounding out the settlement was a saintly old woman who was retained in order to teach Brother Joachim how to cook American dishes. Already waiting for the French brothers was the colorful thirty-three year old candidate named Charles Rother (mentioned earlier), a German immigrant to whom the bishop had formerly entrusted the school at St. Peter's. Thus while the Frenchmen were acclimating themselves to their new surroundings and struggling to learn English, the little school could go forward under Rother's direction. Rother, taking the religious name Brother Joseph, would subsequently have a curious career in Holy Cross. More of him later.

By November 3 another recruit arrived: James William Donoghue, the first of many Irishmen to join. Donoghue was born in New Orleans and was seventeen years old. With the name Brother Thomas, he lasted with the Community until 1852. Michael Disser arrived next, on December 6, and took the name Brother Francis. He was one year older than Donoghue and born in Alsace. He remained only five years. Francis Rees was the fourth recruit that year, arriving on December 8. Born in Germany, he was twenty-nine, took the name Brother Anthony, but remained only one year, not even making it to Notre Dame. The little Community at St. Peter's that fall and early winter numbered sixteen: six brothers, one priest, four candidates, and five young students. Outside of the students, Gatian was the youngest, hardly much older than the boys he would soon be teaching. He found himself in a multi-lingual environment: Brothers Francis and Anthony spoke only German, Brother Thomas only English. Fortunately, Brother Joseph spoke both German and English so he could serve as the chief interpreter.

Although the living quarters were Spartan, the men took great comfort in their chapel where quiet afforded them consolation in the midst of privation. The chapel boasted a beautiful lamp which hung from the ceiling and was kept burning night and day. Sorin noted the lamp was the second one in the entire diocese.[14] At first the only fuel the missionaries had at hand for the lamp was olive oil. As far as the matter of money, Gatian would have had little to do with the wranglings between Hailandière on the one hand, Sorin and Moreau on the other. With the lack of any written agreement between the bishop and Holy Cross in the two years that negotiations were underway to bring the brothers to America, agreements soon deteriorated into disagreements. Not only did the zealous Hailandière have a debilitating ego, he also lacked resources. He himself lived on the poverty level, as did his diocesan priests. Quite naturally he expected the Holy Cross religious to embrace frontier penury, and when they pressed him to reimburse their travel expenses from France, he balked. In the back of his mind he expected to wean the brothers from the French motherhouse and make them beholden only to him, as he was already trying to do with the Sisters of Providence.[15] But he little realized the stubborn tenacity in his fellow Frenchmen Sorin and Moreau. If Gatian were privy to the financial fracas going on around him, and there is little doubt that in so small a community Sorin could have kept finances secret, Gatian would not have let his own status as youngest member of the group prevent him from voicing strong opinions. What we have epistolary proof of five years later, a brash directness, did not blossom overnight. Such a talent is hard to disguise, even in one at a tenuous point in his religious career, dependent upon the good will of his religious superior to be admitted to vows and full membership in the order. In other words, if Moreau chose Gatian for the American adventure because of the boy's brightness, he would have had ample evidence of Gatian's razor sharp judgements before the boy left France. Indeed, Moreau often referred to his own "customary frankness," so he may very well have appreciated in the boy a characteristic of his own personality. There was, of course, a mature stability in Moreau's judgements that the adolescent Gatian never quite settled into, although he did show flashes of remarkable lucidity throughout his correspondence with Moreau and Sorin.

At any rate, the bottom line was that Moreau and Sorin wanted 300 francs per year for each brother. Sorin himself was outside of the stipend because a priest was not part of Hailandière's original vision for Holy Cross in America, but Sorin would have generated income on his own by exercising his sacerdotal ministry. Moreover, Sorin knew that Hailandière had received 4000 francs from the Council at Lyons for Missionary Efforts.[16] The bishop had given Sorin 1500 francs for the trip, but the sum quickly evaporated into needed repairs for the buildings at St. Peter's.

Immediately the bishop began to flex his muscles. He wanted Brother Vincent to come back to Vincennes to run the cathedral elementary school. Vincent had been sent to America by Moreau for the express purpose of training recruits, and thus he was needed at St. Peter's, but Hailandière insisted and Vincent obeyed. His separation from the community at St. Peter's accounts, however, for one blessing: the rich trove of letters he wrote thereafter are our primary resource for understanding the character of this gracious and generous man. His first letter was sent to Venerable Mother Theodore Guerin a few months after the Holy

Cross missionaries had arrived on their new continent. He thanks Mother Guerin for her gift of a carriage and two oxen, noting that the beasts are "very good natured."

> We have to thank you, my dear Sister, for your carriage and the two fine oxen. They have worked well recently, and the Brother farmer has looked for a board carriage at Washington with which he can test their strength a bit. What is better yet, they are very good natured. For all of that we thank you and offer you our wishes for a happy New Year and a big share of our prayers, as feeble as they are, on condition that you give us a share of yours and those in your house.[17]

He points out that he brought a package from Sister St. Bernard d'Arbentre back in France for the Terre Haute sisters and has already sent it to Terre Haute. With Brother Vincent in Vincennes was Brother Anselm, the second youngest of the group. They lived in the bishop's palace. Vincent's bedroom was next to the chapel, an arrangement much to his liking. Since Brother Vincent was the only experienced teacher among the Holy Cross missionaries, St. Peter's School was, in his absence, run by Brother Gatian who, at fifteen, though incredibly bright, was to be a thorn in Sorin's side over the coming years.

In Vincennes at the cathedral school, Brother Vincent would have been in daily contact with Bishop Hailandière, a transplanted French aristocrat ill suited for life in the American wilderness. Imperious by nature and arrogant to a fault, Hailandière was a curse to the missionaries and even to his own diocesan priests, who eventually complained so loudly about the bishop's ways that Hailandière was removed and lived out long years on the family estate back in his homeland, where he continued to veto throughout his life every request made to Rome by the Sisters of Providence in Terre Haute for ecclesiastical approval of their constitutions. Although Brother Vincent never once complains about the bishop, we have plenty of evidence from the diligent young Brother Anselm that the bishop was despicable. When the Holy Cross Community left St. Peter's in November, 1842, to settle north at Notre Dame, Brother Vincent was left behind in Vincennes with Brother Anselm. Then in February, 1843, when Brother Vincent left for Notre Dame, seventeen-year-old Brother Anselm was left alone in Vincennes to run the bishop's school and suffer degradations that he explains in pitiful letters to both Moreau and Sorin. The boy's health eventually degenerated, and after a brief period of recuperation at Notre Dame (where his heart remained), he was assigned alone to run St. Michael's school in Madison, Indiana, far from Notre Dame.

We can only imagine that Brother Vincent's ease with the Vincennes bishop had something to do with both patience and maturity: at forty-four Brother Vincent had seen enough of the world to know that some situations are best weathered by quiet acceptance of reality. The bishop too, no doubt, had more respect for a man his own age like Vincent than he had for a teenager like Anselm. We can only wonder what fireworks would have exploded had it been Brother Gatian rather than Brother Anselm left behind with the bishop in Vincennes. The volatile Gatian would never have suffered the continuous harassment that Anselm endured. Calamitous sparks would have flown between Gatian and Hailandière, a possibility that may very well have helped Sorin decide whom to take along with him on the first wave north to Notre Dame and whom to leave behind with the bishop.

But before the venture to Notre Dame, while most of the Community still remained at St. Peter's, Brother Vincent wrote many letters that give us a good idea of his life in Vincennes. In early March of 1842, he tells Sorin that he is happy at the prospect of travelling to St. Peter's to celebrate the feast of St. Joseph (March 19) with the community there. It is a major feast for the Josephites and Vincent's happiness is appreciable. He has suggested to the bishop that he travel by carriage "like a priest" and the bishop has agreed, evidence of the amity that must have existed between the prelate and the principal. But a week later in another letter to Sorin he announces crestfallen that the carriage plan has unravelled. He gives no reason why. We can guess the carriage was either broken (doubtful) or commandeered by the bishop (more likely), so Vincent writes, "God be praised I still have the legs of a fifteen year old."[18] He plans to walk the twenty-seven miles, leaving Vincennes at 7 AM on the day before the feast. (Brother Anselm would probably have walked with him.) Vincent adds that he has never before had so many children in one classroom: if they all showed up, he would have eighty, and every day there are new faces. By this point in his career, Vincent had taught for twenty years.

A month later Vincent writes a letter to Moreau in France, the first letter we have from Vincent to Moreau. It is a long letter written, of course, in French as Brother Vincent never learned English. He reports to Moreau that the novitiate at St. Peter's does not lack for recruits. His own school in Vincennes is a model of decorum: the townspeople are amazed that the children process two by two to school and to church, never fighting or swearing as they had before Brother Vincent and Brother Anselm assumed control of the school. We learn in this letter of the stock that the early missionaries put in rewards for the children: mention is often made of little medals and crosses given to the students for proper recitation of their lessons. The children, of course, are not perfect yet, and Vincent regrets their lack of silence during class. They could also be rambunctious. When one boy throws a rock at another and the latter takes revenge on the following day, Vincent expels them both from school, over the protests of both the bishop and his assistant vicar Father Michael Shawe.

At this time half of the three thousand citizens of Vincennes were Catholic. Since quite a few of the townspeople were French, Vincent did not lack for company or conversation. He relied on one of the bishop's seminarians to instruct the children in reading and arithmetic. Vincennes was fortunate to have a Catholic high school run by the Eudists. It enrolled twenty boarding students, a typical number for religious schools on the frontier. It was this school that eventually prompted the Holy Cross Community to decamp from St. Peter's where they had hoped to establish their own high school alongside the grade school they were already running. Bishop Hailandière feared that two such high schools so close together would lead to neither's success.

Brother Vincent had an evident zeal for converts and an overt disdain for Protestants. He notes in May, 1842, that "twelve unfortunate blacks were made Methodists" by triple immersion in the Wabash River.[19] In those days when each church guarded its own turf and rejoiced at defections from other churches, success was often counted in numbers, and any soul converted was another jewel in the crown of a missionary. Anxious to speed the work of the Holy Spirit, Vincent was a model of proselytizing for his time. His interest in recruiting, however, never took a nasty turn: we have the distinct impression that his intentions were sincere and his methods gentle. We value his letters rather for information on pioneer life:

> We all eat at Monsignor's table and as well as he does. There are ten students [seminarians] in all, of which only three are in theology, and the others in different courses. The high school of the Eudists is bigger. They have just under twenty boarders. Our cathedral is rather nice. It's the most beautiful I've seen in the United States. Only the Wabash River separates us from Illinois, formerly very barbarous and wild. Our house is situated in a vast plain. One quarter hour by road finds marshes on almost every side shaded by woods. Snakes, turtles of all kinds abound there. There's especially a kind of small beast they call wood ticks (resembling our bed bugs) which pierce the skin in such a way that if you pull them out, they sooner leave their head than let go, and after having pulled them out, there remains a swelling and itching which lasts three to four weeks. Mosquitos are also beginning to buzz loudly in our ears. They're enemies of another kind, more bothersome than the first.[20]

His capacity for hard work and self discipline would have endeared him to fron-
tiersmen who appreciated these qualities in a person. In this same month, Gatian
was sent to the farm of Charles Kennedy four miles southeast of St. Peter's to
open a school for twenty-five boys and girls. Six months after his arrival in America, this bright young brother at age fourteen was teaching children who did not
know a word of French. They must have found this energetic expatriate a fascinating curiosity.

The summer of 1842 found Brother Vincent back at St. Peter's. He describes
the celebration of Trinity Sunday with great care to Father Moreau in France.
Forty men from the church cut a path through the forest (with the permission of
a "pagan" who owns the land) and build an altar of repose in a clearing. The path
is decorated with arches of tree branches and white cloth. The procession itself is
segregated by gender and age: little boys first, followed by little girls, then the
women of the parish and finally the men, including Protestants and "pagans."
The brothers form a rear guard and provide some of the music. The rest of the
music is supplied by two choirs of ladies. It is an ecumenical procession with non-
Catholics happy to be involved. The ceremony in the clearing begins with a sermon two hours long, delivered by a neighboring missionary. The subject matter?
All the possible proofs for the Real Presence, a topic that Vincent notes "would
have bored our Catholics in Europe." Eight days later the group celebrates again
with a ceremony much like that of Trinity Sunday. The sermon, however, is only
an hour long.

Today we may not appreciate how rocky the relations between Protestants and
Catholics were in frontier days, although collaboration between religions was
often necessitated for the sake of children who needed a good school to attend.
The brothers educated all children who showed up at their classrooms. There
was, however, an unfortunate incident in Evansville, part of the Vincennes diocese at that time. The incident demonstrates the disastrous effects that could follow from intense and bitter bigotry and rivalry between frontier religions. Father
Romain Weinzaepfel was accused of raping a woman in his confessional. The
twenty-nine year old Alsatian priest said that a conspiracy was mounted against
him and, in fact, had gotten so far out of control that the conspirators wanted
him in a wooden prison so they could burn it down.[21] Catholics in Evansville hid
him and then helped him get to St. Peter's where he could find refuge with the
Holy Cross Community, away from vigilantes. Eventually Weinzaepfel was tried
by an Evansville court, but during the trial the enraged husband, who had
brought the charges, disrupted the trial, even stamping his feet in the courtroom
to intimidate the jury. His wife gave conflicting testimony, but the priest was

nevertheless found guilty and sentenced to two years of forced labor. The woman had an unsavory reputation, but the frontier jury rushed to appease the brutal husband.

Although Brother Vincent mentions the case in three letters, the most vivid account is given by Brother Mary Joseph writing from Madison:

> The witnesses were proved to have contradicted themselves seven times. The jury were asked if they had prejudged the case and would not answer. One was a Methodist preacher. Mr. Weinzloephen [sic] slept at Princeton jail that night on a bed of ropes with a buffalo skin. He was manacled to a man who was sentenced for stealing. The sheriff took them to the blacksmith's shop, riveted the manacles, and hurried them to the boat. The day was Sunday in Evansville. He had to pass through two rows of persons. Some laughed and mocked. Some pitied him. What surprised him most was that none of his congregation came to see him with the exception of a few Irishmen who shook hands with him. The sheriff then hired a stage. They came to a town line. The sheriff got out and staid about one half an hour. He told the people he had the Catholic priest so they came to insult him. On board the steamboat to Louisville the sheriff ordered him some coffee without milk or sugar and a piece of dry bread for breakfast. Soon after the passengers waited on the sheriff and begged he would allow them to come in the cabin. The sheriff consented, and the passengers treated him kindly and said he was innocent. All the money he had was $1.62. Mr. Delaune [priest] gave him some money, bought a bed for him, agreed with an Irishman to bring his dinner every day as the prison fare was coarse being bacon and cornbread. He seemed to be resigned to the will of God. He will not have time to say his office. The priests of Louisville will bring him the Holy Communion once a week.[22]

The case was sufficiently unnerving to frontier Catholics that Alerding devotes thirty-nine pages to it in his history of the Vincennes diocese. Although Alerding stresses the chief cause of the trial was the bad feelings of Protestants for Catholics, Gollar has shown that the case was fundamentally a grudge between the husband of the alleged victim and the priest.[23] The trial dragged on for almost two years (May, 1842 to March, 1844), and after a year in prison at Jeffersonville, Weinzaepfel was pardoned by the governor at the intervention of Sarah Polk, the wife of President James Polk. Earlier when Governor Whitcomb had visited Weinzaepfel in prison, he explained that he could not pardon the priest because the political fallout would prevent his own re-election.[24] Subsequently, Weinzaepfel wanted to join Holy Cross at Notre Dame, but Hailandière prevented the move. The priest then served in various parishes until he was sixty and almost blind, at which time he joined the Benedictines at St. Meinrad and died there in

1895. Gatian never mentions the priest in his correspondence, but he would have been aware of the case since he was at St. Peter's at the time of the accusation. He would, of course, have known Weinzaepfel personally when the priest was released from prison and went to Notre Dame.

By early October Brother Vincent and Brother Anselm returned to Vincennes for the opening of the school year. Their trip was undertaken in bad weather, and the pair arrived at the bishop's palace wet and exhausted. The bishop was less than gracious and told the missionaries their vacation had been too long. The brothers may have lengthened their stay at St. Peter's knowing that in the following month the Holy Cross Community would be starting its move north. The group was going to be split up for many months. Brother Gatian and Brother Francis Xavier would leave with Sorin and five novices for northern Indiana in November, 1842. Brother Lawrence and Brother Joachim would remain at St. Peter's with eight novices and a postulant. Brother Vincent and Brother Anselm would remain in Vincennes. Then in February all remaining in the south would travel to Notre Dame, except for Anselm who would be left to teach and suffer in Vincennes. For director of the brothers left at Black Oak Ridge, Sorin named Father Etienne Chartier, who had been a Holy Cross postulant for only a few weeks.

The relocation of the Holy Cross Community to northern Indiana was effected for several reasons, not the least of which was the desire to start a high school, a project not favored by the bishop because of the Eudists' school already running in Vincennes. There was also growing tension between the bishop and Sorin. When the bishop, therefore, offered them a tract of over 500 acres at the far fringe of his diocese, they jumped at the chance to go, site unseen. Only three of the original seven went north in November, 1842: Gatian, Francis Xavier the carpenter, and Sorin. They took five novices with them: Peter, Francis, Patrick, William, and Basil.[25] They left St. Peter's on November 16 at a terrible time of the year. The winter would prove to be one of the coldest on record. Traveling by ox cart west to Vincennes, then north along the Wabash River, they took two days just to reach Vincennes and another two days to reach Terre Haute. At Logansport they cut north, and on November 27 reached South Bend.

What awaited Gatian and the other seven was well worth the trip. In fact, it inspired Sorin to one of his moments of poetry:

> Everything was frozen over. Yet it all seemed so beautiful. The lake especially with its broad carpet of dazzling snow, quite naturally reminded us of the spotless purity of our august Lady whose name it bears…Though it was quite

cold, we went to the very end of the lake and, like children, came back fascinated with the marvelous beauties of our new home.[26]

What appeared as one lake under the snow was actually two lakes connected by a swamp, but the name Notre Dame du Lac ("Our Lady of the Lake") was already in place when Gatian and the group arrived so it stayed.[27] The only building on the property was a log cabin too dilapidated to spend the first night in so the colony stayed in town.[28] By early December the log cabin, forty feet by twenty-four feet, was fixed well enough to accommodate the eight men.

Meanwhile, back at St. Peter's, Brother Vincent waited for an opportunity to move the rest of the brothers north. When Father Chartier had a falling out with Hailandière and suddenly left the diocese, Vincent made his move quickly. He told the men to load all their belongings into a large wagon Brother Lawrence had constructed, and off they went under the guise that they could not live without a chaplain to minister to them. Their hostage, left behind in Vincennes to run the school all by himself, was Anselm who, at eighteen, was about to get all by himself the full brunt of Hailandière's nastiness. Why the kindly Vincent would leave Anselm so stranded is a mystery. It was something Sorin would have done in the wink of an eye, but not Vincent. At any rate, on a Monday morning (February 13, 1843), Vincent, Lawrence, and Joachim headed out into the ice and snow with six novices (Joseph, John, Thomas, Paul, Ignatius, Celestine) and two postulants (Samuel O'Connell, Peter Berel).[29]

We have excellent details of Brother Vincent's move that following February to Notre Dame, a journey of almost 250 miles, because a letter from Brother John (Frederick Steber) to Moreau chronicles the trip undertaken by the group of eleven.[30] The primary vehicle was drawn by four horses and contained beds, trunks and kitchen supplies, all to a weight of nearly three thousand pounds. Most of the men walked, along with eight oxen, because the cart could accommodate only three or four men at a time. They left St. Peter's on a sheet of ice since the rain of the previous day had frozen. Why they would undertake such a journey in mid-winter is incomprehensible to us today, but their wish to reunite with the group at Notre Dame was strong. The horses could barely maneuver the ice, and the oxen slid off the road. Heading west to pick up the Wabash River at Vincennes, near Washington they encountered a hill that posed a real problem. Nearing the top, the horses and cart slipped back down to the bottom. It was only with the help of local people that the hill was conquered. The fingers of the missionaries were numb with the cold, and frostbite was a real possibility. In Washington, the horses were reshod to ready them for future ice. Staying at the home of a man named Gallagher, the group was told that no one in the vicinity would consider such a move in the dead of winter, as if they needed to hear that news.

Undaunted, the men left the next morning. After seven miles they came to the west fork of the White River. Being ferried across on a flatboat, the oxen became restless, jumped into the rigid water and swam back to shore through the narrow channel which had been cut into the ice to accommodate the boat. Finally getting their cattle to the west bank, the missionaries moved on, the snow becoming deeper, eventually to a depth of five feet. We can only guess what must have been going through the minds of the three Frenchmen who two years before had known only the mild winters of France, but their American novices and postulants would have been better acquainted with Indiana winters and would have given them good advice for surviving the ordeal.

Every day in the late afternoon, Brother John would take one of the horses and ride ahead to find lodging for the night, generally with pioneers unfamiliar with Catholic missionaries. The brothers and their young recruits would sleep on the floor in front of the fireplace, sharing blankets, until 5:30 AM when they would get up, cook their own breakfast, and go on their way. During the daily trek when one or the other would feel hungry, he would ask Brother Vincent for some bread. Since everything was frozen with the cold, Vincent would take a loaf, put it on a tree trunk, hit it several times with an ax until chunks broke off. This was their only food while on the road for two weeks. No one apparently complained.

One of the simple joys that buoyed their spirits was their dog Azore who never flagged. When John would go ahead of the group to find a place for the night, Azore would go along, then run back to the other missionaries. After supper, he would go outside and sleep in the cart. John opines, "Many a time have I envied him his bed." The wish was probably as much a desire for Azore's good natured vitality as it was a desire for privacy.

Part of the journey would have been undertaken on the Wabash River, navigable as far north as Terre Haute for large boats and as far northeast as Logansport for small boats. We do not know how much of the trip was facilitated by riverboat, probably no more than half. As they neared South Bend, one of the wagon wheels broke beyond repair. Buying a large sled, the men put the wagon on it and moved forward, covering distances more easily than before because of the ice and snow carpeting the ground. They probably should have tried a sled long before they were forced to try it. Finally on February 27, 1843, they reached Notre Dame. Most were in good shape, but Lawrence had frostbitten toes, novices

Joseph and Paul frostbitten faces. Notre Dame to them was worth the suffering. In addition to being reunited with their St. Peter's companions, they were overwhelmed by the beauty of the place. Brother Vincent walked into the five hundred and twenty-four acres that Hailandière had purchased from the crusty old missionary Badin, who had himself acquired it in 1833 to start an orphanage.

The brothers thrived, and by 1844 they were officially incorporated by legal act giving the Brothers of St. Joseph "perpetual succession with full power and authority to contract and be contractable; to acquire, hold, enjoy and transfer any property real or personal in their corporate capacity."[31] The brothers began making bricks in 1843 from marl found near the lakes. The first building, the "Old College" which still stands today, was not made from this source, but all buildings thereafter until the 1880's were made from Notre Dame marl.[32] When Moreau visited the campus in 1857, he was shocked to see the brothers working in the marl beds and ordered the practice of so using brothers stopped, but it took Sorin ten years before he got around to following the order of his superior general.[33]

At Notre Dame Brother Vincent settled into an active routine. He was in charge of the novices, and he was, as the only certified teacher, in charge of teacher training. In addition, he may have taught courses in French to the students who were beginning to show up at the new high school. There were, of course, breaks in his routine. In April of 1844 he watched at the deathbed of Brother Joachim, the first of the French missionaries to die in America. Joachim, born William Michael André in 1809 at St. Martin de Connée (La Mayenne Province), was a tailor, but in the New World he was used as a cook. His final sickness lasted eighteen months, half of the time spent in his new land. When he died on April 13, he was buried on the island between the two lakes, where a cemetery in the form of a large triangle had been set out: one angle for the sisters, one for the brothers, and one for the priests. A *juxta crucem* scene was placed at the center of the triangle, and a small octagonal chapel would eventually be built nearby. A month after Joachim's death, Brother Paul, one of the first recruits from Black Oak Ridge, died at the age of twenty-eight.

In May, 1844, Brother Vincent set out for France in order to escort a third colony of missionaries to Indiana.[34] Vincent travelled to New York by way of Detroit and Buffalo, using a steamboat on Lake Erie. The steamboat trip for Vincent and his companion Brother Augustine (Jeremy O'Leary), who was heading to Le Mans in order to teach English at Sainte-Croix, cost five dollars for the pair, semi-private cabin and food included. The two-day boat ride took them three hundred miles to Buffalo. From Buffalo to Albany they travelled by canal, a three and a half day trip. Finally on June 6, after a two day stay in a town where Augustine had relatives, they arrived in New York City. They were booked on the *Duchess of Orleans* bound for France.

One month later, Vincent writes from France to Sorin, telling him that he has paid a visit to Sorin's elderly father.

> Your father, who was in bed, jumped up when he saw me. We chatted, but he stopped so that he'd get to morning Mass. Following that, we had lunch together at his place. I stayed there until 10 o'clock, and before leaving I received 20 francs from your brother (he's generous). Your father gave me 10 also, and the curé of La Brulcatte 5.[35]

Not on a pleasure junket, Vincent was under orders from Sorin to solicit money for Notre Dame, so he canvassed in Laval and various towns, including Ruillé. Apparently the trip was a success, and Vincent was able to meet scores of old friends. He had hopes to bring Moreau back to America for a visit, but the founder decided that a visit to a planned foundation in North Africa should come first. For new personnel, Vincent received for Notre Dame one priest (Alexis Granger who would prove to be very important to the colony), Brother Augustus, Brother Justin, and three Marianite sisters. Twenty-year-old Augustus (Arsene Poignant) would live to work over fifty years in America, dying in 1900. Justin (Louis Gautier), almost as old as Vincent was when Vincent first came to America, would die in 1870, a quarter century after his arrival at Notre Dame. Vincent left Augustine in Le Mans where, instead of teaching English, he had decided to study medicine, an interest that did not last since he returned to Notre Dame a year later to study for the priesthood. He did not persevere in that endeavor either and left the Community. The colony of seven were booked on the same boat Vincent had come on, the *Duchess of Orleans*. They arrived at Notre Dame a month later, on September 10.

Back at Notre Dame, Vincent was entrusted with his former duties, still very much needed as trainer of future teachers. Just as he had been used by Dujarié years before to visit schools administered by young brothers, so too was he sent to supervise the work of brothers in their little schools on the American frontier. The death of one of these young men must have touched him profoundly—the drowning of Anselm in Madison, Indiana, on July 12, 1845, at the age of twenty. The health of the young man, who had been left on his own in Vincennes when Sorin called everyone to Notre Dame in February of 1843, deteriorated from the stress he suffered under the bishop, and malaria threw him into a coma in August, 1844. Neglected in Vincennes, he was brought to Notre Dame to recuperate in the summer of 1844, whereupon Sorin sent him alone to run St. Michael's School in Madison. His story will be told in detail in the next chapter.

During the years 1845 to 1849, Brother Vincent remained at Notre Dame absorbed in his duties both to the Community recruits and to the high school students. One of his tasks was not much to his liking, but he undertook it with his customary obedience: appointed to be Sorin's spiritual monitor Vincent was required to evaluate the priest from time to time. How much of what Vincent told Sorin was appreciated we have no way of knowing, but it was to Sorin's credit that he even asked for the frank exposition of the state of his character as it was perceived by another. Vincent, of course, was a safe bet to be an honest and confidential monitor. In a remarkable letter written by Vincent at Notre Dame in 1847 to Sorin at the same location, Vincent itemizes half a dozen shortcomings he sees in his priest-superior.

> It was indeed necessary to make me speak up through obedience because it is so difficult and even dangerous to examine the actions of a superior who can have special motives which make him act, motives which can be known only to himself. I'll tell you then very simply things such as I see them for you to meditate on with the good God during your retreat.[36]

Sorin does not confide in his assistant (Father Granger), and he does not obey his nurses in times of sickness. He makes promises he does not keep, e.g., saying he will dine every Friday at the novitiate, and he overrides the authority of the high school administrators. He keeps the local chapter in the dark about important matters, and he does not give enough Sunday talks on the vows to the brothers. That Sorin kept the letter is testament to his good will. That he followed any of Vincent's advice is doubtful: Sorin was a law unto himself, basically zealous for the success of his fiefdom. An introspective man, he remained to his death absolute master of his own destiny, willing to listen but inclined to follow his own counsel. Yet he and Brother Vincent had a deep and genuine respect for each other that bolstered each other's fortitude during the sixty years they worked together, mostly side by side, in Holy Cross.

Notre Dame was a busy place in its first decade, and the influx of new recruits insured a steady growth. Gatian found his niche very early in the process, and his talents were used in more ways than one. However, among the chores parcelled out, Gatian kept his position as a teacher. In a letter to Moreau, Sorin lists the occupation of all the brothers, including such particulars as:

Justin: shoemaker, carrier of food to the sisters...

Claude: cows and dairy...

Ignatius: refectorian, shoe-shiner...

Cyprian: launderer and wood chopper for the sisters...

Jerome: barber for the high school...

Gatian: teacher of second year English, secretary, and doorman...

Charles Borromeo: regulator, lamp lighter, bed maker in the high school...

James: assistant gardener and wine maker.[37]

Although the list seems exhaustive (in the original letter), there were more tasks at the school than the brothers could take care of, and these were handled by the sisters whom Sorin continued to supervise at both Bertrand, Michigan, and Notre Dame.

Gatian was involved in a very busy schedule at Notre Dame.[38] The boys rose at 5:30, had prayers and Mass at 5:50. Breakfast followed at 7:30. At 8:15 they had a grammar class. A fifteen minute recreation period at 10:00 was followed by an hour of writing class and 45 minutes of reading class. Lunch at noon gave the boys a respite until 1:30 when they sat for orthography or dictation and two hours of arithmetic. A half hour break at 4:00 was followed by an hour and a half of history, geography, or bookkeeping. At 6:00 they had a spiritual conference. These were long days indeed, but Gatian thrived on work, even though he complained about his many tasks. He was a man who enjoyed position, and he demanded that those under him, brothers as well as students, work as hard as he did. Watching him, project after project, was the ever faithful Vincent, without whom Notre Dame could not have become the school it was gradually becoming and the haven of spiritual retreat that Vincent prized so highly. As the years passed, Gatian grew more and more important to Notre Dame. Brothers came and left around him, and some died, but he would persevere for a decade, a scourge to many and a wonder to himself.

4

Readiness to Answer: Brother Anselm in Indiana

When Gatian learned that he was chosen for the American colony, he would have been informed in one of two ways: either Moreau would have told him in a private interview that he was heading to Indiana, or Moreau would have made an announcement of all seven names at a gathering in the house. Perhaps the weekly chapter was the scene, or perhaps the end of the daily Mass. Whatever the method, the effect on the fourteen year old would have been tremendous. The tremors of the Algerian colony were, of course, still fresh in Community minds, and the prospect of an even greater enterprise would have swelled the most adamantine heart. Moreau's plans, as well as those of Hailandière, were at best amorphous, but as the youngest of the group, Gatian needed companionship for the long ocean trip and the uncertain future that waited for him in Indiana. So a suitable travelling companion, someone more sympathetic to the adolescent heart than any adult could be, was selected to help Gatian adjust to the New World. Someone was needed who could be counted on in times of homesickness or anxiety, elements that never totally desert even the stoutest heart, not even the heart of the feisty little Gatian. The travelling companion was Anselm, one year senior to Gatian in age, but not in community rank because they began their novitiate training on the same August day in 1840. Anselm, like Gatian, came from a farming region close to Le Mans, and although Anselm was not a farmer himself, he lived amid the pleasant farms of the area.

At the end of the eighteenth century, the Department of La Mayenne in France saw a radical transformation of its economic base: the linen industry, ruined by war and political turmoil, gradually gave way to agriculture, and farming as an occupation grew by leaps and bounds.[1] In 1815, only 48,000 hectares in La Mayenne were devoted to grain crops, but by 1862, 100,000 hectares were so used. Wheat was exported even to England. Livestock too began to develop as a commodity, and cattle production grew rapidly in the northwest corner of the department. In population La Mayenne grew from 352,486 in 1831 to 360,290 in 1841; France herself grew from 33,218,000 to 34, 911,000.[2] In this idyllic part of the country, near Urbain Monsimer's town of Saulges, nestles Gennes, where Pierre Caillot was born on the feast of St. Joseph, March 19, 1825. From this village, he went at the age of fourteen to follow a new life as a Brother of St. Joseph.[3] Since the Brothers were transferred from Jacques Dujarié to the guardianship of Basil Moreau in 1837, Pierre Caillot, like Urbain, would have been among the earliest religious to be shepherded by the new founder of Holy Cross.

We can only guess at Pierre's gradual transformation into Brother Anselm, the second man to bear that name in the Brothers of St. Joseph, but we know that he impressed Moreau enough to be chosen as one of the seven men for the first colony to be sent to America. Why would a sixteen year old novice, too young even for vows, be shipped to a foreign land? He and the even younger Brother Gatian had impressed Moreau not only with their aptitude for language, but with their energy. Indeed, their subsequent letters demonstrate an exuberance that would be cut short by early death for Anselm and would develop into brash epistolary attacks on Sorin by Gatian. Life in the New World would never be dull for either of these teenage boys.

Of the twenty letters extant by Brother Anselm, only six and a half are in English. The others are in French. All the letters are written to Edward Sorin at Notre Dame, except number 14 (addressed to Father Moreau in France) and number 19 (addressed to Brother Vincent). Two of the English letters (numbers 2 and 3) are dated as early as July, 1843, when the young man was but eighteen years old and had been in America less than two years. The English is remarkably good, but we should not be surprised: Moreau's trust in Anselm and his younger cohort Gatian extended beyond an aptitude for language to a hope that the two teens would do what the older brothers were either unable or disinclined to master. Anselm never became the polished writer that Gatian became, but he penned letters smoothly in two languages. Anselm's twenty letters represent almost fifty percent of the correspondence sent by brothers to Sorin between June of 1843 and July of 1845. It is not that Anselm was a particularly prolific letter-writer, but rather that he was one of the few men not stationed at Notre Dame in the early years. Letters to Sorin came in those two years mostly from two sources: Anselm and Brother Mary Joseph (Samuel O'Connell).[4] Anselm wrote first from Vincennes and then from Madison, Indiana; Mary Joseph first from Madison and then from Vincennes. The two men switched jobs sometime between August of

1844 (Anselm's last letter from Vincennes) and December (Mary Joseph's first letter from Vincennes).

Anselm's first letter is dated June 18, 1843, four months after Brothers Vincent, Lawrence and Joachim had abandoned the foundation at St. Peter's (Montgomery, Indiana) and travelled north with six novices and two postulants to join the rest of the Community at Notre Dame. Anselm, at age 18, was left alone in Vincennes as teacher and principal of the cathedral's grade school. He alludes to some troubles he has had in administering the school, particularly some matter involving Brother Celestine, who had apparently been sent from Notre Dame to help teach in Vincennes. We do not know exactly what the problem with Celestine was, but that this brother had a reputation as a trouble-maker is evident in the Notre Dame chapter books: there he is mentioned in the entry for the Particular Council of August 14, 1843: "After invoking the H.G. the Particular Council took into consideration Bro. Celestine's dismissal and resolved that sufficient money should be given him to defray his expenses to Logansport, unless he could be prudently induced to stay until the reception of his aunt's money."[5] Anselm's first letter is short and already tinged with the poignancy that colors most of his correspondence, a poignancy to be expected of a young man separated from all members of his Community, longing for support and camaraderie.

Anselm's second letter follows the first by one month and begins with anxious assurances that he has been faithful to his religious exercises:

> I was surprized [sic] by the bell and though I have had always a multitude of distractions in my exercises, I have never omitted any one, ex[cept] the particular examination, and that for punishing some boys after school and once the spiritual reading, knowing not w[hat] time it was.[6]

He is overworked: four or five new students have enrolled since Brother Vincent was reassigned to Notre Dame, and Anselm now also has responsibility for eight seminarians. He does not specify the nature of his duties to the seminarians, but it may have included prefecting in addition to after-hours tutoring. The Vicar General of the diocese, Father August Martin,[7] is instructing him in natural history, and Anselm, perhaps counting on Sorin's interest in the subject (Sorin did eventually spend money to build a museum at Notre Dame much to the chagrin of Brother Gatian), uses the moment to force Sorin to a decision about Anselm's vacation at Notre Dame: "I have six different kinds of tortoises and snakes and some insects, which I will bring to South Bend if you juge [sic] it proper...If you want the tortoises I will be obliged to buy some poison to stuff them up."[8] These ingenuous suggestions follow in the same rambling paragraph in which the young man asks his superior when he should take his vacation and if he has to travel north alone. He also writes that he has to know if he will be returning to Vincennes or not for the next school year so he can pack accordingly. School assignments were made late, of course, oftentimes saved for the end of the annual retreat at Notre Dame.

For a first letter in English by this teenager, the style is good but occasionally Frenchified. For example, an expression like "4 or 5 new scholars have come since the Brother's departure" makes use of the definite article where English would not. There are also several misspelled words (but nowhere near the number found in letters by his contemporary Brother Francis). Anselm writes another short letter in English to Sorin a week later; then he corresponds only in French until his final five letters to Sorin in 1845. The short letter written on July 16, 1843, also contains odd expressions ("I have changed of room") and misspellings. It may have been that Anselm tested his wings in writing English letters early on but abandoned the practice for the next year until he felt more comfortable with his new language. Sorin, I suspect, preferred getting letters in French, and Brother Vincent never mastered English, as he admits in one of his own letters.[9]

Within the third letter, there are hints that Anselm is dissatisfied with his living arrangements: he has been shuffled to a new bedroom so his old could be converted into a sacristy, and the new bedroom is so damp that every four or five days his shoes become moldy if he does not brush them. His books suffer the same fate. His new room had belonged to the bishop's valet, and although bigger than Anselm's previous room, it is clearly not to his liking. This room matter will continue to be an issue in Vincennes. Meanwhile, Gatian at Notre Dame was enjoying the relative luxury of a new brick building that the brothers had built at the edge of their lake. We have no letters from Gatian to Anselm, but Gatian must have written to his travelling companion in the first year of their separation, and news about the new living quarters would have been among the best of the news items. Anselm's anxiety in being separated from his community would have been heightened when he realized that his companions were masters of their own destinies while he was living under the thumb of an imperious bishop whom he abhorred and whom most people did not like.[10] To serve a tyrant is worsened by having to live with that tyrant.

By July 26, Anselm has still received no word from Sorin about the starting date for the retreat. The matter leads to a nasty exchange with Bishop Hailandière. Apparently irked by Sorin's suggestion in a letter to Anselm that Father Martin would preach the Notre Dame retreat, Hailandière snaps at Anselm, "The pastor of the parish could not leave his flock to go preach a retreat to Brothers 300 miles away."[11] The previous Monday Hailandière had told Anselm to make his retreat in Vincennes, an eventuality Anselm wanted no part of:

> I replied in a slightly angry tone that that didn't matter as long as I had a Brother to help me next year and that I certainly wouldn't be able to do everything all alone. To that he said that Sister did the free school well by herself but unfortunately I forgot to tell him that she didn't have to teach French.[12]

Leaving the bishop and going to Father Martin's house on the pretense of bringing him an insect, Anselm tells Martin what the bishop had just said, and Martin tells Anselm to complain to Sorin. Hailandière did not enjoy the loyalty of even his own clergy.[13] Several days later the bishop tells Anselm he may go to the retreat at Notre Dame provided he can find a horse to borrow. Anselm breaks down to Sorin:

> My Father, I can't fool you that in learning all this news, I had some resentment against you as well as the Community, because after wearing myself out teaching for a year and having the Community's interests in everything I did, it seemed to me that you'd not hold back six or seven dollars to let me enjoy the benefit of the retreat with my confreres.[14]

Anselm, quite lost in Vincennes and antagonized by the bishop (as almost everyone was), had some support from Father Martin, but nothing near what he needed as a fledgling in the Holy Cross family. Meanwhile at Notre Dame, Gatian was growing religiously in the way Moreau had always intended for Holy Cross novices: Gatian was under the supervision not only of Sorin, but more specifically under the novice master Brother Vincent, who also served to guide Gatian in the pedagogical principles necessary to become a credible teacher. There is no substitute for instant advice: if a vocabulary lesson does not go particularly well with the students on any one day, the novice teacher can ask advice of a master teacher that same afternoon or evening. Anselm enjoyed no such help (except from Martin) in Vincennes where he had to become his own critic at the young age of sixteen. No wonder the pressure mounted. Not only was he pedagogically on his own during the school day, he had to return each evening to live under the same roof with a surly bishop, his only company, aside from itinerant priests, in the episcopal residence.

The problems with Hailandière continue. In letter number 5 (October 26, 1843), Anselm writes that the bishop has accused him of stealing a kitchen brush, not teaching properly, and giving too much vacation time to the students. Anselm runs all three accusations into one sentence, and the effect on the reader is bewilderment: why would a bishop bedevil his own cheap labor-force in such a way? Anselm felt confused in the situation and said nothing to the bishop. One suspects the lad was traumatized by the tongue-lashing. He has other complaints he dare not raise to the bishop, e.g., the coldness of his stoveless bedroom and the fact that the room is so dark he cannot see to draw. He is exasperated: "I'm telling you definitely that if I don't have another room or at least a stove in my room, I will not stay here, because the vow of obedience that I made does not oblige me to kill myself, or to make myself sick to obey the bishop who has at least more than ten rooms standing empty."[15] Anselm mentions the sisters, and it is obvious he is envious of their living quarters, afforded them by the bishop, and their adequately furnished classrooms. His own classroom has been stripped clean of furniture, and all the books were mildewed when he arrived. Toads and caterpillars had taken over the classroom, and someone had turned the room into a temporary dormitory for girls. Moreover, at the beginning of the school year, most of the furniture from his bedroom was missing along with his mirror and brushes. The grievances grow: he has to chop his own wood, mend his own clothes, and "do all sorts of things that have nothing to do with my contract." In short, Anselm feels exploited, probably no worse than religious throughout the nineteenth century in America, but nonetheless the situation rankles this young man. He rages: "I beg you in the name of Mary to get me out of here soon." Then he relents, "But meanwhile your will be done." The above letter ends with a note that school has started: twenty students have shown up for his class. It is late October. It is easy to admire Anselm, even in the outbursts of anger we find in the letters. Sorin was his safety valve: by writing about his anger, Anselm defuses himself. At Notre Dame, when Gatian fulminated against Sorin, he could, of course, confront the priest to his face.

In letter #6, we learn that the lost mirror and brushes have turned up, but the bedroom is still cold. In this letter we have the first strong indication that Anselm is an artist: he boasts that he is adept at oriental painting and hints that with a few lessons he could be perfect. This talent Anselm will use to try to finagle his way out of hated Vincennes:

> As a good teacher of this kind of painting can't be found in America, I'm going to propose to Father Rector [Moreau] to return to spend a year in France to learn all of it, which is hard because it includes landscape and portraiture. I would learn at the same time linear and academic drawing, etc.[16]

Today we would call this process the method of discernment, but given the times and situation, it seems opportunism. Anselm continues:

> Don't believe, Father, that I wish to defrock. No, truthfully, but as Father Rector promised I could return sometime to France, I prefer to go there now while I am yet young because I would have much more facility in learning drawing, and I'd be more able to give service to the Community. Otherwise I'd prefer to go only after a long stay in this country—or not to go at all. I won't nag. (But you know the usefulness of drawing and painting in a college [secondary school]).[17]

He is, of course, using the threat of leaving the Congregation to force Sorin's hand for a move out of Vincennes. He appeals to authority (Moreau) above Sorin's head and suggests long term benefits to the Community for his leaving Vincennes. He demurs and insists he will not "nag," but then he attaches a coda: a trained art teacher would be very valuable at Notre Dame. Anselm is desperate and surely sly. We can imagine Sorin's reaction to this ruse, a young fox writing to an old fox, the master of ruse. Sorin, of course, was already beginning to have his hands full with the rebel that Gatian was becoming. The last thing he needed was another French teenager bedeviling him on site. An American novice he could summarily dismiss and send home, but a compatriot he would have a much more difficult time to get rid of, given not only the distance from the boy's home, but also the fact that Moreau had already approved the boy, guided his initial religious growth, and endorsed him for the American colony.

Anselm, however is soon upbeat in spite of troubles: the bishop has given Anselm a quilt and offered to move him to a new room (colder and darker!). Father Martin has given up on the bishop, or so he tells Anselm, and Brother John is causing scandal at St. Peter's and Washington by passing himself off as a philosopher and a former Brother. Although he lives in the bishop's house, Anselm has to walk to the seminary for his meals where only the bishop and his priests are allowed to eat at the bishop's table. Anselm would rather eat in the kitchen than walk to the seminary. His class is up to forty students including two black boys whom Anselm would like to dismiss. He gives no reason. As he mentions that the black students were placed in the school specifically by the bishop, it may be another show of the bishop's authority that upsets Anselm, or it could be that Anselm is simply prejudiced.[18] He ends the letter to Sorin asking if Moreau has said anything about Anselm's returning to France to study drawing for two years. In a letter we no longer have, Anselm himself apparently wrote to

Moreau requesting the change. The complaints in the extant letter are obviously mitigated by the hope Anselm has for a brighter future.

Two months later, Anselm is in despair: Father Martin, his trusted support, has turned against him. Anselm calls him "my greatest enemy" and outlines his grievances against the priest:

1.   No longer coming to visit my class.

2.   No longer speaking to me.

3.   Refusing to ask for anything from the bishop for me...

4.   Depriving me sometimes of my meals, etc., etc., etc. because, as I told you in my last letter, he told me that when I'd arrive at the dining room after the others, I'd have nothing to eat, and that I could go eat wherever I wanted, that I'd have no privilege here. On that point, having told him that I had rules to follow, he replied that that meant nothing to him, but that it was necessary to follow the rule he gave me, and if I weren't happy, I could go elsewhere.[19]

It is no wonder that Anselm is being given the silent treatment if we remember how he had used Martin as a go-between previously, Anselm jockeying with the bishop for a position in the house pecking-order. He is an outsider and now feels total devastation, a state of isolation and final degradation for bucking authority. Either Martin tired of the complaints or he saw his own bread was buttered by the bishop, possibly a little of both. In any case, Martin could fall back on a local clerical support system that Anselm was denied. Having been told in a letter from Sorin that Martin still likes Anselm, the young brother is unable to accept the fact and doubts he will be able to approach Martin. The friendship has soured that badly. Anselm uses the situation to beg a new assignment:

Reverend Father, once more, please call me away from here for my own good, because I'll perhaps lose my vocation here. I don't doubt but that Mr. Martin seeks to prejudice you against me, but, if you still have confidence in me, be assured that I will do all in my power to remove the bad opinion they have about the Brothers.[20]

He does not specify at this point in the letter what bad opinion "they" have against the brothers: he will save that salvo for the finale of the letter. But first he has one further atrocity to report: Martin is starving him. Apparently there is a rule about being late for meals that may or may not have applied to all members at the seminary. On several occasions, Anselm has no food all day long because, he insists, he could not hear the meal bell and his clock is irregular: "How can you expect me to like Mr. Martin who is the cause of all that?" Earlier in the letter Anselm complains that Martin publicly humiliates him when he shows up late for a meal by demanding to know why he is late. Martin has apparently labelled Anselm "proud" in a letter to Sorin that Anselm here mentions. In closing his letter, Anselm remarks that a rumor is circulating that the sisters and brothers sleep in the same dormitory. He does not name the clergyman who repeated it to him, but it was probably Martin since the letter circles around Martin from beginning to end. The sisters and brothers in question are undoubtedly those at Notre Dame, not in Vincennes, because Anselm lives in the bishop's house. If there were such a rumor, it is a nasty instance of ecclesiastical gossip, but whether there was such a rumor or not, Anselm uses the very idea of a rumor as another wedge in his argument to leave the den of lions he lives among. In a state of persecution, the mind grasps at anything for relief.

Two months later, Anselm is subdued. He seems formal to Sorin as he writes in an April, 1844, letter that he will attempt being kind to Father Martin. There is no allusion to the meal problem, but now it appears that he has been barred from recreating with the seminarians. Although he notes he was previously apt to join the seminarians only rarely, sometimes weeks passing between visits, he is now forbidden their company entirely. The noose tightens. Anselm suffers in April with an unsettling cough which lingers because, he notes, the meals at the seminary have not been very nourishing since Martin became superior. Anselm looks forward to the summer retreat at Notre Dame and goes over his options for travelling north with Brother Mary Joseph, via horse or cart. He makes no mention of a new assignment. As if a letter of remonstrance from Sorin, which we presume Anselm had received, were not enough, we learn in another letter (#11) that Moreau had written Anselm a letter (received May 23) which pained the young religious. Sorin no doubt had told Moreau of Anselm's difficulties with the Vincennes clergy, and although Moreau is in favor of Anselm's return to France (Anselm quotes him to that effect), Moreau defers to Sorin's judgement in the matter. Would that Anselm had saved the letter. His own letter to Moreau in February does not remain either, but if his sentiments to Moreau were as desperate as those we have seen to Sorin, it is not difficult to imagine Moreau's being touched by the situation, more than Sorin apparently was. Sorin, of course, knew Anselm better than Moreau for the boy had been under Moreau's care at Le Mans for only one year before the emigration of the first colony to America. Anselm speaks of his bargaining with Moreau to teach English at Ste. Croix for a few years in exchange for the chance to study art under Brother Hilarion. He again suggests to Sorin that Sorin needs an art teacher at Notre Dame, and he is just the man for the job:

> Since I've been here, I've sold almost all the flowers that I did, and the men and women who bought them have framed them as masterpieces. Although I've had only a single painting lesson, which Brother Vincent gave me, I have gained a reputation as a painter here.[21]

In this letter we have the first mention of Anselm's new friend Tourneux who is helping Anselm find a horse to ride up to the retreat at Notre Dame.

In July, Anselm chides Sorin for not letting him know of Brother Vincent's trip to France since Anselm wanted to send letters along. He asks Sorin to get art supplies for him from France as his are depleted. He continues to speak highly of his own artistic talents. He is happy the year is almost over, and his one regret is that he may be sent back to Vincennes after the retreat. By August, Anselm is sick with a debilitating fever. He had left the classroom at 10:30 on a Wednesday morning, unable to continue teaching, instructing the boys that school would resume the following day. It did not. No one in the house bothers to look in on him as the days pass. Only Tourneux visits him:

> Father, I can no longer continue the subject. I'm too weak to tell you more. What I can tell you in truth is that they don't take as much care of me here as a human being would of a sick dog. I can't stop crying in telling you this, my well loved Father, but it's the truth. I take God as witness: during the two and a half days I was so sick, no one came to ask "Do you want anything" except Tourneux who came three times after work, etc.[22]

It is strange that none of the bishop's staff take an interest in the young man, especially as Anselm is running the boys' school singlehandedly, but we must believe Anselm. It is interesting that he makes no case for a new assignment, but the sickness undoubtedly cleared his head of any thought of manipulation. We can only wonder how Gatian would have reacted if it were he instead of Anselm left behind in Vincennes. No sickness would keep Gatian from speaking his mind, and if local clergy were to make his life difficult, Gatian would have given back as much as he got: he was not one to suffer fools gladly. Hailandière and Martin would probably have met their match in Gatian. Perhaps Sorin knew that sacrificing Anselm to the Vincennes wolves would save the community any headaches that Gatian would have precipitated in locking horns with the bishop or his vicar.

We have a gap of five months in the Anselm correspondence until he does write again on January 14, 1845, and the letter is sent from Madison, not Vincennes, to Father Moreau in France. In the letter we learn Anselm had been dangerously ill for two months, during which time Sorin came to hear the young man's confession. We presume Sorin travelled to Vincennes although the letter is not clear on this point: Anselm's previous illness may have abated enough for him to make the trip north to Notre Dame. At any rate, Anselm was in a coma or near-coma: he could not "hear or speak or see." When Sorin asks Anselm if he knew that he had made his confession the night before, Anselm says "No." Sorin tells him he must make a deathbed confession, and Anselm does so that evening. The exercise revives him. On November 17, he leaves Notre Dame for his new assignment in Madison, changing places with Brother Mary Joseph who is sent to Vincennes. It seems unconscionable that Sorin would send Anselm off on his own again to run a school hundreds of miles from the Community when the young brother had recently been deathly ill. For Sorin, however, obligations to mission often superseded concern for individuals. Again Gatian is torn away from his young French comrade. We can only imagine how he must have felt seeing Anselm broken down by solo missionary work. The two boys must have had some heartening talks and no doubt gentle Brother Vincent helped soothe the distraught Anselm.

Fortunately the situation in Madison was salubrious for Anselm: the pastor, Father Delaune, was kind, and Anselm was across the State of Indiana from Hailandière.[23] The work, of course, was heavy. Anselm was the only teacher for sixty boys who were at all levels of education. But he thrived. His schoolroom still exists, the basement of St. Michael's Church. It is long and well lit by windows running the length of the west wall. He had a small room off the east wall that served as his bedroom, but he probably took his meals with Father Delaune across the street in the rectory (now a private home). He loved the children. He took up painting pictures of flowers which he sold to local people. With six thousand inhabitants, Madison was not a small town, boasting eight elementary schools and two high schools. Two of the elementary schools were Catholic. St. Michael's was the only Catholic Church, but there were twelve Protestant churches in town. Anselm did not lack for pupils, both Catholic and Protestant. In spite of the overwhelming work, Anselm makes no repetition of his desire to study in France. One can sense his relief to be away from Vincennes. Who would not be? Hailandière was the poorest excuse for a bishop and administrator the territory would ever see, and he terrorized the local church, including Mother The-odore Guerin whom he locked in the episcopal residence for several days in an attempt to get the deed to St. Mary-of-the-Woods. After his resignation in 1847, he returned to France, where he lived comfortably another thirty-five years, not dying until 1882.[24]

Anselm eventually becomes impatient with his situation. He wants Sorin to direct Mary Joseph to ship to Madison all the things that Anselm had left behind in Vincennes. In leaving Madison, Mary Joseph had left not so much as a prayer book for Anselm, but in spite of the hardships of working without supplies, Anselm reports he is "delighted" to be where he is. His exuberance continues. He comments on the town, remarks that he has been to Cincinnati on St. Joseph's Day to get the holy oils and meet the bishop there. Then he asks Sorin about reports he has received from Vincennes that Father Martin is spreading slander about him:

> He charged me, if I rightly understood you, to have had bad intercourse with a woman but that as falsely as 2 and 2 are 10. Indeed I don't know how a priest like Mr. Martin who pretends to be good can fabricate such stories. I would have justified myself sooner, but before, I wanted to know if it were true that some designing men had started stories or *lies* on me in that place.[25]

This segment of Anselm's letter is problematic. The manuscript does say "bad intercourse," although the eye might read "bad" as "had." The latter reading, however, makes no sense ("to have had had intercourse"), and Anselm would not have been sloppy in so important a segment of the letter, especially as he is writ-ing in English. One may wonder how "bad intercourse" differs from "good inter-course" or any kind of intercourse for a celibate religious. It is probably not an attempt to discriminate between fornication and adultery as Anselm would have little reason to discriminate the two. He probably means that he was accused of "evil," possibly only talking with a woman ("communication" being another nineteenth century meaning for "intercourse"). The matter never comes up again, nor does the name of his nemesis Martin. We have no reason to believe that Anselm would have had an active sexual life in Vincennes. If he had, Sorin would have recalled him to Notre Dame. A wakening sexual drive, of course, in the twenty year old young man would not be out of the question. Like Gatian, Anselm had been sequestered from women for six years, but his sexual matura-tion, unlike Gatian's, would be taking place in isolation from the Community and the helpful advice of his mentor Brother Vincent. Gatian himself would head into some rough sexual waters at Notre Dame, but Anselm, from all we can tell, navigated his own sexual voyage successfully on his own in Madison.

In April, Anselm asks Sorin about a trunk that he is still waiting for and notes that the fever that laid him low the previous year returns now and again. Anselm's disease was probably malaria.[26] This time the fever has lasted six days in spite of his daily medications. He already is making plans, however, to travel north for the summer retreat. By mid-June his supplies have finally arrived, but his fever has returned and has lasted three weeks. He makes further plans for the retreat. On the same date that he writes to Sorin, he writes to Brother Vincent, rather curtly, chiding his mentor for items missing in the received package.

Anselm's final letter is dated July 10, 1845, two days before he drowned in the Ohio River. It is a letter full of excitement about the coming retreat at Notre Dame. Gone are the complaints about living conditions or local people. He is so totally happy in Madison that he wants to know what date he can tell the pastor Father Delaune to expect his return. He brags a bit about his successes:

> I had a great dinner here on the 4th. More than 100 children were admitted to it and behaved very well. The most respectable ladies of Madison helped me to serve at table, and before the dinner sent me pies, cakes, and crackers of every kind. They appeared to take a great interest in it. I dare say, Dear Father, that you had not such a dinner at the Lake. After the dinner we marched 2 by 2 through different streets of the city. Three girls of about 16 or 17 years of age carried the banner which I had made the night before, and which though made in hurry, was, I have been told by several, finer than any of those the other schools had.[27]

The obvious affection he felt for the parents and students is reflected in their cooperation at the dinner. That affection would be repeated, sadly enough, a few days later when his body was recovered from the river. Protestants and Catholics alike took to this vibrant young man who died far from the Community he had joined only five years before. The details of his death we learn from a touching letter that Father Delaune sent to Father Moreau. It bears reprinting in full because its heartfelt sentiments could never be captured in summary or paraphrase:

> I have sad news for you. Sudden death has taken Brother Anselm away from us. He came to see me Saturday afternoon, July 12, to tell me he was going swimming. After hesitating a bit, I agreed to accompany him. He went into the water about seven or eight hundred feet away from me, in a place which did not seem the least bit dangerous. He went out more than five hundred feet

without finding water deep enough for swimming. I was in water about three or four feet deep, a little distance off the bank. All of a sudden, while he was swimming, I noticed an expression of suffering on his face. He went down, but I thought he was doing it on purpose. He came up, then went down again, while uttering a cry for help. What a moment for me! I was more than three hundred feet away from him and did not know how to swim. We were two miles from the city, with no houses nearby. He came up again and then sank. A moment later he lifted his arms and I saw him no more.

All aghast, I hastened to give him absolution. He had probably received it that morning for, as usual, he had gone to confession, and he went to Communion at least every Sunday. I ran to a cabin. A child told me that there was an old man not far away. I ran to him and brought him with me and pointed out from afar the place where the Brother disappeared. "He is lost for good," he told me. "Right there is a drop-off at least twenty feet deep, and the current all around is very swift. Anything I could do would be useless." I went home, got some good swimmers together, and procured boats and nets.

All our efforts proved useless. It was ten o'clock in the evening before he was found, five hours after he had drowned. An inquest was held by the civil authorities, and then we brought him back to the church at one-thirty yesterday morning. He was laid out in the basement chapel. Some of the Irish settlers watched beside the coffin until daybreak. I clothed him in his religious habit and he remained exposed in the Chapel until yesterday afternoon at four. Everyone was dismayed by the event. Thank God for having borne me up throughout this trial and its accompanying fatigue. Sleepless, and almost without having tasted food, broken-hearted and yet forced to stifle my grief in order to look after all the details, I suffered more yesterday than I ever thought I could.

At four in the afternoon we brought him to the church. The coffin was uncovered, and the calmness of his features made him look as though he were only asleep. Protestants and Catholics alike gathered to the number of more than a thousand. The choir sang the Vespers of the Dead. With painful effort I preached on Chapter Four of the Book of Wisdom, beginning with verse seven. ["But the just man, if he be overtaken by death, shall be in rest. For venerable old age is not that of long time, nor counted by the number of years...He was taken away lest wickedness should alter his understanding, or deceit beguile his soul."]

I had the thirteenth verse written in English on a black banner: "Being made perfect in a short space, he fulfilled a long time." After the *Libera*, the children from his school kissed his forehead; then the coffin was closed and covered with the funeral drape. The two schools led the funeral procession with the banner and the cross. The hearse followed, and then the people, two by two. I marched between the school children and the carriages. We crossed the city to the cemetery, which is a mile from here.[28]

There are curious points in this narrative. First of all, why were the two swimming so far from town?[29] Secondly, why would Delaune let Anselm swim out so far into the river? If Delaune, who had lived in Madison since August, 1842, did not know the treachery of the river in this particular spot, he should have exercised more caution with his companion. Delaune is silent on this point.

If Sorin wrote a special letter to Moreau announcing Anselm's death, the letter no longer exists. It would be interesting to know Sorin's immediate reaction to the loss of this promising young man and one of Sorin's bread winners. He did write to Moreau about the death in some context because in a subsequent circular letter Moreau counsels the brothers against swimming alone. Sorin mentions this death in his *Chronicles* under his consideration of deaths at Notre Dame for the year 1845, but the sentence has an odd addendum: "It is true that the Society this year had to mourn the premature death of Br. Anselm, who drowned in the Ohio while bathing with Mr. Delaune; but no one thought of charging this death to the unhealthiness of Notre Dame du Lac, as was done the two following years."[30] This is indeed objective reporting when one juxtaposes it with Delaune's tearful report to Moreau. Everything for Sorin, of course, was seen in the context of Notre Dame. Sorin is more concerned with the rash of deaths that plagued his foundation in the early years than he is with Anselm's loss, and although Sorin wrote his *Chronicles* years after the events themselves (the Anselm entry has to be dated beyond 1848 since Sorin uses that year in a subsequent paragraph), it is difficult to accept his unfeeling journalese as paternal.

In June of that fatal 1845 summer, Anselm had looked forward to the annual retreat when he could go to Notre Dame in August to spend time with his confreres in Holy Cross. Those his own age, like Gatian and the new recruits, would have given him a companionship he lacked in Madison. Who would have told the boy's parents back in Gennes, France? His father, a weaver, had already lost his only other two children to fever. Moreau himself may have made a trip to Gennes to inform the parents. Vincent does not document his own grief for the young man, but he had visited Madison in the previous October on one of his supervisory trips, and he must have felt the loss as if it were the loss of a son. He had known Anselm in Le Mans when the sixteen year old boy was a novice at la Charbonnière. Vincent crossed the Atlantic with him, lived with him in the episcopal residence in Vincennes when Gatian, Francis Xavier, and Sorin moved to Notre Dame. Vincent taught with the boy in the Vincennes cathedral school and guided him in the first years of his career. Vincent's grief must have been deep.

Today Anselm rests in Springdale Cemetery, Madison.[31] The same river that took his life may have inundated the cemetery in 1937 and buried his stone marker, but fortunately the grave was rediscovered in 2000.[32] Before the discovery, the inscription on the stone was known only by way of a postcard in the archives of the Midwest Province, a postcard mailed from Brother Marius Bednarczyk to Brother Lambert Barbier at Sacred Heart College, Watertown, Wisconsin, and postmarked June 18, 1936.[33] But today visitors to Springdale Cemetery can read the inscription on the stone itself:

> BROTHER ANSELME
> of the Society of St. Joseph
> Born in France
> 1826
> Died in Madison
> July 12, 1845
> "His soul pleased God:
> therefore He hastened
> to bring him out."
> PRAY FOR HIM.

The year of Anselm's birth is incorrect: he was born in 1825. The grave is all we have left of Anselm besides his remarkable letters, but possibly in some farmhouse around Madison there is a painting hanging on a kitchen wall, a painting of flowers, a painting signed "Brother Anselm." That possibility, of course, lies only in the realm of speculation. He was proud of his ability to paint. It was one of his few joys in very difficult teaching situations. It is doubtful that Gatian ever travelled to see his friend's grave, but if he had, he could have thought only kind thoughts about the lost man. In a late letter, Gatian does indict Sorin for Anselm's sufferings, and that is where judgment should remain. The quiet and swift waters of the Ohio River wash away much in Madison, but seas could not wash away the guilt of a neglectful superior. Anselm at least died knowing that he had finally succeeded in his teaching, won the love of his students, fulfilled the hopes of Madison townspeople, and established himself as a true son of Moreau's Holy Cross. The young man deserved better than he received.

5

The Letters Begin

The first letter we have by Gatian was written in February of 1846, a full four years after he arrived in America. The letter is postmarked from Notre Dame to Father Moreau in France and is written entirely in French. It was not, of course, the first letter he had written to Moreau. This loquacious and talented young man could hardly have kept his pen silent for a long period. His gift for interpreting the activities around him would have boiled over earlier into letters to his homeland. We do not know if he ever wrote to his parents. He may have, but none of those letters survive. The first letter to Moreau suggests that Gatian had been seeking counsel from his spiritual father in Le Mans, but whatever letters he received from Moreau are gone. Although he is the youngest of the expatriates, at the time he is not shy about his independence in spite of his being only nineteen years old:

> Father Superior's journey doesn't make me uneasy although there's no one here who can replace him and human prudence expects only disorder and ill fortune, because since only I myself of the entire council voted negative, one can piously believe it's the will of God. Father Superior, better than anybody, will be able to make you understand the urgent needs of the house, to come to an understanding with you on the interpretation of certain passages in the Constitutions and on the founding of establishments, and to explain the confusion which the contract with Monsignor de la Hailandière often puts us in.[1]

He is almost boastful of the fact that he alone in the Minor Chapter voted against Sorin's journey to France, but he accepts the overwhelming majority vote as a sign from heaven that the journey is necessary. Or does he? There is a hint of cynicism in his phrasing: "one can piously believe it's the will of God." Since the French "on" can be variously translated as "one" or "they" or even passively as "it can be," there is plenty of room for reading into the phrase a nasty swipe at those who voted to sanction Sorin's trip abroad. How sad, at any rate, to see this young man already so out of tune with those around him. He must have sensed the group was generally behind Sorin's trip. Why would he persist in casting the only negative vote? He is a stubborn young man, almost prideful, unwilling to admit he is wrong. We can see him in the Minor Chapter meeting, the youngest member, speaking up in the discussion, voicing objections to the trip, hearing the others defend the trip, and when the vote comes, rather than admit he is wrong, he bullheadedly votes the only "no." The chapter meetings were often contentious, and many of their minute books have survived.[2]

In February of 1846 Gatian is serving as secretary for the Particular Council of Brothers because he so initials the notes twice on February 11. This Council was apparently begun as a way of giving admonitions and directives to the brothers. A typical entry is that for December 12, 1845:

> 1st Bro. Dominic shall go to the kitchen & shall help Bro. Charles Borromeo in the slaughter house when the latter has to kill.
>
> 2nd Bro. Michael shall study.
>
> 3rd Bro. Benedict shall not teach any longer at the Novitiate, but shall prepare himself for a foundation to be made at Lafayette. Mr. Healy shall take his place at the Novitiate & attend to the various classes of the studying Brothers.
>
> 4th Bro. Jerome shall cut wood instead of Mr. Koch who, with the young man from Madison shall study. Brother Benedict shall teach them.
>
> 5th Mr. O'Brien shall help Bro. Charles Borromeo in leading his cattle to drink.
>
> 6th Bro. Gatian asked whether he should work at the new grammar; he was answered in the negative.
>
> 7th Bro. Vincent said a method of instruction should be adopted & followed at the Novitiate even at present. Bro. Gatian replied that both were impracticable for the present but that after short time when we would have experience, we could form a better plan, taking Mr. De La Salle for basis.

Only Sorin signs this entry, but later entries have signatures by Granger, Cointet, and Vincent. This assembly served as a kind of "Chapter of Admonition" during which specific assignments could be given in a public forum, as the entry for June 18, 1846 indicates:

> 1st Bro. Mary [Francis Xavier] must make some more cells for the privy of the Brothers & they shall be whitewashed.

2nd Bro. Lewis & Mr. Sullivan shall kill the bedbugs next Monday.

3rd Mr. Hobeck shall speak to Mr. Shawe about his uncle & the affair of his family.

4th The two little boys offered by the Bishop of Vincennes, though too young, shall be received.

5th The Brothers of the Novitiate must be sent to work but as seldom as possible & Mr. Hallinan must be treated kindly.

6th Bro. Vincent will be allowed to retire from the Council of Agriculture at 5 o'clock in order to assist at the Catechism.

7th Bro. Joseph must again be told not to print anything without having it corrected as many times as may be necessary, until there be no more errors.

8th F. Cointet will explain the method of meditation to the Brothers every Monday.

9th Bro. Joseph must submit to the regulations which may be made for his garden.

10th Bro. Patrick, having but little to do, shall sweep the portico.

11th The Brothers in order to suit Mr. Healy shall have class on Wednesday both in the morning & the afternoon & they shall work or take a walk on Tuesday & Friday in the afternoon.

Although these meetings aired some infractions, the Particular Council apparently had no Constitutional authority to mandate penance. That was reserved to the Minor Chapter, the official body set up by a local house and approved by the motherhouse in France. For example, an entry for July 9, 1846, in the Particular Council reads: "Brother Vincent complained of Bro. Thomas's irregularity and it was resolved he should be proclaimed in the next chapter." By August, 1846, Gatian was serving as secretary to all councils except the Particular Council of the Priests.[3]

Some of the minutes books may be lost. For example, the Council of Trades book ends November 21, 1846, but an entry in the Minor Chapter book for September 17, 1847, indicates that the Council of Trades was still meeting on Saturdays.[4] Some councils were officially started and stopped by the Minor Chapter: for example, both the Particular Council of Brothers and the Particular Council of Priests were abolished by the Minor Chapter on October 11, 1847.[5] The minutes of the Particular Council of Brothers had stopped the summer before (on June 29, 1847).

The insights we get about Gatian from the meeting books dovetail nicely with what we learn about him from his correspondence. Something about him surfaces in his first letter quite disturbingly: he seems to be a stickler for the Constitutions, a kind of hard-line interpreter of the letter of the law. This adherence to rules does not bode well for a pioneer in a wilderness where crises and interruptions can challenge the rigorous dynamism of spiritual laws fashioned in a gentler climate for cloistered men and patterned in the walled security of Benedictine monasticism. The Indiana frontier was a lively and engaging area, even in the relative seclusion of the Notre Dame paradise where farming concerns and active little boy-scholars tested the rigidity of prayer schedule and quiet time. But Gatian pledged himself to an iron-clad Rule, and he never showed much tolerance for those who did not buckle under to its dictates, and if he were hard on others, he was naturally hard on himself, incapable of appreciating the spirit behind the letter of the law.

Gatian's rancor takes a particular spitefulness when he lists Sorin's shortcomings:

> Father Superior's great kindness or his timidity or lack of vigilance lets him be easily fooled in his moves and in his dealings with hypocrites and flatterers who get from him everything they want. For example, there's been little concern for three postulants or Brothers, never giving them the least public reproach, although their scandalous conduct merited expulsion, but instead of believing them guilty, he preferred to imagine that those who complained were mistaken. They're no longer in the house. One was since married without a priest at the door of the university. Another revealed Council matters from when he had been secretary. Thus jealousies and complaints are created. I have to add, however, that Father Superior is more on his guard this year.[6]

One gets the distinct impression that Gatian was itching to have given the three lax postulants a piece of his own mind, but such comments would have been forbidden by the Rule: only the brother in charge of postulants would be permitted to correct the young men. Gatian, however, undoubtedly made his mind known locally: we can hardly believe he would hold back from the superior or the postulant director the harsh insights he conveys to Moreau by letter. Of special interest here is Gatian's references to one postulant who left and then caused a local scandal by being married without benefit of church blessing somewhere on or near the Notre Dame property. (It is difficult to know whether Gatian's "at the door of the university" is literal or metaphorical.) It may very well have been this incident that would later inspire Gatian to threaten a similar scandal around 1850 when his own ties to the community would become very thinly strung.[7] A curious segment in this part of the letter is the information that the secretary of the Minor Chapter had divulged council matters. Since Gatian was secretary of this chapter a good deal in these early years, we can conclude that Gatian is either turning himself in or patting himself on the back for his own sense of secrecy. Gatian does not name names here, and the anonymity of all the sinners seems studied, indicating all the more that Gatian held no one to the Rule more than himself if indeed he were thinking of his own position as secretary of the chapter. He is becoming a most unusual and troubled young man.

Unusual also in this letter is the way in which Gatian writes of himself in the third person. After listing Brother Vincent's many jobs, he notes:

> Brother Gatian is director of studies, prefect of discipline, head of the accounting office, secretary of four weekly councils, and in the boarding-school, professor of the upper division course in which the students know as much as the teacher, supervisor of all recreations and of a dormitory, and professor of French to boot. You can guess how the jobs are done.[8]

It seems as if Gatian is writing through Moreau to the Major Chapter in Le Mans at which gathering he probably hoped the letter would be read. The third person narrative would then seem objective and not so self-serving as if it had been carried with the first person pronoun. The job list, of course, is overblown. Since the college had but a dozen students, the job of "director of studies" would have been negligible. "Prefect of discipline" would have meant dealing occasionally with a boy who stepped out of line and could not be handled by one of the other brothers. Still, we cannot begrudge Gatian the insight that his talents were stretched. Pioneer brothers, especially talented ones like Gatian, were expected to fill many shoes, and as a result the quality of their job performance was often less than satisfactory. Many high school teachers today can recognize the same situation: tight school budget, minimal staffing, but great expectations. "Burn-out" is not uncommon among people pushed beyond their capacity. In nineteenth century Indiana, the pie was sweetened by religious motivation, an impetus sometimes stronger than salary, and by the family-like support of the brothers' community: living together twenty-four hours a day, on and off their "jobs," they afforded each other instant camaraderie and solutions to problems, an *esprit de corps* that cannot be so present in most of today's educational institutions where the end of the school day scatters the staff hither and yon.

That Gatian appreciated his community is apparent in this letter when he begs for reinforcements: had he despaired of Notre Dame's potential, he would not have wasted his energy asking for more religious, not that Moreau had any to spare for a foundation that was already making great demands on his available personnel and his finances. Gatian, moreover, wants young men: he specifically asks for "Brothers fifteen years old who can learn English to perfection and be other Anselms." This is his first written reference to Brother Anselm, his companion on the trip from France, lost sadly to the Ohio River in the summer before Gatian's February letter to Moreau. It is good to know that Anselm was still on Gatian's mind, even though the two had minimal time together during the previous four years. Separated when Gatian moved north to Notre Dame in November, 1842, the two young men must have experienced great joy in those weeks during each summer when Anselm could rejoin his religious family at Notre Dame for the annual retreat. It is curious that Gatian specifies men "fifteen years old," because that was his own age at emigration. Gatian is projecting himself into his wish list.

He was, of course, a brilliant young man, and he knew it. Anyone today who reads his letters should marvel at their style and grace, the ease of his language skills. By the time he is twenty, he writes flawless English, with barely a trace of French idiom. He has mastered both the letter and the spirit of his American tongue. He had fulfilled Moreau's every wish in sending Gatian and Anselm to America. Moreau believed (as Gatian notes in this letter) that young boys can more easily than older men master a foreign language: witness, Brother Vincent who never mastered English, gave up trying to learn it, and was quite honest in saying so. At the same time, Gatian believed he was suited for a different calling—ordination. He would be willing to study for the priesthood, he tells Moreau, if his superiors would so direct him, but he can only hint at his change of vocation because as a religious under vowed obedience, he cannot make the change on his own volition. Being as intelligent as he was, Gatian was very much in touch with his own short-comings. He appreciates the fact that his temperament is "somber and irritable," and he tells Moreau that, coupled with his exhausting schedule, he is concerned that his duties "sometimes make me want to play the fool." This is a phrase that Gatian uses from time to time in his writings, and it seems a code phrase for sexual lapses. To "play the fool" probably meant sexual play of some kind, play that Gatian here tries to explain away as a stress reducer. It is a not so subtle attempt, perhaps, to blackmail Moreau into pressuring Sorin to relieve Gatian of some of the multiple duties Gatian had. Not that the young man disliked positions of authority. He craved them. But the multi-plicity of jobs gave him an excuse for "playing the fool."[9]

It is very difficult to determine exactly what Gatian's sexual life was actually like. We can, however, attempt to understand his psychosexual attitudes and inclinations if we look at religious manuals of discipline under which he would have been trained. There was a great uniformity among churchmen about matters sexual in the nineteenth century, all of the religious attitudes being shaped by relatively few tracts, all based on the same puritanical foundations of self-abnegation to train the will to combat temptation. We can get a closer look at how church discipline in sexual matters affected a young man if we study the notebooks of Gerard Manley Hopkins, a contemporary of Brother Gatian. Although he was born a country away and a generation after Gatian, Hopkins exhibits much of the scrupulous attention to rule that Gatian had, except that Hopkins was healthier in that he never castigated others for their lack of scruples pertinent to rules. He was, in fact, plagued by his own scruples, and perhaps it was the anguish he felt in his own soul that prevented him from wishing others to sub-scribe to his own tough expectations. In his juvenile notebooks we find meticulous lists of "sins" that he recorded daily. Following are entries for June, 1865:

> [June] 11. Inattention at chapel. Idling. Self-indulgence. Making an unclean joke. [June] 12. Inatten. at C[hapel]. No evening lessons. Waste of time in evening and not sending Coles from my room, so as to be late to bed. Temptations. Conceited thoughts more or less self-indulgent. Repeating to Garrett what Coles said of him. Looking at Fyffe. [June] 13. Unkind talk to Coles probably. Looking at Mitchell.[10]

All of the references to "looking" at men indicate the shame and guilt that Hopkins had just for being aroused by attractive human beings. Some of these feelings are generated by schoolmates ("Looking with terrible temptation at Maitland"),[11] some by choirboys ("Imprudent looking at organ-boy and other boys"),[12] and some by grown men ("Temptation in meeting man at Godstow").[13] There is no doubt these temptations were sexual in nature rather than, say, references to anger or envy. Hopkins writes at one point: "Looking at temptations, es at E. Geldart naked."[14] Geldart was a schoolmate at Balliol.

As if the looking were not anguish enough, masturbation must have been catastrophic. So embarrassed is Hopkins even to record these experiences, he renders them in Latin: "I fear mortal sin, effluximina nulla adhibita mora [night emissions to which no restraint was applied]."[15] And on another occasion, "I remember being doubtful at the time whether nocte ei diei quo...[It happened on the night preceding the day when I noticed the stains, or earlier]."[16]

Although Gatian kept no sin lists that we know of, his attraction to boys is similar to that of Hopkins, and he reveals it both in his letters and in a personal journal.[17] Both Hopkins and Gatian lived in a time of great prudery, when sexual mores were harsh and unrealistic. Well intentioned religious boys were confined and sometimes destroyed by the strictures. Unwilling or unable to laugh at or ignore the prohibitions to either masturbation or shared sexual experiences, Hopkins and Gatian grew twisted in their slavish adherence to the expectations of their religion. Lesser boys grew up healthy, but Hopkins waxed ascetic, and Gatian waxed cynical. Lucky today are boys who do not have to torture themselves with the following code from an 1861 pamphlet entitled "Questions for Self-Examination":

Commandment VII.—Duties of Purity.

Purify, O Lord, and cleanse my heart by the inspiration of Thy Holy Spirit.

Have I been quite pure in thought, word, and deed?

Have I kept the example of our Lord and Blessed Virgin in this respect before me?

If there is any special line of thought, or circumstance of life, or mode of speech which tempts me, have I avoided it as I would the fire of the pit?

Have I joined in talking of such sins in a worldly way? Have I looked at immodest pictures or other objects of the kind?

Have I been vain of my person or anything belonging to me?

Have I been fond of dress? Thought of it more than so as that it be decent, modest, and unobtrusive?

Have I sought to be noticed, especially by the opposite sex? Have I taken undue notice of them? Not "made a covenant with mine eyes"?[18]

Scrupulous self-examination can lead sensitive souls into paroxysms of mental torture and needless anxiety, producing obedient little boys who can grow up dysfunctional, unless they are rescued at some point by clear sighted adult mentors who see beyond the rigors of Augustinian-Calvinism to the sweet charity of the gospels. Hopkins was saved. Gatian was not. And so both Hopkins and Gatian were caught up in the swell of religious fervor. One persevered as a priest and an honored poet. The other died broken and estranged from the religious community that trained him in monastic fundamentals of prayer and work.[19]

By the fall of 1846 Gatian writes to Moreau from a position of established power: as a member of the administrative council at Notre Dame, he feels he has an obligation to report on the general state of affairs. He first enumerates more jobs assigned to him: in addition to the previous list, he adds "secretary of four weekly councils and one monthly council, which take up the whole night."[20] He reminds Moreau that a decision has been promised about Gatian's inclination to ordination, and he adds with a touch of paranoia, "He [Sorin] who ought to communicate it [the decision on ordination] to me no doubt has his reasons for not doing so." Of course Sorin would have been in contact with Moreau over the matter, but by this time, having lived on a day to day basis with Gatian for five years, Sorin would have appreciated that Gatian's lack of tact ill-suited him for an ecclesiastical career, especially in a religious community that was trying to establish itself credibly in a new land. The last thing Sorin needed was an irascible young priest antagonizing the frontier bishops and diocesan clergy. Keeping the young man busy at multiple tasks was the method Sorin used to channel Gatian's energy into areas for which he was very well qualified: bookkeeping, prefecting, and secretarial chores. The strategy would work for nine years, but eventually, as we shall see, Sorin had to resort to more drastic measures to keep Gatian occupied.

The young man never seemed too busy to monitor other people's spiritual lives. In this letter Gatian gets right to the point: Sorin is power hungry and considers himself equal in authority to the motherhouse in France. Secondly, Sorin keeps sloppy financial records. In fact, Gatian notes, in preparing the records for his trip to France, Sorin created them from memory (with the help of Brother Lawrence), and passed them off in Le Mans as authentic. On learning the purpose to which they were put, Gatian cuts his signature off the bottom of the records. He now cites for Moreau's benefit some of the errors passed off on the motherhouse: the Indiana Community actually owes local merchants some 4500 francs more than Moreau was told. They also owe a defrocked brother [possibly ex-Brother Mary Joseph] 3500 francs. Gatian does not specify the reason for the latter debt, but since religious who leave a community are not paid for services rendered over the years, the money was probably money that the man had brought with him when he entered the Community at Notre Dame. In addition, Notre Dame, according to Gatian, would soon have to spend 30,000 francs to purchase more land.

At this point in his long letter, Gatian becomes methodical and begins to outline Sorin's faults.[21] We can recognize in Gatian an extremely tidy mind, one that thrives on organization, even in letters of complaint. He is logical to a fault, but unfortunately his logic is mired in anger, and hostility blurs any advantage he may have hoped to gain with the founder in France. Rancor appeals to the rancorous, and since Moreau was a man devoid of vengeance, he could not have received Gatian's outpouring with the seed bed of rapt admiration that Gatian expected. If anything, the letter would have confirmed in Moreau's mind any insights he may have received from Sorin about Gatian's volatility. But the two priests were not in any kind of secret plot to destroy Gatian. Moreau especially would have been the most patient of listeners and the kindest of counselors. Gatian's fevered brain lashes at Sorin whom he perceives as a local incompetent. Sorin was not, of course, incompetent. He knew how to use people, and he may have been a bit untidy in his record keeping, but his spirit was always bigger than his organization. He could get people to work for him, generally more out of respect than fear, and he was not one to be intimidated by Gatian and his outbursts. Moreau thus becomes the ultimate appeal. Gatian has no one to turn to in America above Sorin. Since frontier bishops had little interest in how religious superiors treated their subjects, Moreau was thus in the unenviable position of having to listen to Gatian and having to somehow let Sorin deal as best as he could with the outspoken young man.

It is difficult today to realize not only the love that Moreau had for his subjects but also the love they tendered to him. Separated by years, we have also been separated by the calculated rancor of wayward men and stiff clerical biographies, both making Moreau seem unapproachable. Of the two, books are the easier to deal with because we can return to them and read through the veneer of mid-century crustiness, but sincerely good men like Sorin who plotted against Moreau to further their own apostolic agendas are more difficult to assess.

Gatian divides the remainder of his remarkable letter into three parts: 1) "Father Superior does everything by himself" 2) "Probable reasons for Father Superior's conduct" 3) "Remedies." Each of these sections has subdivisions, following classic outline form. Gatian must have put much thought into this letter before he actually began to write it. The first flaw in Sorin's character, his assuming too many jobs when subordinates prove incompetent, may have been simply the expeditious route for a superior who wanted things to run smoothly but was either frustrated by poor performance or lacked the manpower to shuffle responsibilities, but Gatian, nevertheless, reads Sorin's actions as simply the priest's being anxious to do everything himself. The example provided by Gatian involves the loss of a sugar loaf from the infirmary, the bailiwick of Father Gouesse, Gatian's confederate in the Minor Chapter. The priest-infirmarian sent a note to Sister Mary of the Cenacle: "A loaf of sugar was taken from the infirmary; if it has fallen into your hands, please have the courtesy to send it back." Whether he knew it or not, Cenacle was the actual culprit, and whatever her intentions for the sugar, she was angry enough to complain to Sorin who removed Gouesse from the supervisory position. Sorin, as we will later see, disliked Gouesse immensely, probably for good cause, and eventually tried to force him out of the Congregation.[22]

The second charge against Sorin is more serious: Gatian gives evidence that Sorin acted without the permission of his council on matters of grave importance. Sorin, in fact, realizing a matter would be voted down in council, would not bring the matter up but would simply act on his own. Thus several enterprises, including a hospital, a home for elderly priests, and a boardinghouse, had to be abandoned for lack of resources. Gatian is not clear on whether or not these institutions ever got out of the planning stages. A museum, however, was established on the campus at the cost of 4000 or more francs, and its revenues for the first two years were 150 francs. Gatian had it on the best authority (a former member of the council) that the proposal to create the museum was actually voted down in council. It should be said to Sorin's credit, however, that the concept of a museum was sound pedagogically, in the best tradition of French education. There are several references in early letters to the wonderful sense of natural history among the pioneer Brothers, particularly in the letters of Brother Anselm who wrote with great enthusiasm about the bugs and things collected in cooperation with one of the local priests. This quest for hands-on knowledge of creatures and their habitats would have been certainly more refreshing than dry textbooks for little boys studying science. Nothing like a field trip to take the dull edge off a tedious class. Gatian, of course, saw only the bottom financial line: the museum did not support itself, no matter its educational pluses.

Another item in Gatian's 1846 catalogue of Sorin abuses affords us a rare opportunity to get another side of the story. Gatian complains to Moreau that Sorin sent two brothers off to teach in an Indiana school before the pastor had offered an invitation. The exasperated pastor refused to accept the brothers, one of whom "disgusted with management of our house, instead of coming back here, defrocked." Gatian thus loads the event totally to Sorin's discredit, but if we look at the situation from another point of view, we can gain a more objective appraisal of the events. Fortunately we have a letter sent to Sorin by Brother Mary Joseph one month before Gatian's letter to Moreau.

The most pugnacious of the early brothers in America had to be Brother Mary Joseph (Samuel) O'Connell who was born in Ireland in 1819 and joined the community at Montgomery, Indiana, in December, 1842, when he was twenty-three. By that time, Brother Francis Xavier and Brother Gatian had already settled into life at Notre Dame with five novices, prepared to face the northern winter in a log cabin on the banks of what they presumed was a single lake under the snow. Brother Lawrence and Brother Joachim remained at Montgomery with eight novices and the postulant Samuel O'Connell. Brother Vincent, in nearby Vincennes with Brother Anselm, served as novice master for the southern foundation in spite of the fact that he was teaching full-time at the cathedral's grade school. In the February following Samuel O'Connell's arrival, all of the brothers headed north to Notre Dame, except, as noted earlier, Anselm, who remained in Vincennes. Samuel was the first postulant to become a novice at Notre Dame, an event which happened on the feast of St. Joseph in 1843.

What was this Irishman like? How wonderful it would be to have a picture of him, but photography was in its infancy in the 1840's, and if he had his picture taken after he left the community in 1846, we shall probably never know. We can, however, get a very good portrait of him from the letters that the brothers wrote in those early days. Brother Mary Joseph was apparently a fearless kind of fellow, as we can surmise from the following incident that Brother Francis witnessed on a ride in November, 1845:

> The first day of our traveling was good enough, but Brother Mary Joseph was too full of gab with the driver. This it is that caused some dissatisfaction for when we came on the other side of Lafayette, we came to be going in the night, not knowing where to stop when Brother Aloysius spoke to the driver to drive faster, but in place of doing it did much harm. The driver spoke harshly to Brother Aloysius and said to him, "None of your lip," etc. Brother Mary Joseph spoke then very roughly, etc. I was silent. Brother Mary Joseph scolded me for not speaking.[23]

Brother Mary Joseph seems here a kind of protector of gentler brothers; he was not about to take abuse from some cheeky coach driver. This same Brother Francis had a kind of awe for the tough Mary Joseph. In a later letter he complains about not having wood for the school in Vincennes: "and as for Brother Mary Joseph we were informed that he went in the river frequently when the water was high to get wood."[24] Mary Joseph was not about to freeze in his classroom when there was wood to be had floating in the nearby river. He had a reputation in Vincennes as a severe disciplinarian and in Madison, Indiana, as a truant teacher. He was, apparently, his own man.

Mary Joseph was one of the two Brothers sent to Madison, Indiana, to St. Michael's Parish where Anselm had worked happily and effectively a year earlier. In the fall of 1844 Anselm had been shifted from Vincennes to Madison after his ʕul sufferings under Hailandière in the cathedral town. Anselm's death by ing in July, 1845, left Madison without a brother for the school year. As beloved as he had been, Anselm needed to be replaced if Sorin hoped to maintain the good will of the bishop and the people in Madison. Sorin should have, of course, consulted with Maurice de St. Palais, the priest who had replaced Father Julian Delaune, Anselm's pastor at St. Michael's, in June, 1846, but Sorin apparently just sent the two brothers without consulting St. Palais. One would think that a pioneer pastor would have been delighted to be given two religious teachers for his school without having to beg for them, but St. Palais was not delighted. Mary Joseph fills in the details:

Reverend Mr. St. Pallais was in the sitting room. I presented to him your letter and he asked me who had told Father Sorin he wanted Brothers. I said that I had, that the people were asking me everywhere when I passed through, when they would have two Brothers. I said that if they would write, that they would have either one or two from South Bend, and that the representations I had made to you induced you to send two. When we arrived in Madison, the people were glad to see us all except two persons who wrote against Reverend Mr. Delaune to the bishop and one of them, Mr. W. Griffin, has circulated through the town that Reverend J. Delaune had taken the people's money from Madison to buy the college and farm in Kentucky.

These men boasted on Sunday that we would not be received by Reverend Mr. St. Pallais. I asked Reverend Mr. St. Pallais if he would permit us to teach catechism on Sunday. He said it was not necessary. I said, very well. On Sunday we went to High Mass. Everyone welcomed us to Madison. They asked us when the school would commence as their children were running wild for want of a school. Others told me they were sending their children to Protestants' schools, but would send them to us as soon as we should start the school. There were over 40 children in gallery at Mass and there has been a increase of several families since I left. All told us they would assist us. Some offered us rooms if we would accept of them. I told them I would wait till I would know what the priest would tell us.

Brother Francis and myself went to Mass on Monday morning after we went to see Reverend St. Pallais to ask him if we should start school as the children were at the school door waiting for us. The school and desks were all ready. He talked with us some time, then told us that his house was not ready yet and he wanted to ask you about the terms. I told him the terms were $50 for each Brother for 10 1/2 months schooling. He said he wanted to see the people about it. I told him the people had sent their children to school and that they had paid well last year and said they would do the same this. He then said his house was not yet finished and he wanted us to live in his house and he would rather we would return to South Bend. He would pay the expenses back and would send for us when he wanted us. He wished us to leave Madison, and I said we could not leave untill we had an answer from the Superior.

He said he would take that upon himself and would give us a letter to you which would be satisfactory.

Brother Francis and I thought it would be best for us to write to you and wait untill you should tell us what to do in this matter. The members of the congregation are very much displeased. They say that Mr. Griffin and Mr. Blenkinsop have prevailed with Reverend Mr. St. Pallais to send us back. You will not believe this possible perhaps, but if you knew these men as well as I do and how they have troubled Reverend Mr. Delaune since his first arrival in Madison untill this day and even now are trying to blacken his character by saying that he took the money of the congregation away with him, but no one believes them because they knew Reverend Mr. D. too well.

You perhaps will say what has this to do with the school? Why when Brother Anselm was here, Mr. Griffin went to him and wanted him to make more of his children than the rest. Brother Anselm refused. He [Griffin] sent them to a Protestant school. When I came here a year ago, he did not like to send them, but Reverend Mr. D. said he must. He sent them. They came to school 7 months, behaved bad, would not conform to the rules of the school. Reverend Mr. D. told me to punish them. I did so. He [Griffin] took them from school and sent them to Protestant schools. He refused to pay Reverend Mr. Delaune his school money that was due, but abused when he was asked for it. Mr. Blenkinsop has no children.[25]

Thus the truth of the matter emerges: a local tussle between Brother Mary Joseph and a disgruntled parent had poisoned the well. Mary Joseph was no Anselm, and although Mary Joseph may have worked in the Madison school with some success under Delaune, he met his match under St. Palais. A postscript to this letter continues the saga:

Since writing the letter in which this [is] enclosed, Brother Francis had an attack of the fever and ague. About 4 o'clock we heard that Sr. Liguori was dying, so I went to enquire how she was. Whilst I was there, Reverend Mr. St. Pallais sent for me. I went. He told me he had written a letter to you and that he believed all would be settled. I told him that Brother Francis was sick. He seemed to doubt it, said he would send the doctor to see him, and he would know whether he was able to travel. I said also that I wished to have a letter from you before I left Madison regarding something which I wished to ask you. (This was whether you would allow me to go [to] Kentucky as I had not settled the matters we agreed to.) He said he could not see why I wanted to stay. He said it appeared that we did not want to leave Madison. I deny'd wanting to stay in Madison. I said that I thought it was necessary according to our Constitution to write to you before leaving any place. I told him I had done so regarding Reverend Mr. Delaune. He then said in a angry tone, "I as parish priest of Madison and as Vicar General of this diocese order you both to leave Madison immediately." He said that he "would defray the expenses." I said that perhaps you might have some other destination for us. He said that "he would defray the expenses back." He said these were his last words. He said that "he had nothing against us but that if we were to stay 6 days waiting for your answer, the people would want to detain us to keep school and he would not do it."[26]

It is possible that St. Palais did not disdain all religious teachers so much as he had aversion for this particular one. In the previous year Mary Joseph may very well have proven to more than Griffin and Blenkinsop that he was ill-suited to fill the place of hard-working and beloved Anselm. It is not easy to replace an idol. So the real culprit in this case may have been Mary Joseph who could have mis-represented the Madison situation to Sorin. Mary Joseph, the replacement for Anselm two years earlier in the hot-bed of Vincennes, may have seen a way out of Hailandière's town and knowing the wondrous goodwill enjoyed by Anselm in Madison, may have engineered the switch himself. Then for a year in Madison with Delaune as pastor he had annoyed two influential local laymen. St. Palais, already number two man in the diocesan clergy and destined to be consecrated bishop three years later when Hailandière was sent packing, was nobody's fool, and he undoubtedly took umbrage at the outspoken Mary Joseph, who had proven himself confrontational. Mary Joseph's poor little companion, Brother Francis (Michael Disser) was caught between the mighty egos of his travelling companion and the feisty future bishop of the territory.

In his letter to Moreau, Gatian spells out none of the mitigating circumstances about the Madison affair: no mention of the poisoning of the atmosphere by the two disgruntled Madisonites, no mention of Mary Joseph's inventiveness, no mention of St. Palais' imperiousness. Everything is Sorin's fault. We cannot, of course, let Sorin off without some fault—he was, after all, assigning men to an institution without an explicit invitation from the pastor, and although Sorin may have conjectured that once established, a foundation remains running on its initial invitation, his decision to send Mary Joseph and Francis looks at least impolite and presumptuous. Moreover, St. Palais was not Delaune, and it was Delaune who had been pastor in Madison when Holy Cross first began its work there. Of course, the bishop was ultimately responsible for the acceptance of all religious personnel, but it would be foolish to imagine a local pastor could be overlooked in the renewal of a contract. Sorin may very well have negotiated with Hailandière, and Hailandière may have neglected to bring St. Palais into the loop, but we must remember Hailandière was himself careening towards his own downfall and did not enjoy the full respect of even his own diocesan clergy. It was they more than anyone who brought about his ouster in 1849. At any rate, the debacle as it unfolded was laid by Gatian at Sorin's feet, and there it would remain had we not Mary Joseph's letter to help clarify the actual events in Madison.

Mary Joseph's defrocking was not the result of his disgust "with the management of our house" (as Gatian put it to Moreau), but was rather the result of a series of things, not least of which may have been his ill-success as a teacher-replacement for Anselm and his disgust with being a ping-pong ball between Vincennes and Madison. His disposition, whatever it was when he first joined Holy Cross in 1842 at age twenty-three, could not have improved after a year teaching in Vincennes and living with the prelate who had bedeviled Anselm into sickness and acute mental agony. One would like to think, however, that Mary Joseph could have given as much to Hailandière as Hailandière gave to others. It may have been, in fact, such a chemistry that could have induced Hailandière to be less than unhappy when Mary Joseph left for Madison. There must have been hot times in the episcopal palace when the French bishop crossed swords with the hot Irish Brother. No long-suffering Anselm, Mary Joseph could give back whatever was dealt to him. Anselm cried in his room over Hailandière's insults and humiliations, but Mary Joseph would never have cried. No bishop would push him around.

Brother Mary Joseph's final days in the community were not happy ones. In the nine letters that remain from him, he gives evidence of being astute in money matters, but he was also outspoken, and the latter trait did not help him in his final assignments. Instead of returning to Notre Dame, Mary Joseph went to St. Mary's College in Kentucky where a previous Madison pastor, Julian Delaune, was struggling to keep the institution afloat for Sorin. Mary Joseph officially left the community a month later on November 12, 1846. His final letter clears up what has always remained a mystery in histories of St. Michael's Parish in Madison. Those books wonder why the brothers left the parish, but the mystery is no mystery to anyone who reads the early letters of the brothers. The bad blood between the pastor and the confrontational Brother Mary Joseph is all too apparent there. It would be most interesting to know what happened to Samuel O'Connell in later years, but he has faded into the frontier of the Midwest, caught perhaps in some county records in Kentucky, Illinois, or Indiana, records that are still waiting to reveal the further years of a most colorful Brother of Holy Cross in pioneer America.

Meanwhile at Notre Dame Gatian continued his running feud with Sorin. In support of Gatian's contention that Sorin listens to none of his Minor Chapter councilors, Gatian narrates an episode about a fire he attributes to Sorin's authoritarianism. At the end of October, 1846, the matter of stoves versus chimneys was debated with the conclusion that stoves were safer than chimneys, but Sorin on his own had some workmen construct three chimneys in the college building: one in Gouesse's room, another two elsewhere on the second floor.[27] One afternoon at three o'clock, smoke appears in the corridors but is ignored until six o'clock when all the rooms on four floors become smoke filled. Suspecting the new chimneys, residents extinguish all the fires except for the fire in Gouesse's room because that room was relatively free of smoke. But smoke continues to fill the other rooms. Brother Vincent suspects the belfry (for whatever reason), but a delegate to the belfry finds nothing. By 7 PM Gatian, ever the logical sleuth, walks around the building slowly, checking the windows and roof. Seeing flames at Gouesse's window, he alerts several residents who, apparently doubting Gatian's word, go to see for themselves. Gatian himself does not follow but goes rather into his own office (the secretary's office) on the first floor, directly under Gouesse's bedroom, where he discovers a chunk of the floor on fire. He quickly throws his books and papers out the door just before plaster, bricks and water come crashing from above. The fire had apparently started on the second floor under Gouesse's new hearth and crept along in the space between the floor of the second level and the ceiling of the first level. The fire was not totally extinguished until 8:30, an hour and a half after Gatian discovered it. Gatian concludes that the damage to the building will cost 2300 francs to repair, but Sorin insists on keeping the chimneys: further evidence, concludes Gatian, that Sorin listens to no one but himself.

If we were to categorize Gatian and Sorin as risk takers, we would have to note in the matter of this 1846 fire that Gatian is the better man attuned to progressive ideas. He opts for the new and experimental. The Franklin stove, that revolutionary concept in home heating invented by the Philadelphia genius associated with creating bifocals and with flying kites in electrical storms, was not a century old, whereas the chimney had a long European history. Sorin, raised in a French manor, was comfortable with the image of quiet nights reading by a flickering fire. Gatian, the farm boy, was ready for something new, less aristocratic. The stove was highly efficient, wasting little heat. The chimney, on the other hand, uses half of its heat to warm an outside wall. The native Americans had long used fires in the middle of their wigwams and hogans so Gatian was much in the line of New World methodology. Sorin still thought like a European. Gatian, a match for any wits with Sorin, was frustrated, however, by a lack of power, a yearning for Holy Orders, and a temper capable of vicious wrath. His letters of complaint to Moreau were one way he could release steam, and Moreau had to read them, responding as gently and firmly as he could. It is not easy to domesticate a wild flower.

Another matter of concern to Gatian was a supposed gift of land from Father Stephen Badin. The Minor Chapter was apparently never allowed to see the terms of the agreement, and Sorin stalled in sharing with them various conditions for the gift.[28] Gatian notes that the land was non-arable and of little resale value, becoming a useless encumbrance while the Community was required to pay Badin 500 francs quarterly with 125 francs added if payment was not timely. Sorin, of course, had no right to keep from the Chapter the particulars of a major financial transaction. As far as the individual members of the Chapter are concerned, Gatian has little use for any of them. He names them to Moreau one by one and cuts each one down. Granger and Cointet are chameleons: they side with Sorin until Gouesse voices an opinion, at which time they switch to support Gouesse. "Brother Marie [Francis Xavier] is almost a zero."[29] This is a slur on the Community carpenter, apparently a gentle and soft-spoken man who did his duties faithfully and with little fanfare. The irony is that he would outlive Gatian by thirty-six years, dying at Notre Dame after serving as carpenter and undertaker for fifty years. As far as the other members of the Chapter are concerned, Gatian says that Lawrence and Joseph have ideas but cannot express them well. Thus Sorin can manipulate them. Lawrence we remember as a farmer with excellent business sense, much praised at his death in 1873. Joseph, on the other hand, was a different kind of thinker—extremely spontaneous to the point of absurdity. Sorin had to rein him in on more than one occasion when his ideas (e.g., marketing ladies' clothes) proved to be too bizarre for a religious apostolate. Later, off on his own in Indianapolis, he wrote back sometimes daily to Sorin with new schemes: a winery, a land scheme for a proposed railroad station, a cabbage farm. He must have been delightful to live with. Vincent, the final member of the Council, was a reserved man and a staunch Sorin supporter. Gatian could never get him to join a cabal: "Good grief! It's to a Council composed of such members that Father Superior proposes the most important money matters."[30]

Moreau would have known all these men (except Joseph) so he had a very good understanding of the chemistry of the Chapter. One cannot help but sympathize with Sorin, faced as he was with a council of such divergent talent, including erratic Joseph and irascible Gatian. Meetings must have been colorful. No wonder Sorin preferred to act on his own and get things rubber stamped after the fact. The Badin land gift would be a perfect example of his unwillingness to bring important matters to the Chapter. Sorin was not a forgetful man: he was shrewd. Gatian believed, however, that Sorin's major fault is that he is "too good," besides being "forgetful, neglectful and variable, [he] forgives everything and lets himself be led by those who know how to say kind words to him."[31] Gatian prefers Gouesse who is a stickler for rules (like himself) and believes in adherence to the Constitutions. Such inflexibility, of course, does not bode well for men who want to live in a Community and let the laws shape the men instead of letting the men shape the laws. Time eventually proved the error of Gatian's thinking: both he and Gouesse found themselves outside of Holy Cross in the prime of their lives while flexible people (Sorin, Vincent, Francis Xavier) lived to be very old men at Notre Dame.

At this time among the several councils at Notre Dame, the most important was the Minor Chapter (responsible for the entire local Community) and the Administrative Council (responsible for supervision of the college). The Minor Chapter was higher in authority and mirrored on a local level what the Major Chapter in Le Mans represented for Holy Cross worldwide. All money matters had to pass through the Minor Chapter. The system works well and assures an institution that one person will not be running the entire operation and making all decisions without consultation, and the system also offers relief to an administrator who might otherwise feel overwhelmed by the decisions and responsibilities of his office. Notre Dame in 1846 was not a mammoth institution, but it was viable and gave every indication of growing. Moreau himself had difficulties with some of Sorin's unilateral decisions, but he never doubted the man's ability to make Notre Dame thrive.

Once Gatian had exhausted his professional invective, it was time for gossip. He confides to Moreau:

> It seems that you had ruled at Ste. Croix that the Sisters would no longer be seen in the stairways and apartments of the college. Well, you can still meet them every time you turn around, even after nightfall and after supper, sometimes in the stairways where there's hardly any light. Thus a Protestant boarder aged 18, coming back from places at 8 PM, met three of them under the porch. Many are shocked at these comings and goings, but what seems more scandalous is to see the new Sister Superior [Mary of the Cenacle] spend hours with Father Superior, often in his bedroom, although he ordinarily receives nobody except in the office. I'm making you aware of this disorder because I have in mind that you wouldn't tolerate it if you knew about it.[32]

There is in these remarks, besides the youthful wish to titillate, a desire to keep women in their place, and the attempt to smear Sorin with sexual imbroglios is all too transparent. It is not so much the possibilities of sexual contacts that Gatian begrudges Sorin as it is the violation of rules that riles Gatian. Gatian was obsessed with rules. If there were some other evidence that Sorin compromised his vow of celibacy, Gatian's remarks could be taken seriously, but Gatian's mind ran in a gear of paranoia. The suggestion that Sorin and Mother Superior were sexually involved, if it had any merit, would have come earlier in the letter. Tacked on to the end of a long list of grievances, it reads like a last ditch effort to garner sympathy: when all else fails, cast sexual aspersions. Moreover, if Sorin were guilty of clandestine scandal, it would have been brought to Moreau's attention by Gouesse (who was no friend of Sorin's), Granger, Cointet, or Vincent. Vincent was, after all, the oldest and most respected member of the American Community, and he was Sorin's official monitor on occasion.[33] None of these men ever suggests in correspondence that Sorin had a sexual liaison of any kind with anyone. The man was too careful of his power and the image of his institution to risk scandal for anything so slight as dalliance.

If anything is true of Sorin it is that he was careful of his hold over Notre Dame, even to the point of confiscating letters of complaint to Moreau. Gatian claims, for example, that in 1844 he had found at the bottom of an old trunk an unmailed letter from Joseph to Moreau. When he showed it to Sorin, who had ordered Gatian to empty the trunk, and suggested that Sorin had overlooked mailing the letter, "He [Sorin] replied that he hadn't forgotten it, but that Brother Joseph was a buffoon."[34] This incident bears all the earmarks of being true. Its being factual could have been easily verified by Moreau, so Gatian would hardly have made up an incident that could have brought discredit to himself if proven false. After all, in his remarks on Sorin's supposed sexual intrigues, Gatian is careful simply to hint what may have happened in Sorin's bedroom, but in regard to Joseph's suppressed letter, he infers nothing because he was at the scene of the crime, not interpreting facts so much as reporting them. Of course Joseph was a buffoon. A look at his correspondence with Sorin (fifty-seven letters over four years) will lead any reader to the same conclusion: well intentioned and energetic but foolish. The nascent public mail system in 1844 may have had a federal law against interfering with the posting of a letter, but religious communities have often breached such a law, generally with the implied consent of the writers or receivers. As recent as the 1960s, novice masters in Holy Cross still felt free to read mail coming in or going out of the novitiate, especially if an incoming letter smelled of perfume. No novice master today could long survive such a violation of privacy.

As Gatian brings his lengthy letter of November, 1846, to a close, he plays a dire trump card: the Notre Dame Community is doomed. Fever has affected Cointet and the former Mother Superior. Many are in danger of dying and one brother could not work for three months. Brother Anthony, Brother John Baptist, and a postulant have died. Brother Francis Xavier will not live long. (He actually lived until 1896.) Brother Lawrence and Brother Benoit were out with fever. It is a scare tactic designed to have Moreau intervene in the running of the Indiana foundation, as if anyone could do anything against yellow fever. Having lived closely with Sorin for five years, Gatian thinks he knows the priest well, but he miscalculates at every angle the trust that Moreau has in the Indiana superior. Whatever Moreau said in reply to Gatian's remarkable November letter we will never know, but we do know that time would strengthen Sorin's position in Holy Cross while Gatian moved closer and closer to isolation.

During the winter of 1846 Gatian is silent, but at the end of spring in 1847 he writes again to Moreau. April at Notre Dame is usually a wonderful month, especially welcome after any of the harsh winters that choke the land east of Lake Michigan. The winter "lake effect" dumps ice and snow on Michigan City and South Bend because the air that passes over Lake Michigan picks up moisture to deposit on the hapless counties to the east. With spring come daffodils and a lightening of spirits. Gatian, a man sensitive to change of any kind, writes to Moreau with renewed aplomb. Acknowledging reception of a letter from Moreau, Gatian specifies that he has delayed answering until he could see how Sorin would implement the reforms that Moreau has specified in a letter addressed to Gatian, Sorin, and Granger. Sorin obviously did not prevent this letter from getting into Gatian's hands, and we can imagine the delight that Gatian had in seeing some directives issued from the motherhouse in France. Gatian succeeds in getting Gouesse made a member of the Minor Chapter probably because he sensed in the man a spirit kindred to his own, a spirit contrary to Sorin's and Granger's.[35] Two hostile voices are better than one. But Gatian is not satisfied that Sorin is implementing the reforms specified by Le Mans because either "he is a consummate liar, or the explanations given to him at Ste. Croix weren't clear."[36] One can little doubt which reason Gatian believes.

In an aside, Gatian remarks that he has noticed much discontent among the members of the last colony to arrive in America. This would have been the contingent of 1844 that arrived in September with Brother Vincent as chaperon. It included Granger, Brother Augustus (who would live at Notre Dame to the ripe old age of 100, dying in 1900), Brother Justin (chosen later for the disastrous gold expedition of 1850), and three Marianite sisters: Sister Mary of the Five

Wounds (Paillet), Sister Mary of the Circumcision (Chanson), and Sister Mary of the Crucifix (Argot). Two and a half years have passed since their immigration, but Gatian harkens back to their discontent on arrival when they found grave disparity between the way they had lived the Constitutions in France and the way they found the Constitutions followed in Indiana. This theme for Gatian is recurring, and it is a truism that many young people who are sticklers for rules do not survive very long in a religious community because they cannot reconcile rigid prescriptions with the reality of human frailty, their own especially. Rules thus become an unrealistic end in themselves that frustrate and eventually break a vocation into despair. Sensing some dismay among the new colonists, Sorin assembled all the French immigrants and explained that he could not change his approach to administration to suit them. He further explained that, given time, they would see the wisdom of accommodating a French set of rules to American customs. Gatian here gives no specifics on what rules were being bent, but they no doubt included the handling of major money matters without express consent of the Major Chapter in France.

In this 1846 Gatian letter we are afforded a rare glimpse into Sorin's sense of humor. The bishop had proposed that a brother be sent to sell Catholic books door to door and promised two mules for the apostolate. At Minor Chapter, Sorin painted the advantages of the scheme, no doubt all financial, and asked for responses. Gouesse was absent from the meeting and Gatian remained silent "taking everything as a joke"[37] as it really did seem a radical departure for a teaching community. Within two days Sorin had appointed Brother Joseph (the "buffoon") to the job and directed him to buy a cart, eventualities that Sorin revealed at the dining table. Gatian was furious and wrote a "nasty note" to Sorin saying that the councilors did not consider the previous Chapter meeting simply a consultation on the matter. Sorin reconvened the Chapter, proposed the venture, and listened to the debate. Gouesse said nothing because, as Gatian surmises, he did not want to jeopardize his upcoming ordination. Gatian himself raised five objections, one claiming the venture would lose 700 or 800 francs because it was a stupid venture. Sorin replied, "You can only do good by taking risks."[38] The vote was taken: Gouesse and Gatian voted against it, and the other councilors voted for it. Then Sorin pulled a fast move saying, "I vote against it and thus the responsibility rests on those who have voted for."[39] One member objects: "Ah, Father...If you believed the enterprise is useless, you shouldn't have proposed it, and if you believe it bad, you shouldn't undertake it." Sorin's response borders on dark comedy: "Too bad...You've voted: it'll be carried out."

Today we smile at the sly tactics, but the episode does indicate the little regard, if not wry disdain, that Sorin held for his Minor Chapter. The autocrat survives not by suppressing democratic process but by manipulating it to his own purposes. Sorin won this battle, but in the long run, as Gatian is happy to repeat to Moreau, the adventure failed miserably: by the time Joseph reached Indianapolis to begin his sale of Catholic books, his cart is broken, he is sick and penniless. Nevertheless, Joseph has the energy to buy a plot of land for 22,500 francs ($3,000) and send the bill north to Notre Dame. Knowing as much as we do of Joseph, we are not surprised by the revitalization of his creative energies. If nothing else, Joseph was a capitalist at heart, a crackpot in reality.

Gatian's concern over money matters was apparently well founded. In addition to Joseph's Indianapolis land purchase (22,500 francs), the college faced the purchase of two plots adjacent to the Notre Dame property (35,000 francs), to say nothing of existing debts (30,000 francs). Moreover, Sorin was thinking about building a church for 5,000 francs. It was enough to send a worrier like Gatian into convulsions. But he continues to work hard at all his tasks which include being Prefect of Discipline "who alone is loved, respected and obeyed."[40] It is hard to know when to admire or smile at Gatian's self assessments.

In this letter Gatian reveals that he has not written to his family in two years: "I don't like to write to them because I've lost the habit…And because I've received no news from them since I've been in America."[41] This is a sad remark from a young man so far from home. His mother being dead, he may not have been very close to his step-mother, but he speaks affectionately elsewhere of his younger brother August and expresses hope that the boy is getting a good education.[42] It is not unusual, however, for youth to be so caught up in adventure that they lose touch with a previous life, and Gatian was certainly in an environment extremely different from what he had known back in a country steeped in centuries of tradition and racked by war. The American frontier had little resemblance to the tame French countryside he had known, and the lure of quixotic adventure in exotic areas like Louisiana swamps and California gold fields would be enough to dazzle any energetic young man away from home.

In all the acrimony of the early Gatian correspondence, we often find flashes of brilliant insight buried under heaps of character assassination. From his earliest letters in 1846, he went on to continue his surveillance of Sorin's activities at Notre Dame and to report them to Moreau in France. Sorin did need some surveillance, but others at Notre Dame also needed some supervision, for example that unusual Brother Joseph. One of the most colorful of the early brothers, Charles Rother was a layman already teaching in the little school at St. Peter's when the little colony arrived in Indiana from France in 1841. He seemed to be a valuable recruit since he was already at age thirty-three a veteran teacher, and Sorin used him in sundry teaching assignments. Becoming a novice on December 28, 1841, with the name Brother Joseph, he traveled to Notre Dame in March, 1843, where he was professed on August 27. He was then sent to teach in Pokagon, but the minutes of the Council of Administration for December 4, 1843, note that he was to move to Fort Wayne. We lose sight of him for a few years until he begins a barrage of letters to Sorin starting in 1846 and continuing until June of 1849, fifty-seven letters in all (plus one to Brother Vincent). In March, 1846, he writes from Indianapolis where he is running a school, begging for more brothers to help in the school. By July he is having problems with the hired help. His own words are so lively they bear reading:

> Little Henry has left me yesterday. In the morning I sent him to market, and instead of keeping his stand, he run about with a bad fellow after girls. When he came home, I sent him to work in the meadow to shake out hay. There he got at the whiskey jug of the man who mowed my grass. At dinner he came home so drunk that he could not stand on his legs. Then he spent the whole afternoon in the meadow doing nothing. Towards evening he came to tell me that he would not work for me [for] under $4.00 per month and boarding. I told him I would not give him 50 cents, and if he was not pleased, he might go. So he did, but I kept his clothes back. Never a human being abused me and gave me such bad language as this little rascal did. But today he was sorry for it. He waited for me at noon when I came from town. He wanted me to take him back again, but I would not. Perhaps I will, if he humbles himself well.[43]

If this were not factual, it would make very good comedy. Joseph's mismanagement of money so infuriated the bishop that Sorin was forced to move the noviorate from Notre Dame to Indianapolis to keep episcopal good will, but when funds proved meager, Sorin on a visit to Vincennes in December, 1846, tried another way to placate the bishop: he agreed to put a brother on the road selling Catholic books, and that brother turned out to be Joseph.[44]

With two mules (one named Jack), Joseph sets off in good spirits from Notre Dame for Indianapolis in January mud. By Logansport he is experiencing difficulties with rough roads, and Jack has a sore shoulder from an inadequate collar fashioned by Brother Lawrence. Finally reaching Indianapolis by January 11, Joseph wastes no time in reevaluating the property he had purchased from a real estate agent. Joseph believes if he holds on long enough, a new railway line will pass by his property and its value will triple. Within a week an agent named

Phipps is getting him interested in twenty-seven acres of prime land, fifteen acres of it cleared for farming. By February he buys the property for $4000 without Sorin's permission: "Now it is bought, and you have to keep it" he tells Sorin. By March the mules are sold and there is talk of transferring the novitiate from Notre Dame to Indianapolis.[45] Meanwhile Joseph teaches French to locals, including the wife of a judge.

In May, Joseph finds a Mr. Boder ("the richest man in town") who will buy the mortgage notes from Phipps or lend Joseph the money for the land purchase. Boder will charge no interest for a year on any loan, but at the end of the year he can confiscate the property. The Boder plan is probably the one to which Sorin refers in the minutes of the Minor Chapter: "F. Superior informed the council of a means by which Br. Joseph had found to pay out our debt at Indianapolis. Fr. Superior promised to write that that means should be used, unless himself could find money at Niles at a better rate."[46] Joseph is in a corner. By June he gives up his teaching and the Boder plan goes sour. Sorin announces the collapse of the Boder plan to the Minor Chapter on June 24, 1847:

> He [Sorin] informed the council that Mr. Bathe [sic] had disposed of the money he had offered for the payment of the novitiate at Indianapolis. It was unanimously resolved that money should be borrowed at the bank for the payment of the novitiate. It would be impossible, it was said, to refuse to ratify the contract, without exposing ourselves to the danger of losing a law suit. The honor of the Establishment would be greatly injured, a true injustice would be committed against the seller, and the Right Rev. Bishop, who has already sent his subscription would be greatly displeased, and his favorable dispositions would be totally altered. But as this payment will require much money, and in order to spare it and to get some, Br. Vincent will not go to France, as it had been decided in the preceding chapter, but will go to collect money on the Railroad, and he will be accompanied by Br. Stephen.[47]

Joseph, however, writes to Sorin that with prospects for the railway still hot, they could sell half the land within one year for the purchase price of the entire plot.

Meanwhile, bizarre ideas continue to flow. In July Joseph is excited by the prospects of starting a winery to make money. He is tilting at windmills, of course. With one hundred shoots in the ground, he is planning to get six hundred more in the fall. The man was an open-hearted child with no sense of business or farming. If left to his own devices longer, he could have bankrupted the whole Community with his schemes. By the end of the summer Joseph tells Sorin that the bishop has given him a draft for $3000. With it he will close the land deal on September 6.[48] His next letter (December 29, 1847) tells Sorin he is going to write "a treatise on vineyard cultivation" to make more money.[49] He is sure that it will be a masterpiece—this from a man who put his first grape shoots in the ground but six months previous.

In January of 1848 there are eleven men living in the Indianapolis novitiate. Joseph serves as the steward and is quite happy, but in late spring a hailstorm destroys his garden and he is despondent. Moreover, the railroad has not yet made its decision about the location of the Indianapolis depot so Joseph remains in limbo, advising Sorin it may take two more years of holding on to the property before they can turn a profit. A month later he brags to Brother Vincent that he will harvest "500 cauliflower, 3000 cabbages."[50] There is no end to his pie in the sky. He plans to ship four hundred grape shoots up to Notre Dame so they can start their own vineyard.

The fall drags on without a decision by the railroad supervisors. They delay a decision until December. Finally in January Joseph breaks the bad news to Sorin: the depot will not go on his land. Because Bishop Hailandière, Joseph explains, had never transferred the deed over to Joseph in the land office, local investors thought Joseph a poor risk. The new depot, however, is three hundred yards from his property line, and he has hopes this fact will inflate the value of the property. Joseph proposes to divide the land into lots and sell it piecemeal to make more money. Fifty-five or sixty lots, he claims would bring in $6000, doubling their investment.

In March of 1849 Joseph gets a visit from the new bishop, Maurice de St. Palais, who wants the school turned into an orphan asylum. If Sorin does not agree to the change, St. Palais will foreclose on the $3000 debt that Joseph incurred in the land deal. Joseph suggests to Sorin that the bishop simply be given the land: "Let him take his part in land and do with [it] what he pleases."[51] By April, Phipps is pressing for his money as he wants to leave town, and Joseph comes up with another scheme to raise money: he can trade sixteen acres of land with a Mr. McKernan for $4400 worth of dry goods to sell. The items include satin, cashmere, "and beautiful articles of summer stuff for men and ladies."[52] Joseph is as dazzled by gaudy clothes as Trinculo and Stephano are with the trash that Ariel hangs outside Prospero's cave. Fortunately Sorin telegraphs Joseph to stop the new folly. June, 1849, finds the bishop still pressing Joseph to convert the school into an orphanage, but Sorin is not interested in the proposal.

The following February, 1850, Joseph left the Community, but he continued to call himself Brother Joseph while he ran St. Vincent's Male Orphanage in Vincennes (close to the bishop), but his incompetence there forced the bishop to turn the institution over to Mother Guerin. When the orphanage moved to

Highland, outside of Vincennes, Joseph lived nearby as a recluse, died there, and was buried in the cemetery with a gravestone inscribed "Brother Joseph." So would end the life of the first recruit that the brothers had in Indiana. If anything, Joseph was a major distraction for Sorin in the 1840's. He was also a dangerous embarrassment. Curiously, in the various Joseph debacles, Gatian was of a like mind with Sorin in condemning the money making ideas. But battling Joseph's schemes off campus and Gatian's volatility on campus, Sorin had his hands full. Both Joseph and Gatian escalated in their shenanigans during the same years, and both left the community in the same year. Sorin would not have wept over either departure.

In the fall of 1847, Gatian writes to Moreau a remarkable letter in which he forwards a request from the Minor Chapter that Notre Dame be afforded more latitude in making local decisions. Given the distance between the French motherhouse and America, the Chapter suggests a superior be named for all American establishments who would act at the behest of "a chapter formed by the gathering of Minor Chapters from each house."[53] Gatian suggests that what Notre Dame wants is its own provincial superior even though they do not use the word "provincial" in their petition. Gatian, of course, does not think Sorin is the man for the job. What Gatian does not realize is that his days in the Chapter are numbered: he is about to be excluded by Sorin with Moreau's approbation.[54] Not knowing his fate, Gatian writes to Moreau as if he were running the Chapter and Notre Dame himself: he gives Moreau advice on the settlement of St. Mary's in Kentucky, he thinks little of the Canadian superior Saulnier, and he deplores the fact that the sisters have modified their habit. Once Gatian learns of his exclusion from the Chapter, the wind will be taken out of his sails, but if Sorin thought demotion would silence his most vocal critic, he was wrong. Moreover, Gatian's degradation may have furthered his descent into behavior that would, within two years, push Sorin to look for a way to get his fellow countryman away from Notre Dame. Already in October, Gatian had been assigned to the novitiate in Indianapolis, according to Minor Chapter notes, but he did not go.[55] He was a time bomb ticking under Sorin's nose.

6

Off to Brooklyn

One strength of an institutionalized religious life is the use of retreats to stop ordinary work for several days to assess the interior state of the soul. Gatian, like his confreres at Notre Dame, benefitted from the annual event that generally took place at the end of the summer before the beginning of the fall semester. By the time Gatian was twenty-two, he would have enjoyed eight such community retreats, and the 1848 retreat is particularly valuable for our understanding the young man because his annual interior examination is preserved in the form of a letter dated August 20, 1848. In his typically well organized fashion, Gatian enumerates nine characteristics about himself, some of which he elaborates. He admits that he is flawed but insists that he is valuable to Notre Dame because he can accommodate himself to any job. His personality type, he admits, is a blend of "melancholy and sanguine," but the melancholy predominates. To a reader today such self introspection is borne out in the evident unrest Gatian had exhibited for years: he was not a very happy young man. His melancholy has plunged him into paranoia and self-doubt, particularly when he realizes other men his age are already respected doctors and military officers. He questions his vocation and admits that he stays a brother only because submitting to a superior is the only way for him to save his soul. Moreover, he cannot even think about leaving Holy Cross and Notre Dame because he is too exhausted to begin a new lifestyle as a layman apart from the school he loves so well. Nevertheless, he is tempted "to return to the world to lead a philosophical, political and philanthropic life where, away from religion, I could be happy."[1] If he had only a few days to live, he muses, he could be virtuous, but not knowing his longevity, he often wishes for "the madness which would take away all my cares and let me sin innocently: that's why I play the fool."[2] The coded phrase "to play the fool" (noted earlier) refers to his homoerotic sexual desires. Gatian's sexual inclinations will be discussed later since they figure significantly in his eventually leaving the community, but at this point we should recognize that the man was already aware of his proclivities.

If melancholy drives him to distraction, Gatian appreciates that his alternate state (his sanguine quality) is of little help to ameliorate his unhappiness because his thirst for knowledge cannot be satisfied. He vows that he would upset the world if he could, but not in Robespierre's manner. Rather he would choose the style of Lamartine. This is a very significant insight into himself as it shows that Gatian must have measured himself at some point against two very important revolutionary figures. The dark attraction he had to Robespierre is no less important than his light attraction to Lamartine, although he obviously fears the ramifications of the former. Gatian probably never read Lamartine's *History of the Girondins,* but he was bright enough to know that romantic historians had already begun to accept Lamartine as the chief liberal voice of the Revolution while Robespierre lapsed into being the sad mouthpiece of Jacobin reactionary fanatics.[3] Gatian was not a modest man. When most young people select an idol (athletic, musical, or political), they have the presence of mind to realize their idol is beyond their own talents. Gatian, however, measured himself against public figures and concluded he could be them if only he were not saddled by religion.

His frustration to excel, Gatian writes, has resulted in his becoming emotionally attached to individuals. He is, it appears, just beginning to understand his homoerotic attraction to certain students: "I can't teach without loving my students passionately and without my heart requiring inwardly that they love me as well."[4] When students do not return his affection, he punishes them and alienates them. Thus two groups have arisen: his favorites who return his affections and those who have turned against the favored few. It is one of the pedagogical lessons to be learned by every young teacher, that is, keeping affections under control in the classroom, but Gatian was incapable of separating his classroom persona from his personality. He needed a good dose of reality from a mentor, and one wonders where Brother Vincent was at the time. Even though Gatian had long outgrown the need for Vincent's rudimentary lessons in pedagogy, the young man at twenty-two was still in need of psychological guidance.

One has to admire Gatian's honesty, even if it seems self-serving in this letter, an attempt to elicit from his superior some soothing words to endorse Gatian's sexual attraction to his students. He admits that his affections have in fact come to be centered on a student named John Hays: "I can never and I'll never be able to stop myself from loving him, nor from wanting to be loved by him…I've loved other children before him (but never as much as him)."[5] A student from Fort

Wayne, John Hays was sixteen years old at the time and had been at Notre Dame since June 26, 1844, his date of enrollment. He was six years younger than Gatian and had taken several classes from Gatian because the brother taught both mathematics and language courses.[6]

John Hays was a bright student. The notes from the Council of Professors for August 4, 1846, list him as taking four of the five premiums in the first division of studies. He was named second accessit in Religion, first accessit in English Reading, premium in Grammar, Orthography, and Parsing, premium in Epistolary Correspondence, premium in History and Geography, premium in Arithmetic, premium in Writing, first accessit in Purity of Language, first accessit in Public Reading, first accessit in Vocal Music. As secretary for the Council, Gatian must have taken great delight in recording the merits of his favorite student. Why this bright student would later transfer into the Manual Training School is a mystery, unless it were to avoid Gatian. A note from the Council of Professors for 1846 reads: "F. Cointet proposed that Mr. John Hays should not concur in certain branches, lest he should have all the premiums, because he had more talents than the rest & also a better memory." On July 24, 1846, the Council was divided on the awarding of the music premium, two in favor of Gregory Campeau, and Gatian in favor of Hays. Gatian claimed that "J. Hays had sung much better at the examination & 2nd. That his fiddle helped Campeau in learning his notes, beating time & rendering him bolder." Something at this time aggrieved Hays because another notes reads: "F. Cointet shall speak to Mr. J. Hays & threaten him if necessary. He may be deprived of his premiums & condemned to work for his schooling, & then be dismissed."[7] No reason is given for these drastic measures against this boy. Two years later on June 21, 1848, John Hays is excluded from all premiums "on account of his familiaity with A. Collet." Possibly the same kind of affection that Gatian hoped to cultivate with Hays was being lavished by Hays on another student.

During the four years they would have known each other, the two developed an emotional attachment that was probably more heartfelt by the tortured teacher than by his student.[8] Gatian writes, "Nothing but the caresses of John Hayes can quiet me."[9] But Hays does not return the affection sufficiently, and Gatian blackens into despair. He then admits something very curious: he has written a letter to the Blessed Virgin "and I played the fool, and then repenting, I begged again and promised to act better, if I got that." He does not say what he wrote to Mary, but it was probably an appeal for her to soften Hays' heart. Such is the desperation of a Petrarchan lover. Again, the phrase "playing the fool" is used, and we are sure Gatian did something he regrets, but the specifics of the act are vague. He says he repented and promises to act better, but it is obvious that he is no longer talking about Mary but rather about the teenager he is trying to seduce: "the child doesn't hate me now and acts very nicely to me." So Gatian is somewhat happy the situation has been defused, but he renders no thanks to God and instead "began to go no longer to confession and to send everyone to the devil." The man probably figured out that the sacrament did him little good since it did not allay the ardor he felt for Hays. So his contrition is contrived because his repentance extends only to his being grateful he is no longer hated by Hays.

Gatian seems to have no concern for Hays' actual feelings on the matter. There is no indication that Gatian understands in fact what he has done is wrong: using his power as a teacher to flirt with a student. He is simply upset because his maneuvers did not work. One wonders what Sorin did about this rather confessional admission. It surely was one of the warning signs that Gatian was heading into troubled waters. Interestingly, Gatian writes that he has not had temptations "against the sixth commandment for at least two years" even though he is "subject to illusions at night."[10] For Gatian, the sixth commandment may have been limited to adultery with a woman (although confession manuals since the Middle Ages had broadened the range of the commandment considerably) so that his temptations to flirt with John Hays would not be covered by the commandment. It was a convenient ploy to rationalize his sexual attractions to a man which were then released in the nightly illusions that he admits to.

One solution Gatian proposes is that he be taken out of teaching and put into manual labor, but he dreads the prospect because he has found such work deadening. There may be, of course, a hidden agenda for such a request to shift apostolates: John Hays by this time had shifted into the Manual Labor School. But such a suggestion is speculative and would have been transparent to Sorin anyway. We should accept Gatian at his word that the classroom has been the scene of his temptations and leaving it would remove the temptations, a specious argument, of course, because his attraction to men would stay with him in or out of the classroom. He is not yet grappling with his real cause of anxiety. In this confessional letter, he questions his vocation to be a brother and says he would have become a priest except for the fact that his family was too poor to finance a seminary education. Now he thinks less about ordination for three reasons: he has had a near death experience, he is too old, and the careers of the two Holy Cross brothers who had actually transferred into seminary training aborted. Gatian's solution for his melancholy, he thinks, lies in being kept busy (a timeless antidote in religious lore), and Sorin was probably of a like mind because the wily superior soon found a way to keep Gatian occupied and away from temptation at Notre

Dame: he sent Gatian off on a long trip to Brooklyn that Sorin probably hoped would extend to months if not years.

As early as 1847 the bishop of New York had asked Sorin for brothers to teach in his diocese. In the fall of 1848, Sorin and Drouelle visited Bishop Hughes to explore the possibility, and one month later five brothers went to New York. Because of difficulties securing actual employment in diocesan grade schools, three of the brothers returned immediately to Notre Dame, leaving only Brother Basil (thirty-eight years old) and Brother Aloysius (eighteen years old) in Brooklyn.[11] The two brothers were to teach one hundred boys, but the situation was a financial disaster from the beginning since the pastor paid Basil and Aloysius nothing, letting them support themselves on whatever tuition they could get from their students. After Brother Vincent had failed to correct the situation, Gatian arrived in the winter of 1849.

A sizable chunk of Gatian's extant correspondence was written from Brooklyn: fourteen letters to Sorin, two to Moreau, and one telegram. If anything, the young man took his supervisory duties seriously. The first letter is written in English and exhibits some rather grandiose pretention: "I have seen the great city at last, and I have pitched my tent on the seashore in the heights of Columbia Street No. 94 at the Baths of Brooklyn."[12] This is poetic hyperbole. First of all, it is not the first time he has seen New York, although "at last" could be simply a sigh at the end of an arduous journey, which it was. But "pitching one's tent" sounds as if the young man is on some kind of military crusade. He then joshes his audience (the letter is addressed "To Notre Dame du Lac University") as he clearly intends to amuse a wide readership. He says that since he lives in a bathhouse, he will keep clean, and if he becomes suicidal, he will have plenty of water in which to drown himself. It is winter, and he tours the city, often getting lost because of missing street signs.

His actual journey to New York had been harrowing. Riding in a sleigh from Notre Dame north to Bertrand, Michigan, where the Holy Cross Sisters had begun a girls' academy outside the domain of the Vincennes diocese, Gatian had to spend a cold, sleepless night before heading the next morning east to Niles where he caught the train ("the cars") to Detroit. He had another sleepless night because he missed his Notre Dame community intensely. He crossed into Canada and traveled sometimes by rail, sometimes by sleigh. Part of the way the sleigh glided over Lake Erie and occasionally the horses had to leap over two-foot gaps in the ice. He passed through London (Ontario) and arrived at Buffalo, having gone 265 miles in two and a half days. He recounts several accidents, and the worst almost killed him:

Whilst I was sound asleep with some sweet dream about my friend of the Lake, the driver put us in a ditch. The coach upset, and we all came down on top of each other, but I was on the lower side and my head went thro' the window in the snow, and the first thing I knew was that some were standing on my breast. My feet were entangled in the feet of my companions, and it was some time before we could get out of the coach, and I was the last that came out. Luckily the horses stood still. If the contrary had happened, my head would have been severed from my body.[13]

Naturally, his heart remembered his "friend of the lake" John Hays, and the recounting of the incident may have been calculated to soften at least one particular young reader back at Notre Dame. The travellers continued on foot to a hotel where a doctor replaced an ear cut off of one of the men in the coach accident.[14] At Niagara Falls, Gatian elected to cross by the dangerous ferry rather than by the safer wire bridge because he knew the ferry was quicker and would ensure his catching the train for Buffalo. This was not a faint-hearted man: when he set his sights on a goal, he was not afraid to take risks that others would call foolhardy. Passing through Albany, he arrived in New York City one full day before the travellers who used the wire bridge back at Niagara Falls. His first letter ends with special mention of four students: two to whom he had taught bookkeeping (Richard Ferris, John Connolly) and two to whom he had taught arithmetic (Francis Wolke, Thomas Richardville). There is a genuine tenderness in his fond regard for the students he has left behind.

The day after his arrival in New York, Gatian writes Sorin a long letter giving his first impressions of the situation in Brooklyn: it is quite hopeless. Gatian lays the blame on Sorin, Vincent, and Basil, each one culpable for a different reason. True to form, Sorin has opened an establishment without sufficient preparation of the personnel. Vincent was worthless when sent to Brooklyn. Basil, the elder of the two brother teachers in Brooklyn, has alienated Mrs. Parmentier who runs the boarding house where the brothers live. Gatian includes several lists of financial analysis, and the school seems salvageable, but a new teacher will be needed to replace Aloysius who has no training in algebra, geometry, or bookkeeping. Sorin's incompetence in assigning personnel is no idle insight from an irascible Gatian: Aloysius was sent out to teach at age eighteen, one year after he entered the community. He was terribly unprepared to teach the hordes of boys (between fifty and sixty) assigned to him in Brooklyn. Gatian's indictment of Vincent is more unfounded since it does not seem to take into account the mess that Vincent found on his arrival. Gatian, of course, plans to right all the wrongs and prove himself superior to both the Notre Dame priest and the brother patriarch.

After three days, he reports on the rambunctious students: they fight and yell "like so many wild Indians" during Sunday school. These rowdies are not the lads who attend the school during the week (106 boys), but rather the one hundred lads who are dumped by their parents at the church on Sunday and expected to master their religious duties and decorum with an hour or two of pious tutelage. These were not docile boys, and some of them undoubtedly came from the Irish gangs of New York that were gradually clubbing their way out of oppression in the New World. To expect them to behave on Sunday after battles for their lives during the rest of the week was a little naive. The pastor, Father Bacon, has insisted that the brothers accept both groups of boys and has threatened to black-list the Holy Cross community in the diocese if the two brothers refuse the combined duty. As far as Basil is concerned, although Gatian finds little fault in him, Gatian thinks Basil should be replaced as director in order to keep the peace. Gatian suggests Brother Thomas as a replacement, although Thomas too is problematic because he writes poorly and is rather young.[15] Gatian soon discovers that Basil's problem is that he is a bed-wetter and thus has developed a reputation as dirty and slovenly.[16] Basil is thirty-eight years old, and incontinence was clearly a misunderstood affliction in mid-nineteenth century America. Basil will be gone within a month, however, shifted to New Orleans to help Brother Vincent run the orphanage there. Meanwhile, Gatian pitches in and substitute-teaches for Aloysius who is often sick. Gatian plans then to take over Basil's class if Basil can be removed. Father Bacon has lost all faith in Basil and tells Gatian, "I'd gladly have him crucified in the street."[17]

Gatian is, however, beginning to wear down. He is not only supervising the school and teaching almost full time, he has to run around Brooklyn to find a new boarding house. He also has to broker a deal with a printer to have rule books printed for Sorin. He advertises for a science teacher for Notre Dame and interviews a good prospect. He investigates a new organ for the church at Notre Dame. But the factotum is losing energy: "All this time, I'm growing old, etc., etc. I've become hard of hearing, and I can hardly see. Teaching is killing me."[18] He sounds like a man of sixty instead of the twenty-three he actually is. His deafness, however, is an actual problem: it prevents him from having any kind of order in a classroom full of fifty-eight boys who have run roughshod over the teenager teacher Aloysius.[19] Gatian tries, but as the boys talk constantly in class and he is unable to discriminate the source of the noise, he devises a pedagogical plan for Aloysius and leaves the classroom. He does not, however, understand nor admit the cause of his own failure as a teacher other than deafness. He turns to prayer, promising to say a thousand "Hail Marys" if order comes back to Aloysius's classroom. The heavenly bribe does not work, and Gatian flails out again at the root cause of the disaster: Sorin who simply sends people out on mission whether they are prepared or not. It is, of course, a Sorin tactic to extend his province beyond the Vincennes diocese by ingratiating himself with various prelates. The mental well being of his subjects is secondary in Sorin's mind, and Gatian has not only the presence of mind to diagnose Sorin's faults, but he has the nerve to confront the priest as well.

Compounding the problems in Brooklyn is, in Gatian's analysis, Father Bacon who seems zealous for education but has no regard for method: he loads 225 boys (including the hundred from Sunday school) on the backs of two brothers and gives them no teaching supplies. Without desks and blackboards, the enterprise is doomed. Touched by the evident sufferings of his two confreres, Gatian settles in for the long haul. No longer simply an official visitor, he has become a necessary part of the day to day operations of the school.

On March 16, 1849, Gatian writes two letters to Sorin, the first announcing that he is officially closing his three week "visit." He has received no letters from Sorin to help the brothers through what Gatian calls their "terrestrial hell." Gatian then makes three proposals. First of all, Sorin must insist that Bacon free the brothers from the Sunday school duties and purchase necessary classroom furniture. Secondly, Sorin should tell Bacon the brothers will remain only until the end of the school year and each brother will need sixty dollars per month to survive. Thirdly, if Bacon does not comply, the brothers will leave by April 22, the end of the school quarter.

Meanwhile, Gatian has had a chance finally to supervise Basil's classroom where the brother tries to teach math without blackboards or desks. It is hard to imagine such a teaching situation, let alone the fact that Basil faced sixty boys in one room. What did he do? He probably recited problems aloud and had the boys figure them out in their minds. Any teacher would realize that such a technique might work for about ten minutes before boredom and pandemonium would set in.

Desperate to succeed, Gatian turns to his own physical ailments, particularly his deafness which by now is total in his left ear. He has no money to consult a doctor. In the middle of his troubles, he reaches out for his emotional crutch, memories of John Hays:

> Friends I have not. John Hays loves me not. I am intimately persuaded that he does not. I can't take it out of my head. Without him, I can't be happy. Why won't he love me? Oh, if I did but see him come to me with open heart, but

he won't. And when I take the first step toward him, I always think, even if he says he loves me, I always think, I can't help thinking that he says so only to get rid of me. I do not think it proceeds from his heart as long as he does not make the first step and take me by surprise. O, how homesick I am! How I do love the Lake. How I do love the boys, especially the apprentices.[20]

The openness with which he writes about the boy is revelatory, not only of Gatian's para-sexual obsession but also of Sorin's probable motive to get Gatian away from Notre Dame. The infatuation with John Hays, apparently one-sided, simultaneously drives Gatian to distraction and yet has the calming effect that affection, in any form, has on a person cut off from comfortable surroundings. Any number of love poems, e.g., Abraham Cowley's "Friendship in Absence," investigate the idea.

The second letter to Sorin on March 16 is a formal outline of the visit results. Nine points of concern are followed by nineteen "decrees." It is a remarkable production for a twenty-three year old supervisor to promulgate. Its officialese must have brought a bewildering frown to Sorin's face as he sensed Gatian preening in authoritarian feathers and as the letter lays the fault for the Brooklyn mess again at Sorin's feet. Gatian's "decrees" are intended to salvage the school, directing Bacon to buy classroom furniture, release the brothers from the odious Sunday school duties, and have their living expenses paid. As far as the school is concerned, Basil is to be replaced immediately, accounts are to be regularized, and an established curriculum, including specified texts, is to be put in place. The letter was "read in Chapter," which means Gatian assembled the two brothers and read it to them before mailing it. Their reactions could have been only positive: the fact that someone, even if it were the imperious Gatian, was taking their woes seriously must have brought some glimmer of hope into their dismal souls.

Four days later the Brooklyn brothers grow impatient. In the entire three weeks of Gatian's visit, they have had no letter of direction from Sorin and only one telegram. But Sorin at this time had his hands full of other matters. The unflappable Brother Joseph continued to concoct schemes in Indianapolis. Sorin was also deep into plans for his new establishment in New Orleans, indicative of his rashness in setting up a new location even as an earlier one was crumbling in Brooklyn. Gatian has given ultimatums to Bacon, but the poor priest could not agree to any of them. Four days later, Gatian reminds Sorin that the nine letters he has written Sorin have brought none in return. He decides he will close the school on his own on April 22. But finally on March 29, just as he is about to tell Bacon about the April closure, Gatian receives a letter from Sorin (posted March 21) directing Basil to leave for New Orleans. Gatian is furious because there is no mention of a replacement being sent for Basil and no mention of money to finance Basil's trip. On April 1 and again on April 2 Gatian writes a letter in increments indicating that Brother Thomas would, after all, probably be an acceptable replacement for Basil, even though earlier he had doubted Thomas' capabilities. Now Gatian asserts of Thomas: "It would take a soldier like him to manage our brats and face off Mr. Bacon."[21] As for another teacher, Brother Michael might be suitable.[22] Meanwhile, Gatian tries to teach bookkeeping, but only to ten students at a time because of his deafness. However, after trying four weeks in a row to handle the Sunday school, he has given up that aspect of the foundation. He does seem to think, however, that the Brooklyn foundation can be saved, given the right replacements for Basil and Aloysius.

As one might expect, when Gatian received no support from Sorin, he turned to Moreau, probably suspecting that his being sent to Brooklyn as a supervisor was only a ruse to get him away from Notre Dame and John Hays. A letter to Moreau at the end of March expresses his frustration. With a delicious sarcasm, Gatian remarks: "Father Sorin and he [Drouelle] made the arrangements [for New York] so well and examined things so well that, having sent five Brothers in November, three had to go home immediately, and the two that Mr. Bacon wanted to keep preferred Purgatory to being at his place."[23] Gatian rehearses all the Brooklyn abominations: too many students to teach, unprepared brothers, lack of adequate housing, an uncooperative pastor. Then he concludes for the first time that his loss of hearing can be attributed to frostbite suffered on the mid-winter trip from Notre Dame: he has no hearing in the left ear at all and very little in the right ear.

In early April Gatian tries again with a letter to get Sorin to make some decisions about Brooklyn: "Time rolls on, and to our great annoyance, nothing is done to deliver us from the chaos of uncertainty from which we cannot emerge without your assistance."[24] The young man's debilities continue: added to loss of hearing and sight, now his sense of smell is weakening. He misses John Hays and wishes to be at Notre Dame "were it but to enjoy his presence from time to time." He threatens Sorin that if he does not soon get to see Hays, "impatience might well cause an outburst of folly, which would be very scandalous here."[25] The reference can be to nothing else but a sexual tryst of some kind, probably homosexual, given Gatian's recent history, so he tells Sorin:

> I shall probably be able to keep my courage up, if I am busily employed at the Lake, not too far from him, having always some hopes of eventually recovering his friendship. But if all possibility of gaining his affection were taken from

me, or if he died before having showed me this affection, I would be a broken heart. *I would pine away and quickly follow him to the grave.*[26]

The Gatian who feels his senses leaving him is the same Gatian who lapses into the deepest sentiments of broken affection. His hope that Sorin would actually bring him back to Notre Dame to continue his heartaches proximate to Hays is unrealistic.

Gatian's sexuality deserves scrutiny because he himself made no secret of his struggles with celibacy. The French Revolution did more than change the economic face of the country—it also instituted a sexual rebellion that should be recognized for the force that it was. Sodomy, for example, was decriminalized in 1791 by the French National Assembly and was never reclassified as a crime in the Napoleonic code, but little is known about the deliberations that led up to the vote because the papers from the Committee on Criminal Investigation no longer exist. We do know, however, that the Committee got rid of all crimes (like sodomy) that were defined in religious terms.[27] Of course the secular sway of morality could not totally dislodge the ecclesiastical mores of a thousand years. As late as 1848 sexual expression was still considered best when restrained. Thus Debay in 1848 could write, "Pour conserver longtemps l'intégrité et la vitalité des organes génitaux, il ne faut jamais les fatiguer par de trop fréquents exercices"[28] ("To keep your sexual organs healthy, you should not wear them out with too much sexual activity"). And the church was reluctant to let go of its time-honored dictum that sexual participants must have procreation uppermost in their minds: pleasure secondary to progeny. Manuals to prepare the faithful for sacramental confession stressed the necessity of purity, and to the question "What are at present the most widespread habits of mortal sin?" a manual from Châlon-sur-Saône replies rhetorically, "In the case of young people, they are improper thoughts, and the sins of impurity" [erotic daydreams and masturbation].[29] As church fathers read the situation, the problem with masturbation was that it would give sufficient pleasure so that addicts would never marry. Marriage was thus a remedy against selfish pleasure. Antoine Blanchard's extensively used list of questions to examine the state of one's conscience dwelled with a pathological intensity on the act of masturbation. Such a mindset would cause terrific inner struggle in a young man as bright as Gatian who, opting for celibacy, would have to reconcile his passionate tendencies with devotional rhetoric. For many religious men of the period, the answer was Mary, an untouchable symbol of virginal purity who was both mother and icon. To someone like Gatian who was attracted to members of his own sex, the rift was painful. Nature and idealism: never happy bedfellows.

The matter of Gatian's homoerotic attractions can be substantiated by reference to a very curious document that survives among early records. In his capacity as secretary for various councils at Notre Dame, appointments undoubtedly given to him because of his excellent writing skills, Gatian was in a position to assess not only other people but also himself. Thus he speaks of himself in the third person in council minutes as he "officially" attempts to evaluate his own actions. From February, 1847, to January, 1849, Gatian kept the chronicles for Notre Dame, a document which contains some bizarre entries about his own infatuation with John Hays. An early entry in his *Chronicles* decries the presence of "particular friendships" between students.[30] Another bemoans the relationship between a thirty-six year old ex-postulant named Hobeck and Brother Charles Borromeo: Hobeck returned home to Louisville to settle certain affairs and Brother Charles "followed him, but death has now separated them."[31] Gatian narrates the episode with a kind of Gabriel and Evangeline touch even as he attacks the moral failing. He is a writer torn between romantic reportage and a moral sense infused into him by spiritual mentors who recognized that even if such emotional attachments did not end in sexual trysts, they usually jeopardized the harmony of a community in which all members should share the support and acceptance of each other. Pairings, spiritual directors always cautioned, lead to exclusivity and the undermining of common life. What solidifies a marriage, in other words, destroys a religious community.

On May 30, 1847, Gatian again writes of the matter of "particular friendship." Two officers (the vice president and the secretary) of the St. Mary's Association ("having for its primary object the honor of the Blessed Virgin") "contracted a dangerous familiarity and particular friendship." In spite of their liaison, Gatian notes, they were elected to their positions by their fellow students. Moreover, they are "the smartest pupils of the college." Here Gatian's torn soul surfaces again: on the one hand he has to point out the boys' moral lapse while on the other hand he emphasizes their intelligence and popularity. It is as if Gatian is consciously or unconsciously demystifying male bonding, setting himself up for his own infatuation with John Hays. Today, educators see the attraction of two male students to each other as something perfectly acceptable, but in the middle of the nineteenth century in a Catholic college run by Jansenist tinged priests and brothers, homoerotic attraction or activity was never tolerated, much less encouraged. One month later, in June, 1847, the St. Mary's Association runs into trouble: six boys go into South Bend without permission and one boy swims naked in the river. One of the six is dismissed, but not the naked swimmer "because he had not paid for his board." (Morals bend to economics—a reason to delay paying one's tuition perhaps.) The secretary of the Association is publicly degraded, and John Hays is elected to the office!

At this point the Gatian *Chronicles* begin to focus on Gatian himself, principally his insistence on strict enforcement of rules. On July 18, 1847, he drags a student out of a pew during Sunday vespers. At the annual retreat he confronts Sorin about the changing of rules set down by the Le Mans motherhouse. So freely does Gatian speak up that he is expelled from the Minor Chapter on November 15, 1847. He continues to flail away at Notre Dame's poor discipline:

> The discipline is exceedingly mild this year: Pupils may do anything with impunity. There is indeed no other law than that of nature. Yet [a] great many pupils have abused the authors of this laxity, such as Bro. Vincent who has not the least authority and who has been several times positively disobeyed and whom they have hissed two or three times.

Gatian does not exhibit here much concern for the venerable Brother Vincent as he indicts the patriarch for not being as vigorous as he should be in maintaining good order. There is a pulling inside of Gatian, an overwhelming sense of moral rectitude that is coming up against his homoerotic attraction to John Hays. He notes that one apprentice "has been secretly dismissed for some immoral actions" but he adds that the teachers believe "there exists a good deal of immorality among our boys, especially the pupils." The supposedly high incidence of moral weakness thus argues against the high road of purity that Gatian would like to espouse as a norm. Gatian will return to this theme in a letter to Sorin ten years later.

Finally the tension inside him by early summer, 1848, is so intense that it erupts into public displays of despair that Gatian captures in his *Chronicles*:

> The following incident shows how carefully every one ought to watch over the affections of his heart and also that too great a severity is blameable. Bro. Gatian was laboring for a whole year in desperate agony (and his soul for the same cause is still languishing) on account of the alienation of John Hays's heart from him caused by Bro. Gatian's too great severity. For the latter, strange to say, who idolizes and still idolizes J. Hays, was exceedingly harsh and unjust towards him. At last, Bro. Gatian became so desperate, at the beginning of June, that he began to play the fool and determined rather to go to hell than to give up the idea of obtaining an interview from J. Hays. The Superior threatened him and said he would have him taken up. But he heeded

not. At last, the Superior sent him John Hays who forgave him and Bro. Gatian promised to play the fool no more. But B.G. is not at rest until he has received some testimonies of affection from J. Hays and I am afraid he will never be saved if he does not obtain said feelings from J. Hays. Then B.G. was crazy; he would break the panes of glass, swear, not say any prayers, go to the lake up to his neck and by various ways attempt to kill himself.

Sorin, in attempting to handle the problem locally, is trying to keep the peace. Having the student, however, agree to a private interview with the love sick brother was probably not the best way to defuse the situation: if a wolf has problems with a lamb, the lamb is not sent in to listen to the wolf without at least a third party present. Sorin gave Gatian what Gatian wanted: a private meeting with the object of his affections under the guise of apologizing for perceived harshness in the past toward the boy. The interview, of course, was a failure because Gatian did not get from Hays the signs of affection that he wanted. What follows is Gatian's radical behavior, including destruction of property and attempts at suicide. The latter, of course, were half-hearted and calculated to elicit attention rather than death because death, of course, would bring separation from his beloved.

One final incident six months later serves as another danger signal that Gatian is losing control. The final entry of the Gatian *Chronicles*, dated January 10, 1849, does not mention Hays by name, but the details indicate that the object of Gatian's affections, bringing the brother to "play the fool" during public prayers, is probably Hays since the Gatian letters later from Brooklyn are still obsessed with Hays:

> Last Saturday, January 7th the Institution was greatly scandalized by Bro. Gatian who, pushed on by an irregular affection and his violent passions began playing the fool during the Litany of the Blessed Virgin and continued at supper when Mr. G. Campeau, a boarder of muscular strength, by the orders of the Superior, endeavored to seize him, but it required six men to take him out of the room. He swore most horribly. Mr. Campeau came very near breaking his (Bro. Gatian's) neck—however Bro. Gatian calmed down and the next morning having obtained of the Superior what he desired, took the resolution of correcting himself. He also begged pardon of the Institution on the 9th Inst.

It is important that Gatian recognizes his "irregular affection," but it is also important to understand that he must have had an equally strong sense that his homoerotic tendencies were genuine and natural to him. It is thus that the inner conflict between what he has been taught is proper conduct (no same-sex affection) and what he senses is good and natural (same-sex attraction) boils up to precipitate his mental breakdown. The tension is more than he can handle: an intelligent and energetic young brother is destroyed by an inability to sacrifice his natural tendencies to societal dictates.

All of this sexual baggage Gatian carried to Brooklyn where he attempted to save a school, and where Sorin hoped Gatian's sexual tensions would be expunged by hard work. Gatian's final letter from Brooklyn is a reply to a letter Sorin posted at the end of March and a telegram which simply read: "Is Basil gone to New Orleans—teach yourself."[32] Gatian becomes furious: he has not sent Basil to New Orleans because there is no money for the trip and there is no one to replace Basil in the school. Gatian repeats that he himself is too deaf to teach and he remarks (with underscoring): "*Truly a Brother must have an iron vocation to stand the trials you make him undergo.*" Gatian then adds he will send Basil to New Orleans, but he himself will try to teach for only one week. At the end of that time, if he finds himself unable to continue in the classroom, he will give the boys a week's vacation. Then with the end of the quarter looming, it will be up to Sorin to send a teacher. As for Brother Aloysius, the young man has vowed not to teach more than half a quarter longer. Gatian's visit ends in disaster, and he returns to Notre Dame.

Meanwhile, Brother Vincent was travelling south from Notre Dame to take over St. Mary's Orphanage in New Orleans. Although Vincent met challenges greater than those met by Gatian in Brooklyn, the patriarch's response was mature and deliberate. In spring of 1849 at the age of fifty-two, Vincent was presented with this great challenge: he was sent with four brothers and three sisters to assume direction of an institution founded in 1835 by a young diocesan priest who died in 1837 of typhoid incurred from his heroic efforts to save his orphans during a hurricane. St. Mary's had languished for a decade under lay supervision, and the prelate of New Orleans, Anthony Blanc, was very anxious to have a religious community take the children under its wing. When Vincent arrived on May 1, 1849, he found ninety-eight boys in pitiable condition.[33] The miserable blankets they had were quickly burned by the sisters. Thanks to the generosity of the Ursuline Sisters and the Sisters of Charity, Vincent and his staff were able to turn things around.

Nature, however, assailed him. Spring flooding in New Orleans was an annual problem, and two weeks after Vincent's arrival, a dike broke in the city and water in the downtown area stood at four feet:

The Mississippi broke its dike, which we here call a levee. Water rushed in and is still rushing like a torrent in a large part of the city, from there into the sugar and cotton plantations. The inhabitants have to save themselves. The loss is immense. It is thought that the water won't reach us. It's still half a league away. Two or three thousand workers are employed to fix the levee, but in the evening they aren't any more ahead than in the morning. They made the water run into ditches. Although these ditches were reinforced with stones and bricks, they haven't been any less carried away by the current. God sometimes shows men His power before which all ingenuity and knowledge can do nothing.[34]

Fortunately the orphanage, five miles distant, was spared. Cholera, however, plagued the city and sixteen orphan boys had died in the two months before the brothers arrived. Water was unhealthy to drink, so they drank only the water collected from downspouts.

Gradually Vincent had to deal with problems among his staff. Brother Theodulus, the cook, came down with a fever, and Brother Louis developed an open sore on his hand.[35] The cook proved to be a particular problem. Theodulus was a man who could complain at length, and he did so in several letters to Sorin. Brother Vincent went out of his way to accommodate the man, but Theodulus' whining was chronic. At the same time, young Brother Basil started to be a problem. Having recently gone through the trauma of teaching in Brooklyn, New York, under poor circumstances, he seems to have brought his unhappiness to New Orleans. He threatened to return to Notre Dame if Vincent did not procure a priest to live in the orphanage and help with the ministry. Then, as if problems among the brothers were not enough, two of the three sisters came to be at odds: Sister Mary of Calvary and Sister Mary of the Five Wounds, the latter described by Vincent as "a little busy-body or at least too moody." The sisters may have resented taking orders from a brother when they had been answerable only to a priest in their positions before. Within two months of his arrival, Vincent is busy reshuffling his staff to make up for their weaknesses.

Ever the kind man, he was not well suited to be a superior since he lacked the knack of making people do what they did not especially want to do. Although he could maneuver students admirably in a classroom and guide novices through their formative years, he was never able to command his peers with the steely resilience that men like Moreau and Sorin could muster to rein in their subjects. His heart must have been excessively kind. He was certainly sensitive to a fault and absolutely devoted to his vow of obedience. For example, although he could not abide wine because it made him ill, Sorin once ordered him to drink a glass of wine. Sorin had secretly told some visitors that Brother Vincent, an old man at the time, would do anything he was told to do. Sorin ordered, and Vincent raised the glass. Then Sorin stopped him before he could drink and told him to leave the room. Sorin had proved his point. It seems to us today a deplorable act.[36]

By July Theodulus' health had improved, but he wanted to return to Notre Dame anyway. Basil was beginning to show promise as a prefect. Vincent himself took charge of doing the steward's job. He rose every day at 4:30 and hitched a horse to a little cart which he drove through the hotel area of the city to collect leftover food for the orphanage. Sometimes he had to pick old cigar butts out of the food he was given. By 7 AM he was back at the orphanage. During the day he gave relief to Louis, Basil, and Francis, who supervised the boys seven days a week, all day long, and needed occasional breaks.

> The Brothers in charge of the children get up at 5 AM, and the children at 5:30. As you see, no prayer for them, no more than for me. Then one hundred children on their backs all day long. They can't leave them alone for a minute. No particular examen for the Brothers who teach class, and very often none for me either, because with Brother Theodulus being incapable of doing his job, I have to replace him as much as I can. The two Brothers are very glad that I take part of the recreation supervision, because they're tired of always being with the children and have their studies and classes to prepare.[37]

Vincent thus supervised the boys' recreation periods, and he took responsibility for one of the dormitories.

Francis was, by August, starting to chafe. Vincent agonized, and by August he himself was begging Sorin to be replaced. He sent Brother Louis back to Notre Dame in order to save Brother Basil: the two had irreconcilable differences. Then Sister Five Wounds started to make demands on Vincent. It seems he could satisfy no one. The subjects saw a power vacuum and rushed to fill it. Had Vincent been stronger, he might have calmed some of these people, but he agonized instead of guiding firmly. His subjects smelled a weakness. The New Orleans atmosphere was, of course, no help: Yankees and Frenchmen were unused to the horrible heat and humidity, and they were susceptible to recurring plagues of cholera and yellow fever that threatened the city. Theodulus did little work. Five Wounds was flexing her muscle. Basil and Francis worked like slaves as did Mary of Calvary and Mary of the Nativity. Theodulus complained to Sorin that Vincent chose Francis as a spiritual monitor and that Francis thus took it upon himself to tell Vincent how to run the orphanage. Theodulus thus gets orders from two people, and he bristles, faulting Vincent for weakness and Francis for arrogance.[38] It was, of course, a smoke screen for his own indolence. Vincent, at the end of August, was still asking to be replaced.

By October 5, Theodulus had settled into some work as sacristan, and Vincent was pleased. Basil continued successful in his work but neglected his spiritual exercises: Vincent worried about the young man's long-term effectiveness. Francis, on the other hand, seemed to be doing fine. The need for a permanent chaplain had become so acute, however, that Basil and Theodulus threatened to leave if a priest did not arrive soon from Notre Dame. Eventually Vincent got his wish. The Minor Chapter Book at Notre Dame contains a note for May 24, 1850, that Brother Vincent "shall be called back if possible, and Brother Ignatius sent in his place, that is, to take the employment of Brother Theodulus who shall succeed Brother Vincent in his charge of Director of the asylum." But Vincent remained in New Orleans for at least another half year as an entry in the Chapter book for November 15, 1851, documents once again a resolve that Brother Vincent will be called from New Orleans. Finally an entry for September 27, 1852, indicates that Vincent "will replace Br. Eleazar and Alexander on Saturday morning, to give them time to go to confession." Thus Vincent was back at Notre Dame when a terrible crisis occurred.

On September 13, 1852, Sorin was appointed by Moreau to become superior of the Holy Cross mission in Bengal. Under the pretense that he was unworthy of episcopacy, an honor that would follow the move to Bengal, Sorin refused the obedience. One month later Moreau wrote again to Sorin commanding him to take the position in Bengal. Moreau also responded to a letter from the Minor Chapter at Notre Dame which had protested Sorin's transfer. Brother Vincent would have, of course, been part of the Minor Chapter during this entire affair. In January, 1853, the Minor Chapter decided that Father Cointet "should go to the motherhouse as the legal deputy of this establishment [Notre Dame] for this year, and should try to settle there the difficulties actually existing between both houses." The language of the resolution is brash, pretending to a kind of equality with the motherhouse, an equality which it legally did not have. A month later Sorin delivered to the Minor Chapter a decree of separation from Le Mans, had them sign it, and mailed the document to France. Curiously there is no entry in the minutes for the Minor Chapter concerning this event. An entry two days later treats of small matters, including the purchase of some cows. The rebellion by Sorin was, in fact, a secret kept to himself and the few members of the Minor Chapter, including Brother Vincent, who apparently could be browbeaten. Sorin had the encouragement of two American bishops who felt that European missionaries should break their ties to their motherhouses, but Sorin lacked the backing of his bishop friend Purcell of Cincinnati and a canon lawyer whom Sorin consulted on the matter.[39] Within a year Sorin went to France and was reconciled to Moreau: Sorin got his own way and stayed at Notre Dame.

Brother Vincent must have been ripped apart during the year of this unfolding drama. He was born in France a few miles from Sorin's home town. He had worked side by side with Sorin for a dozen years as his trusted mentor, through the hardships of St. Peter's and the early years at Notre Dame. He had guided Notre Dame people to New Orleans and worked to save that apostolate for Sorin in trying times. At the same time, he was trusted beyond a doubt by Moreau who had worked with him as far back as 1834 to transfer the Brothers of Saint Joseph out of Ruillé. Moreau selected Vincent for the foundation in Indiana and relied on Vincent's religious values to shepherd novices in America. When the Sorin crisis peaked, Moreau sent word that Brother Vincent was to submit to Le Mans a quarterly report on the state of affairs at Notre Dame, indicative of the lack of trust Moreau held in Sorin. Thus Vincent was torn between two allegiances. That he signed the decree of separation in 1853 merely reflects the power Sorin had to terrorize his local subjects. Vincent signed the document, a document written entirely in Sorin's handwriting, created before Chapter discussion. Vincent was not a man who confronted crises well. He was a man of prayer who sought refuge with God and let others fight over worldly particulars. Unlike Gatian, Vincent was not a fighter. Sorin and Moreau both needed the good will of such a man as Vincent in their respective camps. That Vincent survived the power struggle is testament to his conviction that such a matter was something he was not supposed to arbitrate. He chose the line of least resistance. Moreau, fortunately, knew the cause of the rebellion and never faulted Vincent, as demonstrated by his appointment of Vincent as quarterly auditor.

A few years later, Brother Vincent was on hand at Notre Dame to welcome Moreau on the only visit Moreau made to America. On August 27, 1857, the founder arrived for a three week visit to Holy Cross institutions in Indiana, Chicago, and Philadelphia. Returning to France with him on the *Arago* was Brother Vincent, just as a financial crisis hit the United States and threatened the property at Notre Dame. Holy Cross in America survived, but Vincent, who was always at the heart of Notre Dame, must have been missed. Later, back in America, Brother Vincent fell ill in February of 1859 and was very sick for a month and a half. In charge of the Notre Dame budget and accounts at the time, Vincent was sorely needed as the local chapter scurried to ready the annual report for Le Mans. Throughout his life he was a valuable contributor to his community, and people were able to sense in him a special significance. Late in his life,

Brother Vincent made a trip to Rome with Sorin. At their papal audience as Vincent started to kneel in front of the pontiff, Pius IX raised him up, proclaiming him a "patriarch" too worthy to kneel in front of a pope.

As Vincent aged, so did Sorin, who never lacked for ideas. In the chapel of the novitiate at Notre Dame a double burial vault was dug on Sorin's orders in late spring of 1861. He intended it to be the final resting place for himself and Brother Vincent. Sorin's further plans were lugubrious: he wanted Moreau's right hand to be enclosed in a reliquary, suspended as if in blessing over the graves. Supposedly Moreau approved of the scheme. Sorin wrote in his *Chronicles*: "The right hand of the venerable founder and the body of the pious patriarch of the Brothers of St. Joseph will be two of the most precious relics possessed by the Congregation."[40] It was the idea of a man desperate to associate himself with men of virtue. Seven years later, however, it is doubtful that he still wanted Moreau's hand at Notre Dame. As part of the 1866 cabal that forced Moreau out of office, Sorin was no longer attempting to feign a love for the founder. He recanted, naturally, on his death bed and proclaimed himself a fool for distrusting and disgracing Moreau, but that was in 1893, twenty years after Moreau's own sad death. As Moreau's fortunes fell, Moreau was hounded from office and the motherhouse sold in France, along with the boarding school that Brother Vincent worked in as first director. Could the high school in Le Mans have developed like the high school in Indiana into a great university? We will never know. Fate, ever ironic, saw Sorin elected in 1868 as Superior General of Holy Cross, a post he held until his death. From that election on, Holy Cross became beholden to Notre Dame.

Of the seven men who came to America in 1841, Vincent, eldest of the missionary colony, outlived most of them. Joachim died in 1844. Anselm drowned in 1845. Gatian left the community and died on his family's farm in 1860. Lawrence died in 1873, much lauded for his contribution to the success of Notre Dame. Only Sorin and Francis Xavier outlived the patriarch Vincent. Francis Xavier was the last to die (in 1896), his grave dug by a novice named Brother Bernard Gervais, whom many members of Holy Cross still remember today. How very different were the fortunes of these seven immigrant brothers: Joachim the cook, Anselm the energetic young teacher, Gatian the rebel, Lawrence the farmer-businessman, Francis Xavier the carpenter-mortician, Sorin the potentate, and Vincent the patriarch.

Brother Vincent was never buried in the pretentious crypt envisioned by Sorin for the novitiate chapel, nor was Sorin. They both rest in the quiet Community cemetery near St. Mary's Lake at Notre Dame, Vincent with the brothers, Sorin with the superiors general and the Indiana provincials. Death came to the patriarch Vincent on July 23, 1890, at the age of ninety-three. Fortunate those who knew him, who lived with him, who cared for him in his final days.[41] If he ever longed for his homeland, he never said so in his letters. Content to follow his spirit to America, he gave a total gift of himself to his church and his community, never looking back. The joy he knew endures in those who revere his memory. What a contrast were the last years of this man to the restless years of Brother Gatian. Burned by his lust for John Hays, frustrated in his attempt to salvage Brooklyn, driven to distraction by a superior who could not tolerate his passion, Gatian headed day by day toward destruction. Sorin felt he had to do something to get rid of this young man.

7

California and Dissolution

By the time that gold was discovered in California on January 24, 1848, Gatian was already heading into spiritual chaos. When he returned from Brooklyn to Notre Dame early in the summer of 1849, he had not changed in his attachment to John Hays, so Sorin would have been looking for another way to remove Gatian from the area. Given Gatian's complaints about hearing loss, he would not have been useful in any of the schools like those in Vincennes or Madison. In fact, by 1849 the brothers had already left Vincennes and Madison, as well as Washington (Indiana), and their only apostolates (outside of Notre Dame) were at Pokagon and New Orleans. Sorin was stuck with Gatian. Then as the gold rush fever began to accelerate, touching the South Bend area, Sorin saw a way to dispose of him. In fact, he says as much in his *Chronicles* where he specifies two reasons for his having sent brothers to California: "1. That of preventing a terrible scandal which might ruin the work [Notre Dame]; 2. That of trying a means of paying arrears of indebtedness."[1] It is significant that Sorin puts the scandal ahead of financial needs, indicating his primary motivation was to get Gatian out of Indiana. He elaborates: "Br. Gatien was going to leave the Society to marry and to settle down near the college. He consented to depart for those distant regions."[2] The matter of Gatian's threat to get married seems odd in view of his strong homoerotic attraction to John Hays, but he would not have been the first homosexual man to believe that a heterosexual marriage would be just the remedy needed to settle his sexual confusion.

The Minor Chapter notes for September 28, 1849, do not indicate that a reason for the gold expedition was the Gatian scandal. In fact, Gatian is not even named as one of the three brothers (Lawrence, John, Michael) for the expedition. The only reason given in the Minor Chapter notes is the need for money. Sorin, of course, may not have shared with the Minor Chapter his intention to use the expedition as a way to get rid of Gatian. A more likely explanation, however, is that the idea to add Gatian to the expedition did not occur to Sorin until after the September 28 meeting of the Minor Chapter. In fact, it may have been Gatian himself who suggested adding himself to the expedition, but this explanation is doubtful given his previous grief at being separated from John Hays. In a letter written on August 15, 1851, to Sorin after the collapse of the gold expedition, Gatian apologizes to Sorin for forcing the priest to send brothers on the expedition: "I am sorry that for my sake you have sent Bros. to California."[3] But since the Minor Chapter decreed the expedition months before Gatian was added to the company, we should distrust Gatian's remark unless, as mentioned above, Sorin intended all along that the expedition would be a way to get Gatian out of Indiana, Sorin suppressing this motive until after the Minor Chapter had voted on the matter for the expressed purpose of getting riches. Gatian himself may have been in on such a ruse with Sorin, as Gatian may suggest in his August 15, 1851, letter, but we cannot read Sorin's mind on the matter except to repeat that in his *Chronicles* Sorin does list Gatian as the first reason for the expedition.

By February, 1850, Sorin had determined the members who would form the "St. Joseph Company." Originally he planned to send Brothers Lawrence (John Menage), John (John Thornton), and Michael (James Flynn). But in January the latter two were replaced by Brothers Alexis (Patrick Day) and Placidus (Urban Allard). Then Alexis was pulled from the expedition, possibly because he had entered the community only in 1848 and had been a novice less than three months. Sorin would have had difficulty explaining the man's presence among the group even though Alexis was thirty-one years old. Placidus, unfortunately, was not pulled from the group and would meet his death in California. He was an uneducated man who signed his name with an "X" and was included in the group because he was having a difficult time controlling his temper around both the brothers and the Notre Dame pupils.[4] The oldest brother prospector was Brother Justin (Louis Gautier), also a simple man, a cobbler who was forty-nine years old at the time. The religious leader of the group was Brother Lawrence. Sorin must have had a good deal of faith that the expedition would unearth riches because he spared a man who had proven himself essential to the financial well being of Notre Dame. Lawrence's official title for the expedition was "lieutenant," the office of "captain" being reserved for the layman George Woodworth who had lived in South Bend since 1843 with his family, including four children, two of whom were then students at Notre Dame. Rounding out the company were two students, Michael Dowling and Gregory Campeau. The latter figures several times in Gatian's *Chronicles*, most notably as the muscular student ordered by Sorin to subdue Gatian on that fateful day one year earlier when Gatian had broken down at supper and required physical restraint. One has to wonder about the chemistry of this gold expedition group, particularly when it included Gatian and a student who "came very near [to] breaking his (Bro. Gatian's) neck."[5]

On February 28, 1850, Gatian set off for California with the St. Joseph Company. It was winter, and the trip would take over four months, the group travelling about twenty-five miles per day. They used a large supply wagon pulled by six horses and a small wagon pulled by two. The adventure was ridiculous from beginning to end. Gatian kept the books, and of the $335.17 he lists as receipts, $259.55 had gone out as expenditures by the time the group reached Goose Neck, Missouri, on April 16, leaving them $75.62 for the remaining (and longer) part of the journey. Expenses included not only purchase of food but also repairs to the wagons and the shoeing of horses.

Gatian's first letter en route was posted from Burlington, Iowa, on March 15, 1850, and he notes they have travelled 189 miles through Illinois by way of Joliet, Morris, Ottawa, and Galesburg. The toll across the Mississippi River at Burlington was $1.50. Gatian is exuberant: he comments on the stories being told about the diggings in California. There is no mention of John Hays in Gatian's exuberance. Lawrence is not so delighted: in a note he attaches to Gatian's letter he says that Captain Woodworth is a lax leader and the brothers are neglecting their prayers. To Lawrence's remarks Gatian then adds a "postscript" to the effect that they have had no opportunity to hear Mass although they have passed three priests. Mass obligation, it seems, has had to be sacrificed for their need to move on. As far as the brothers neglecting their prayers, Gatian writes that when the horses ran off with the big wagon, Lawrence promised that the brothers would say a thousand "Aves" if the wagon and horses were retrieved unharmed. Gatian remarks that the brothers have no time to say the thousand prayers and asks Sorin "to say them for us." The brash presumption is quite evident, to say nothing of the fact that Gatian obviously read Lawrence's note written to Sorin and felt he had to counteract the older man's gloom.

A long letter in Gatian's hand but written on behalf of and signed by all seven was posted from Goose Neck Creek, seven miles west of Independence, Missouri, on April 9, 1850. They cannot push on before the end of the month or the beginning of May because of the lack of grass for the horses, so the men encamp on the frozen ground, biding their time. They eat well each evening on pork, sausage, or codfish, but they sleep in a tent on whatever hay, straw, or leaves they can manage to scrape together. Gatian notes that the roads had been muddy, and on March 20 they had broken the master bolt on the small wagon. Some creeks have been problematic, and settlements have been sparse, some settlers being less than helpful: "We had to entreat an old woman for a half hour for a bushel of corn and yet we had to pay one dollar in advance for it." On March 30, they behold a wonder: they pitch their tent on the property of a Mr. Atchinson who turns out to be six feet and six inches tall and weighs 350 pounds. After a week with the Atchinsons, the company lightens its load by selling its dishes, stove, trunks, and many clothes. They jettison the oars to Brother Lawrence's canoe but keep the canoe. They have learned from local lore that each pound of freight costs at least one dollar to haul, but they load up on hams and cross the Missouri River by ferry. By the end of April, they are well on their way again, the grass along the way finally being plentiful enough for the horses.

Although Gatian wrote to Sorin on May 5, we no longer have the letter. A letter dated May 19, 1850, however, notes the weather has been good and the scenery "rich though monotonous." Coming to the Platte River, Gatian is struck by its grandeur: it is over four miles wide and has islands in it fifty miles long. They pass through Pawnee territory and see the prairie strewn with the bones of dead animals. They also pass graves, seven in one day, of men who had been heading west. After crossing the Vermillion River, some men in this caravan of fifty-two wagons think they see an Indian crouching to fire at them. They shoot, but coming nearer, they discover, in Gatian's words, "the Pawnees were metamorphosed into prairie hens." The St. Joseph Company also sees wolves and antelope. This must have been exotic fare for the twenty-four-year-old Gatian. No wonder that he is so distracted by the excitement of new things he has no time to pine for his lost love back at Notre Dame.

Although Gatian had continued to write almost daily in a kind of diary form at this point on his trip, we have no entries after May 20. His next letter to Sorin is dated August 4, 1850, from Hangtown (Placerville), California, so we can only guess at the probable route that the St. Joseph Company followed in their last month of travel.[6] "Hangtown" was named for the hanging of three men, according to Brother Lawrence, by vigilante miner,[7] and the tree on which the unfortunate men were executed still stood in the town. Because their funds are running low, the St. Joseph Company decides to sell all its horses except one and to ration their remaining food. The men also stop drinking whiskey and drink coffee only in the morning, and "spruce or mountain tea without sugar" at noon and at night. They settle in on the South Fork of the American River near the John "Cockeye" Johnson ranch about six miles northwest of Hangtown.[8]

At the beginning of August, the St. Joseph Company begins its quest for gold with pan and shovel. It is difficult and generally unrewarding work in spite of Gatian's assertion that "California is as rich as the imagination can represent it.

There is more or less of the precious dust in every inch of ground."[9] Realistically, he does admit, "A man may in half a day dig a hole which will make his fortune, another may toil for a month and be unable to pay his board." It was every miner's dream, of course, to be the former. Since previous miners have already raked the best areas, new miners, including the St. Joseph Company, find themselves working through areas that have already been worked two or three times: "The conclusion I draw from the chances I see around," Gatian writes, "is that for the future people ought to stay at home."[10] Some men from South Bend have already gone home rich while others are broke. Gatian's prospects are bright, however, because he has made some valuable contacts: he may return to Hangtown with a speculator named Good, and he has found a former Notre Dame pupil named Garrett prospering on his own ranch. Obviously, Gatian is pulling away from the St. Joseph Company, and his days in Holy Cross are numbered. At this point in mid-September the St. Joseph Company, Gatian writes, is doing moderately well and is worth a thousand dollars. This news must have warmed Sorin's heart, as well as the knowledge that Gatian was distracted enough to have made peace with his passions.

By the beginning of November, however, the fortunes of the Company begin to sour due to sickness which afflicts all the brothers. Lawrence tells Sorin in a letter that he would like to start raising dairy cows in the area since he figures he could clear fifty dollars a day, enough to float the entire Notre Dame community.[11] Five days later Brother Placidus dies, and Lawrence writes Sorin with the sad news, including the fact that there was no priest on hand for Placidus' passing:

> It was useless for us to think of it for one [a priest] was not closer than San Francisco [about 150 miles away]. He had a burning fever; he did not speak two words for three days before dying; he had been sick eight days and had a completely edifying death ending like a candle.[12]

Thus died the brother with the bad temper, unable even to speak, if he still had any rage to voice. He was thirty-eight years old. He was buried quickly, as he probably died of cholera, in a hastily dug grave near the Company's tent, his marker, if there was one, a simple wooden cross.[13]

The effect of Placidus' death on Gatian must have been devastating. In a letter dated November 29, 1850, he writes:

> I am sick,—I am unable to work,—one of my acquaintances has just died,—is the talk of nearly every group in town and out of it. The St. Joseph's Com-

pany have not been spared. William Lucas, John Menage, have been in danger of death; and Bro. Placidus is gone, I hope to a better world. Their Doctor's bill is not far from *six hundred dollars*. I have also been very sick for four weeks, and have run $60 in debt. The majority of miners are in the case of the St. Joseph Company, unable to work and in debt.[14]

Whatever exuberance Gatian had entertained for California is now gone. He notes skirmishes between soldiers and Native Americans around the Placerville mines. He records the hanging of an eighteen year old gambler: "So Placerville is truly *Hangtown* again." After working for a full week, he is able to pay only two days' board.

Although there is no record of Gatian's request to break his religious vows and leave the Congregation of Holy Cross, it is apparent from this letter that the break is already finalized. He tells Sorin that he is leaving Placerville to head sixty-five miles north "with my partner who has discovered good mines in the late expedition against the Indians." They will encounter these hostile Native Americans and will have "to sleep out in the cold rain," but apparently the drive to get away from the troubles in Placerville is enough to fuel his energies for the new adventure. He does not here identify his partner, but in a later letter he will allude to their less than happy relationship. His outgoing personality was never hidden under a basket, so that to encounter him was to receive a strong impression either for good or for bad. He could make friends or enemies quickly. As far as the nature of his partnership, there is nothing to indicate it was anything other than business that linked the two men. Gatian is, however, becoming secularized rapidly:

> Gambling is the great occupation of everybody during leisure hours. No group of miners is without a deck of cards. At the grocery of the St. Joseph's Company, they are going to have a table for the better accommodation of players. I gamble also for the fun of it, but I hope I will never risk any money. However, I have won a mince pie from Capt Woodworth and half a pound of walnuts from William Lucas playing *seven-up*.[15]

As innocent as the winnings seem, they do indicate that Gatian is comfortable with the other laymen in the St. Joseph Company, of which he is still legally a member, and he has other things to do with his time than fulfill his religious exercises. There is no reference in fact to any kind of prayer in the entire letter, not even in the reference to Placidus' death. Gatian tells Sorin gold mining is a "worthless endeavor" and there is "not more than one out of three hundred that would not wish himself home again." Moreover, ten percent of the prospectors have died in California, and only one in a hundred will make a fortune, only one in five hundred the coming year, because "the mines are exhausted." He ends this sad letter with some sort of hope for a new life for himself:

> If my feeble body, which is now a mere skeleton and the picture of death, can go through the hardships I have already mentioned, and if the Indians spare my life, I hope to do well on Jackson Creek. I would like to have you exact a certain sum in the latter case, and to set me free [from his legal obligations to the St. Joseph Company] instead of requiring that fulfillment of my agreement, for I want to go home to the States as soon as possible.[16]

In spite of his determination to try mining further north, he does intend eventually to head back east, an announcement that could not have pleased Sorin as the last thing the priest needed was to have the volatile Urbain Monsimer (as he will now be called) sniffing around the Notre Dame area.

Other members of the St. Joseph Company held on in the Placerville area, although Brother Lawrence and Michael Dowling left mining in 1851 to run a kind of transport service between Placerville and Sacramento.[17] Brother Justin kept prospecting with Captain Woodworth who had, however, left the company along with Gregory Campeau.[18] Sorin eventually admitted defeat and called Justin and Lawrence back to Notre Dame where the two remained until their deaths in 1870 and 1873 respectively, Justin a Community cobbler and Lawrence a farmer-businessman highly respected in the South Bend area.

The response from Le Mans to the gold mining mission had never been positive. Moreau was aghast that Sorin would authorize such a foolish venture without the approval of the French motherhouse, and the General Chapter in August, 1851, condemned the gold rush mission totally.[19] In a circular letter dated December 8, 1851, after a list of the recently deceased, Moreau adds, "The death of Brother Placidus caused me all the more grief because I had not been informed that he had been sent to California. I would never have approved of such an undertaking."[20] Privately, Moreau was more understanding of Sorin after Sorin wrote to explain his motivation for the California expedition. Moreau softened his tone: "Following your account I can no longer condemn you and I am writing a few words to Brother Gatian to lead him to come to an understanding with me sooner or later."[21] This letter, however, was written before the November death of Placidus, so that Moreau was reacting principally to Sorin's explanation for getting Gatian and Placidus out of Indiana, the one for his dalliance with a student, the other for his uncontrollable temper. However, Moreau does not mention Placidus so his change of mind is based only on what Sorin had told him about Gatian. He may not have known about the motive for sending Placidus. Moreau, as much as Sorin, feared what a scandal could do to the increasingly good name of Notre Dame.[22]

Thus the matter of gold fever tainted the early history of Notre Dame, although Sorin weathered the storm and, outside of his *Chronicles*, never wrote of the subject again. Gatian and Placidus were the surest victims of the enterprise: they who were supposed to be cured by the adventure turned out to be the ones lost to Holy Cross. O'Connell sums up Gatian's fate:

> And Gatien—that brilliant, ill-starred young missioner, that stormy petrel, that hard, Jansenist conscience of early Notre Dame—Gatien had discovered in California, not gold, but the courage to admit that the call to religion he had harkened to as a boy had somehow gone silent. Whatever his inner turmoil, withdrawal from the Congregation of Holy Cross had become for him a moral imperative.[23]

Perhaps it was indeed the shock of new surroundings in California, new challenges, new acquaintances, that propelled Gatian out of Holy Cross, but whatever the reasons, he came at last to forsake the spiritual security of a religious community to strike out on his own.[24] Don Quixote did not do better.

In January, 1851, Urbain and an unnamed partner head north taking three days to reach Grass Valley where, carrying a sixty pound pack, Urbain suffers from vomiting and diarrhea. His partner runs off, leaving Urbain to convalesce with a Mexican man who speaks no English. After a week, Urbain heads back south for Dry Town, passing through Jacksonville.[25] He arrives in Dry Town in Calaveras County without a penny but is soon making two dollars a day. A local blacksmith recognizes him and offers him fifty dollars a month to work as a smithy, a job Urbain accepts, giving up on mining because of his weak health. Out of nowhere, however, Gregory Campeau shows up with two partners, John Green from South Bend and Charles Ebner from St. Louis. Urbain informs Sorin that Campeau had broken away from the St. Joseph Company when Brother Lawrence took a new man (William Lucas) into the company in violation of the company's original contract. Campeau had been correct in his anger because article 23 of the contract specified, "New members will not be admitted into the Company unless two thirds of the Company Members should vote for their admission."[26] A new member admitted into the company would, of course, get a share equal to the others. Moreover, the contract specified (article 10) that any member who died during the two years that the contract was valid (it would expire on February 28, 1852) would get a full share of the profits to be distributed to his heirs. Thus, the dead Brother Placidus' full share would go to Sorin at Notre Dame, so naturally Campeau would resent Brother Lawrence's bringing a new member into the company to further erode Campeau's share. Campeau plans to go home in the spring, but Urbain is determined to stay in California for another three years.

By the summer of 1851 Urbain, with Campeau as his partner, has relocated in Shasta County (250 miles north of Placerville) where they live in One Horse Town on Clear Creek. Later called simply "Horsetown," One Horse Town was as far up the creek as wagons could go and was so named "because a miner came in early driving one horse [hitched] to his wagon, which amused the miners gathered there."[27] The town was located two miles west of present day Shasta, seven miles west of Redding. Sorin has written to Urbain and apparently absolved him of his religious responsibilities and his financial obligations to the defunct St. Joseph Company. Urbain is still mining, and in an August 15, 1851, letter he tells Sorin that he will never return to Holy Cross because "as a man I don't know what it is to go back." He assures the priest, however, that he has remained a "practical" Catholic, by which he means "practicing" Catholic, "abstaining from whoring, gambling, and drinking, from swearing, from meat on Fridays and mining on Sundays." He adds that he still misses his beloved Notre Dame apprentices.

We then hear nothing from Urbain for three years, and when he writes to Sorin again on June 20, 1854, he is back in Kelsey near Placerville where he started out. He writes about California politics and religion in general terms. Sounding more and more like a self-satisfied businessman, he gives Sorin advice on some trouble Sorin is having with a man named William Huncheon. Two months later, Urbain writes again, decrying the laxity of Catholics, particularly in regard to adultery. He specifies six heretical doctrines of the wayward:

> 1st. It is no sin to have carnal communication with an unmarried woman that has attained the age of puberty, if she be willing.

> 2nd. It is no harm for married people to exchange beds where parties are all agreed.

> 3rd. It is a sin to refuse a man or woman badly in want of copulation, because it is a sin to burn in the flesh.

> 4th. It is no harm to go to prostitutes, if you pay them for it.

5th. It is no harm to procure the death of a child before it is born, provided you are not found out.

6th. It is highly meritorious to procure abortion before the germ is six weeks old, that is before quickening, because then you destroy no human life and you save the honor of the young lady.[28]

It is noteworthy that the rigorous moral code that Urbain had endorsed for himself as Brother Gatian has not deserted him as a toughened miner. Urbain tells Sorin that many at Notre Dame "practice all the above abominations," but Urbain is unwilling to name names even though the culprits have confessed to him themselves. Poor Sorin must have paled at the thought that under his very nose all sorts of sexual promiscuity and abortions were going on at Notre Dame without his knowledge. Urbain concludes that priests should do more to instruct young people in refinements of the sixth commandment and parents should let opposite sex affection proceed unchecked because it will eventually blossom into wholesome matrimony. He boasts of the advantage he had at Notre Dame to observe things Sorin never saw:

I know you cannot see things as they are from the inside of your walls. I on the contrary must necessarily pass thro' Society where being and having the reputation of being a singularly sedate fellow, of extraordinary moral doctrines, but still never middling with other people's doctrines and practices or being the less friendly on that account, they naturally want to find out what I think of these subjects and sometimes enter into friendly arguments. Some I convince and more I do not. But as I do not try to force my opinions upon any of them, they all remain friendly and communicative.[29]

It is hard to imagine a more smug person, and whatever he meant by "singularly sedate fellow," Urbain certainly prided himself on being a confidante to many.

At the end of this August 15, 1854, letter, Urbain refers to money that a certain Henry Kennedy is to have sent to Sorin. Kennedy, a local Placerville businessman whom Urbain gets to know very well, had three children named Sarah, Ann, and James, who are in Indiana, the girls at St. Mary's and the boy at Notre Dame. Urbain has strong romantic feelings for Sarah, apparently ignited before she left for Indiana, and he will pursue her affections for four years to no avail. She did inspire Urbain to sit for his daguerreotype. It was sent by Henry Kennedy to Sarah Kennedy sometime before April, 1855, because Henry mentions it in a letter to Sarah dated April 8, 1855. The daguerreotype is mentioned again in Henry Kennedy's letter for December 12, 1855, Sarah not yet having received it. Unfortunately, no trace of the daguerreotype remains.[30]

The following months bring four more letters to Sorin from Urbain who mentions again the ominous William Huncheon who has contributed surprisingly to the Catholic church fund in Placerville, although he is not a member. Huncheon plans to return home to Indiana in the spring when he will patch things up with Sorin. We never learn the nature of the problem, other than that it was financial, and we can only speculate that it may have concerned the St. Joseph Company. In addition to working, Urbain is in charge of collecting money to build the church at Placerville, but there has been no priest locally for five months. Urbain mentions that the archbishop has written to him about thousands of dollars in reserve for priests who are yet to materialize. In a November letter Urbain refers repeatedly to Henry Kennedy, his health and money woes in particular, and Urbain sends "Mr. Kennedy's love and mine to his children: Sarah, Ann, and James."

Fortunately, Urbain's letters did not stop. In early March, 1856, he adds a postscript to a letter written by Henry Kennedy to Sarah. The letter is posted from Kelsey in El Dorado County, California, to St. Mary's at Notre Dame. Urbain writes what seems to be a genuinely affectionate proposal of marriage to Sarah:

> My Dear Sarah, you are aware that I esteem you highly & love you affectionately. Should your feelings towards me be similar & should you accept of my heart and hand which I now offer you, we could very well obviate all the difficulties your father speaks of. You & I would give him a home here where Ann could also come & stay with all safety after her schooling. I would gladly spend to further your education & thus help your father, even if you chose to learn a trade. But if you chose a studious life, then I would let you know what branches to study during your two years, as there are many branches [things] that I could teach you myself after our marriage & your return here. I would not have made this premature proposal, had not your present circumstances convinced me of its propriety. For you see, if we fully understand each other at once, we can make our plans so as to more highly adorn your mind & heart & thus enhance your own happiness, your father's & mine also, if I prove acceptable. If you reject me, I will still pay for your music as I promised; but if you accept me, I will do everything in my power for you & strain every nerve for your happiness. Answer this, Dearest; pray to our good Mother the Blessed Virgin for me & for yourself; & meanwhile rest assured of my best & sincerest love.[31]

On the surface, the man's sentiments seem natural enough, and Urbain had surely met Sarah before she went east to Indiana for her schooling, but the postscript becomes problematic when we realize that Sarah is only twelve years old at the time. She was born on January 14, 1844. The date of the letter is not incorrect, nor are the data on Sarah, who eventually became Sister Columba at St. Mary's, Notre Dame.[32] We can draw several conclusions, therefore, about Urbain's sentiments. First of all, he may be teasing the girl like a grandfather teasing a favorite granddaughter or a bachelor uncle teasing a niece. But the tone of the postscript does not sound like teasing, especially lines of sentiment like "if we fully understand each other at once, we can make our plans...& thus enhance your own happiness, your father's & mine also, if I prove acceptable." On the other hand, Urbain was capable of great tonal subtlety in his prose style, as we have seen earlier in letters to Moreau about Sorin. The teasing may simply be beyond the comprehension of modern readers. If, however, we assume a darker intent, we have to conclude that Urbain was really proposing a future marriage to a child, and the projected liaison of a twenty-five year old man and a twelve year old girl seems odd.[33] We would deduce from such a reading that Gatian is psychologically disturbed, but if he were, it did not make much of an impression on Sarah's father who continued to forward Urbain's love and good wishes to the girl in letters posted in September 1854 and December 1855.[34]

What the postscript raises again is the question of Urbain's sexual orientation. If he were serious about his marriage proposal to Sarah Kennedy, how can we reconcile his heterosexual sentiments with the vividly homoerotic attraction he had for John Hays and wrote about to Sorin? The nature of the two sentiments are, however, quite different. His expressions of love (if actually real) to Sarah are formal and artificial. His sugary longings for Hays, on the other hand, are expressed time and again with persistent energy. Moreover, his love for Hays led to wild physical expressions of lover's melancholy and despair (e.g., going into the lake up to his neck, breaking panes of glass) six years previous to the Sarah postscript. Furthermore, the proof is in the pudding: the fact of the matter is that Urbain never did marry, and early letters to Moreau indicate a hostility toward women beyond boyish bravado. He never married, we conclude, because he could never seriously relate to a woman.[35] Thus the March 2, 1851, postscript to Sarah Kennedy is a kind of sad joke in the life of a sexually disturbed man who could not accept his homoerotic inclinations.

After a two year hiatus in his extant correspondence, Urbain writes to Sorin in April, 1858, of his continued interest in Sarah Kennedy and another woman

Sorin knows. However, Urbain has been courting a local girl, who, he claims, is head over heels in love with him:

> It is unfortunate that Sarah did not sooner communicate her disposition in my regard for the week which preceded the reception of her letter, being pressed for a decisive answer in regard to an amiable Catholic young lady only five days older than Sarah, I could no longer keep her in suspense and I informed her that there was no hope, expecting daily to receive an answer from Sarah whom I am unwilling to give up as long as there is the least prospect of success. I am now in consequence of this mishap rather in a fix and do not know what girl I like best or which I ought to prefer. I am rather inclined to make duty my rule and to marry, whether my head and heart approve or not, that girl who may think herself best entitled to my hand. It is on this account that I write to you and if you will help me in making a choice, your advice shall be welcome even if not followed. I want to write about Maria G. Lincome. If the lady thinks I have not used her well and if she would gladly make it up by marrying me, I would like to know. But if you cannot ascertain her dispositions without letting her find out that I have written on the subject, it is not best to let her know anything. Because as long as Sarah is single and does not belong to the Sisters, I will probably not marry, for I would drop the prettiest girl in the world to marry Sarah, if she were willing.
>
> I love Sarah, I love Maria. I love this girl out here whose parents are so anxious to get me. This girl out here loves me dearly. Sarah pretends neither to love nor to care for me and I never could make out what Maria wanted of me. I find the girl out here full of defects: she is not learned nor healthy; her feet are too large and I shall have to prepare her for her first communion. I object to Maria's Indiana [Indian?] blood and to her age. Sarah is in my eyes perfect and a saint, for this reason I would readily marry her for I would like to lead a holy life with her and it is perhaps on account of my unworthiness that God does not incline her heart to mine. The Catholicity and salvation of the girl out here would probably be rendered easier to her, if I accepted her offer of marriage.
>
> On the other hand, there is not a Catholic girl in the congregation who would not rather marry me than any other Californian and this encourages me to believe that if I had a chance of paying my addresses to Sarah personally, I could win her. There are two or three girls here who are also in deep love with me (one a Protestant), but as I never gave them any reason to fall in love, they should not be considered as competitors against the first three. Now which as a matter of duty to myself and to them should I marry? I ask your advice and if I do not follow it, I shall certainly take it into consideration.[36]

It is painfully obvious from this letter that Urbain is incapable of loving a real woman: he continues to pursue Sarah Kennedy who, as he describes her, seems a substitute for the Blessed Virgin, chaste, holy, and otherworldly. But just as the Virgin in his closing days at Notre Dame was incapable of answering his prayers, prompting him to blasphemy, we suspect that were he to have any real contact with the real Sarah, she would become as unworthy of him as the dewy-eyed California girl with the big feet. Separated from Urbain by thousands of miles and about to join the sisters, Sarah remains the mystical chimera of womanhood that dazzles Urbain only because she is beyond his grasp. Meanwhile, Urbain falls in love with himself as he fancies himself the paragon of masculine attraction for various local girls, including one Protestant, swooning at his feet.

In the following November, Urbain is a changed man, sick and embittered. He first blames his weakened constitution on his sedentary life at Notre Dame, implying that had he continued the outdoor life he knew as a young farmer in France, he would not be the broken man he has become. Unable to work for a month, he can stomach only bread and milk. Bronchitis has infiltrated one lung, and Urbain opines that a change of climate might help him. He thinks he will try either the Sandwich Islands (Hawaii) or Chile, a voyage to either of which would cure him or kill him, the latter outcome preferable, so he says, to a slow death by bronchitis and consumption (tuberculosis). Things are not looking good for Urbain. At the same time, poor Henry Kennedy has lost his business in a flood and gone temporarily insane.

The final letter from Urbain was written from San Francisco on April 23, 1860. It is the most pitiful of all his letters, yet he begins it by giving Sorin advice on why Holy Cross should start a foundation in California. Reminiscent of the old Gatian writing from Brooklyn, Urbain neatly outlines five points why Sorin should send brothers west. First of all, the area is ripe with vocations for the brothers because so many hopes have been blasted by the false lure of easy riches in the gold mines. Secondly, Archbishop Alemany, having been disappointed by talks with the Christian Brothers over opening a school, is anxious for brothers to come into his diocese. Thirdly, the archbishop is burdened with male orphans that the brothers could train. Fourthly, the vicar general has been wanting a commercial college (high school) to educate Catholic youth who cannot afford the tuition at the Jesuit school (which tops out at $670 per annum). Finally, the Monterey diocese is full of possibilities since it has many Catholics, including several influential politicians. Sorin, of course, ignored Urbain's suggestions since by this time in addition to Notre Dame he had to staff schools in Madison (Indiana), New Orleans, Makinac (Michigan), Michigan City (Indiana), Cincinnati, Mishawaka (Indiana), Toledo, Zanesville, Chicago, Philadelphia, Columbus (Ohio), Fort Wayne (Indiana), Alton (Illinois), and Baltimore. All these schools were operating in 1860 with Holy Cross personnel out of Notre Dame. Sorin was stretched as far as he could be.[37]

Urbain is dying. He weighs but one hundred and five pounds. He has the use of but one quarter of his lungs. Doctors have given up on him, and he says that he wishes to see his father in France one last time before he dies. He blames Holy Cross for his debilitation:

> I die, I think, the victim of the wretched system followed in your Institution and so many others. No attention is paid to health. Your subjects have not enough of exercise in the open air and they dress alike summer and winter, buttoning tightly across the breast as if the intention were to choke them as soon as possible. Why not dress according to the Rules of Science and common sense?[38]

His logic is gone, and he does not acknowledge that hundreds have dressed as he dressed, including the robust Brother Lawrence and the aging Brother Vincent. The venom is fierce, but then he has suffered much, mostly at his own doing. With his closing thoughts, he invokes the Virgin Mary:

> Now, Revd. Father, pray for me that I may not die during the voyage and that I may carry my cross patiently. Pray to God and the Blessed Virgin for me, when I am dead. My greatest sins were committed at Notre Dame du Lac. There I blasphemed God in my heart and publicly insulted the Blessed Virgin. There I was guilty of unnatural impurities. I repent chiefly of one thing, namely that I ever was a Brother, for with God's grace and the protection of Mary, my Blessed Mother, I have been preserved from any grievous sins among the general corruption of California. Pray to Mary for me that I may obtain pardon for my blasphemies, especially of the 6th of January, 1849, and my insults to Mary in 1848.[39]

The reference to "unnatural" sins of impurity, occasioned ten years before, is to that period when Gatian was obsessed with John Hays. Still unable to reconcile his homoeroticism, he fingers his sexual meanderings at Notre Dame, and instead of accepting his sexual inclination and failings, including blasphemy, he repents of only one thing: that he was ever a Brother of Holy Cross.[40] This sentence must have bought a dagger into Sorin's heart and the heart of anyone else who was given the letter to read. All of Urbain's recriminations fall not on Urbain but on the persona he had assumed as Brother Gatian. If Sorin misused the young man's talents, there had been many good men around Gatian in his formation whom Gatian loved and who taught him much, including Moreau himself and the grand old men at Le Mans who carried with them the simple and unselfish spiritual riches of Dujarié and André Mottais. In his dying grief, Urbain turns against the one object that was the shining lure of his soul at age thirteen: the lure of being a Brother of St. Joseph. Inspired by his brother teacher at Chéméné-le-roi, nurtured by the brother teachers at Le Mans, encouraged by his confreres in America, he still ends up bitter and pathetic. But in the heart of this sad finale, there still beat an energy to complete a task, and with the same determination he had to master the English language, with the same sense of purpose he had in trying to save Brooklyn, and with the same drive he had heading west to California, he now, heavy hearted, travels east, first to New York and then to France.[41] Abraham Lincoln would soon become president. South Carolina would soon secede from the Union.

The paper trail for Urbain ends here, except for the notice of his death in the parish records in Saulges, France. He did indeed return to die on his father's farm, in the same house of his birth. Nothing remains today of that house but a cement slab. On the outskirts of town, in a little cemetery surrounded by a stone wall, nestled amid wheat fields, Urbain lies buried with the Monsimers, but the exact location of his grave is unknown because the marker has disappeared. One can imagine the moment of his passing, in the quiet of the summer on the farm he had not seen in over twenty years, attended by the family he had left in 1839. The strong heart of this passionate young man stopped when he was thirty-four.[42] His father would live on to die in 1872 at age seventy-two.

Although Urbain had left the Congregation of Holy Cross, in one sense he never did. Thoroughly devoted to religion, he remained essentially a religious as he made his way around the gold mines of California. He never accumulated wealth and established no homestead, content with a peripatetic life as sparse as any missionary's. He remained devoted to his local church, was in charge of collecting money for a new house of worship in Placerville, corresponded with the archbishop, remained convinced that moral rectitude is essential and must be enforced for salvation. He never married, unconsciously realizing that as a homosexual man, a heterosexual marriage would be a lie to himself and an offense to a woman, so he lived celibate, the only answer his church at the time had for homosexuality. And his call to obedience kept him tied to his previous religious superior at Notre Dame, if only to offer occasional advice and reminisce about life at Notre Dame. He was obedient to his heart, trudging the California landscape and ultimately returning to his earthly French father just before he returned to his heavenly. If his love for his students were too strong, it was still love that made him a great teacher, and his students revelled in the attention, both those who suffered the lash of his tongue for their laxness or boyish pranks and those who touched deeper recesses in his heart where the carnal twines with the altruistic, the one feeling absorbed into the other. Gatian took himself out of Holy Cross, but Holy Cross never really took itself out of Urbain Monsimer. What entered his soul, when he was a perky farm boy of twelve sitting in the classroom of Brother Vital, was ossified by the brothers in Le Mans where the combined spirits of Dujarié, André Mottais, and Moreau created in the boy a religious sensibility he would never shake loose. Whatever moral commitment his parents tutored into him was further shaped by the great men of Holy Cross into an unshakable sense of what was right and what was wrong, even when his anger blinded him or his passion shook him to his roots. He did not die dramatically like Robespierre for the history books of France, but he died as much a man, dedicated to the fire that burned within.

An embarrassment to his community at Notre Dame, he survived in some minds as a brilliant teacher. One former student wrote of him: "Brother Gatian was a genius, an incomprehensible Frenchman! He was capable of doing anything and everything. He was at that early day the intellectual soul of the institution [Notre Dame]."[43] Such is the one-sided view of a gushing former pupil. The real Urbain Monsimer was complex and interesting, a fiery hot bed of academic potential gone awry because the same fire that drove him toward greatness fueled the demons within him. In the end they seemed to win, although we can hope that his final weeks on the Monsimer farm brought to his soul the calm that he deserved more than not. He was an important part of Holy Cross and Notre Dame, and his name deserves to be remembered. He was part of that force in Indiana that Americanized the French brothers and drove them to try to separate from the Le Mans motherhouse, their energies fueled by the one imperative: after Holy Cross, only Notre Dame.

Notes

GA = General Archives, Congregation of Holy Cross

IPA = Indiana Province Archives, Notre Dame

MPA = Midwest Province Archives, Notre Dame

Introduction, Part I

1. Schama, 180.

2. Pétion narrated the event:

> Madame Elisabeth gazed at me with soft eyes and with that languid air which unhappiness engenders and which inspires one with lively interest. Our eyes met now and then with a kind of understanding and mutual attraction: night had come and the moon began to shed its gentle light. Madame Elisabeth took Madame [the king's daughter] on her knee, half on mine. Her head was supported by my hand and she fell asleep. I stretched out my arm and Madame Elisabeth stretched out hers over mine. Our arms were interlaced and mine touched her armpit. I felt a hurried movement of her heart and a warmth passing out through her clothes. Madame Elisabeth's glance seemed to grow ever more touching. I noticed a certain abandonment in her attitude, her eyes were moist and her melancholy appeared to be mingled with a sort of pleasure. Perhaps I was wrong, because it is easy to confuse the sensibility caused by sorrow with that deriving from pleasure. All the same, I believe that if we had been alone, if by some enchantment all the others had disappeared, she would have fallen into my arms and abandoned herself to the promptings of nature.

Pétion in Pernoud, 96. One wonders what Mrs. Pétion thought of this part of her husband's memoirs—if she read them before or after his being guillotined.

3.   Catta, *Dujarié*, 14.

4.   They were beatified in 1955 as the "Martyrs of Laval."

5.   The cellar is used today as an apartment. It is ground level and enjoys light from wide windows that may or may not have been there in Dujarié's day when it was used for storage.

6.   Vanier, 136.

7.   Brother Adrian (Louis Legeai) was the son of Louis Legeai and Françoise Maillet. Born February 26, 1803, at Rahais, he entered the Community at Ruillé January 1, 1825, and received his teaching certificate September 13 of the same year. Professed in August, 1839, he died April 14, 1873, at La Faye.

8.   Mottais, 1. Brother Jerome (René Porcheré) was born January 1, 1800, at Le Fuille. He entered the Ruillé community March 16, 1824, but died Mary 25, 1826, at Ruillé, before taking vows. Brother John Mary (John Mary Gauchet) was born February 7, 1824, at Fougères. He entered the religious community on January 5, 1824, but died before vows March 12, 1826, at Mayenne.

9.   Mottais, 15.

10. The two sets of signatures, on the pact and on the vow formula, do not match, but some of the signatures are difficult to decipher. Lack of penmanship skills as well as the emotional state of the men undoubtedly contributed to the quality of the handwriting. Some omissions are inexplicable. For example, Brother Vital, the man most responsible for bringing Urbain Monsimer into Holy Cross, appears at the end of the vow formula but not at the end of the pact.

11. Mottais, 18.

12. Qtd. in Catta, *Dujarié*, 266.

13. Qtd. In Catta, *Dujarié*, 227. Catta does not name the brother, another faceless brother in this very clerical biography.

Introduction, Part II

1. Various references to Brother André give his birth name as simply "Pierre," but the General Matricule lists his legal name as "André" with no mention of "Pierre." His birth is officially recorded in Larchamp as "Andrée pierre" [sic]. Why the feminine form of "André" appears in the official birth record is a mystery. It is probably an error that only the recorder would have noticed and would not have considered important enough to emend. All of the material on André's relatives was discovered by M. Yves Guilimeau who has generously shared all of his work on the Mottais heritage.

2. Jean's father was also named Jean, and it was with his second wife Marie Laize that André's father was born. André's grandparents were married on July 10, 1743, five years after the grandfather married his first wife Julienne Lepentier on February 11, 1738. André's great-grandfather was likewise named Jean Mottais, and his second wife was Michelle Davy. André's great-great-grandfather, Olivier Mottais, died January 1, 1701, a century before André was born. Olivier married Julienne Sibelle on October 10, 1674, one month before the English poet John Milton died and thirty-one years into the reign of Louis XIV, who reigned until 1715. André's own father died at the age of 78 in Larchamp on July 12, 1847, three years after his Holy Cross son. André's mother had died earlier than her husband, on August 30, 1845, one year after her son André. She was the daughter of François Blot and Jeanne Caillère.

3. André's brother Jean died on March 6, 1830, long before his Holy Cross brother or their parents. He was married twice: first to Marie Fleury on May 8, 1815, and then to Louise Lottin on January 21, 1826. André's sister (named for her mother and possibly the first wife of her grandfather or the wife of her great-great grandfather) married Jean Grégoire Chevillé on October 25, 1834, when she was twenty-nine, ten years before her brother André's death. She died in 1879. André's younger brother Joseph died December 14, 1878, one year before his sister. He was married to his cousin Michelle Caillère on November 10, 1841.

4. Vanier, notes of Brother Rémy, *Rec. Doc.*, 544.

5. Dujarié managed to get André presented to the prefect of La Sarthe, Count de Breteuil, by General Coutant's uncle, the pastor of the historic Le Mans church Notre Dame de la Couture. See *Chronicles*, 10, qtd. in André, 39.

6. Mottais, 16.

7. *Ibid.*, 16.

8. *Ibid.*, 16.

9. The *Chronicles* give the date as November 25, 1821. Since André wrote these early *Chronicles,* we can trust his memory for the precise date.

10. Brother Stephen (Etienne Gauffre) was born in 1792 and was the fourth man to join Dujarié's grou He came to Ruillé in November, 1820, at the age of twenty-eight, one month after André. He received his teaching license in May, 1822, and persevered through all the troubles that visited the Brothers of St. Joseph. He died in 1851 in Le Mans two days shy of his fifty-ninth birthday.

11. The event has been captured in an oil painting by Brother Harold Ruplinger, CSC, who put three brothers (plus Dujarié) in the picture. He used as models three brothers of the Midwest Province (Bernard Platte, Michael Becker, Thomas Moser) because there are no photos of any of the earliest brothers: photography was not invented until 1829 and did not come into any wide use for another two generations. For Dujarié, Ruplinger used Brother Raymond Dufresne as model. In Ruplinger's painting one brother is actually taking off his habit because Ruplinger wanted to show that the man would not persevere as a Brother of St. Joseph. Ruplinger tried to depict three types of brothers: the brother to the left is intellectual, the brother in the middle a farmer, and the brother on the far right unsure of his vocation. There were, of course, only two brothers at the actual event in 1821.

12. *Chronicles*, 11, qtd, in Mottais, 39.

13. *Ibid.*, 11, qtd. in Mottais, 39.

14. *Ibid.*, 12, qtd. in Mottais, 39.

15. Mottais, 7.

16. *Chronicles*, 13, qtd in Mottais, 39.

17. See note 7 for Introducion, Part I.

18. Brother Francis (Pierre François Blanchet) was born February 3, 1793, at Le Chapelle Genson. He came to Ruillé on December 15, 1821, and left the community in 1832. He had been the tenth man to join Dujarié's brothers and thus knew André for eleven years.

19. Mottais, 1.

20. Of the first fifty young men to join Dujarié's community, only ten received teaching diplomas: 1822 (André, Etienne), 1823 (Augustin, Vincent), 1825 (Dominique, Marie-Joseph), 1828 (Pierre, Martin, Marin, Romain). Dujarié may not have accepted "non-teaching" brothers, so the other forty of the first fifty would have been sent out to teach without licenses (or left before being assigned).

21. Catta, *Moreau*, I, 292.

22. See note 8, Introduction, Part I.

23. *Chronicles*, 16, qtd. in Mottais, 39.

24. Vanier, "Brother André's Project," rpr. Mottais, 46.

25. *Chronicles*, 22, qtd. in Mottais, 42.

26. Mottais, 11.

27. Catta, *Dujarié*, 202.

28. *Ibid.*, 212.

29. Mottais, 8.

30. Catta, *Dujarié*, 238, n. 5.

31. It may seem that Moreau was influencing such matters four years earlier, and André's document may hint that Moreau was already determined to head-quarter the brothers at Le Mans, not at Ruillé, but the sale of the Ruillé boarding school was not effected until 1835, so André must have amended

his 1831 letter years after it was written to reflect the fact that M. Laguette from Masle-sur-Sarthe would buy the property four years after the financial separation of the brothers from the sisters.

32. Mottais, 11.

33. *Chronicles*, 42, qtd. in Mottais, 43.

34. André died in 1844 at age 44, Leonard Guittoger in 1887 at age 84, and Vincent Pieau in 1890 at age 93. Henry (Michael Taupin) left at age 42, a few years after signing the oath of allegiance.

35. Mottais, 18.

36. *Ibid.*, 18.

37. Mottais, 24.

38. *Ibid.*, 19.

39. *Ibid.*, 20.

40. The most thorough analysis of André's plan is that by Philéas Vanier. He has carefully reconstructed André's plan and compared it point by point with both Dujarié's plan for an organization of auxiliary priests to work alongside his brothers and Moreau's plan that eventually became the Congregation of Holy Cross. See Mottais, 47-53.

41. See Mottais, 45.

42. Catta, *Moreau*, I, 326.

43. Bouvier had in fact pledged himself to join such a group when he was a seminarian. See Catta, *Moreau*, I, 320.

44. Catta, *Moreau*, I, 343. Maddix suggests (79) that Dujarié never had manual labor brothers and that Moreau created the practice of using them, but Dionne notes that Dujarié did use brothers for manual labor, following the practice of both de Lamennais and Deshayes, founders that Dujarié had consulted in the establishment of the Brothers of St. Joseph. See Dionne, 96. What is not clear is if Dujarié had brothers who were devoted totally to man-

ual labor or if he simply used the novices part time for manual labor before they went out to teach in parish schools. André's reference elsewhere to "brother carpenters" (Mottais, 43) suggests that there may have been brothers who did indeed do manual labor full time and never taught. André names, for example, one brother carpenter: Alphonsus, who was eventually to accompany André to Algeria where Alphonsus worked as a joiner, not a teacher.

45. Moreau left La Chesnaie after three days, but Brother Leonard stayed several days longer in order to visit the schools run by the Ploërmel brothers. Leonard then went to Ploërmel itself where he spent three weeks at the motherhouse. See Catta, *Moreau*, I, 345.

46. In one volume Catta notes that Brother Vincent was left in Ruillé to run the boarding school there. See Catta, *Dujarié*, 268. In another book Catta writes that Brother Vincent was put in charge of the new school at Sainte-Croix. See Catta, *Moreau*, I, 353. Vincent could not be in two places at once. André must have been in charge of one of the schools. As the *Chronicles* mention that André was novice master in both Ruillé and Sainte-Croix, he probably supervised the Sainte-Croix boarding school, and Vincent stayed behind in Ruillé.

47. Catta, *Moreau*, I, 353.

48. Catta, *Moreau*, I, 351.

49. Maddix, in Mottais, 78.

50. Catta, *Dujarié*, 259.

51. Qtd. in Catta, *Moreau*, I, 369.

52. André could not even comment on his own role in saving the brothers without Moreau's finding fault in him. When André in the *Chronicles* writes about his own work to save the brothers as Dujarié weakened, Moreau writes in the margin: "I am pained to see this note by Brother André, which is not the fruit of humility." See *Chronicles*, 42, qtd. in Mottais, 43.

53. Catta, *Dujarié*, 261-262.

54. *Chronicles*, 265, qtd. in Mottais, 44.

55. Brother Léopold (Pierre-Nicholas Putiot) was born in 1804 and entered at Sainte-Croix in 1830 at age twenty-five. He died in 1864 at age fifty-nine. Silvin-Auguste De Marseul was born in 1812, was ordained in 1835, and became a novice at Sainte-Croix in 1836 at age twenty-four. He left in 1842, re-entered in 1857, but left again in 1868 at age fifty-six. Pierre Chappé was born in 1809, entered at Sainte-Croix in 1837, and died in 1880 at age seventy.

56. Another chore André had was to travel to Auvergne where the bishop of St. Flour wanted to start a community of brothers. The bishop had sent three young men to Sainte-Croix to make their novitiate under Brother André, but when André took them to Auvergne, the planned community never did materialize. See *Chronicles*, 147, qtd. in Mottais, 43.

57. Catta, *Dujarié*, 281.

58. The novice Ignatius (Théodore Feron) was born October 20, 1820, making him nineteen at the time of the Algerian announcement.

59. Mottais, 23.

60. *Ibid.*, 24.

61. *Ibid.*, 25.

62. *Ibid.*, 26.

63. Julian Leboucher left the community in late 1843. We do not know the date of his birth. He came to Sainte-Croix as a priest in October, 1839, and was sent six months later to Africa. The other priest sent was Victor Drouelle who was born in 1812 and entered the community as a priest in 1837 when he was twenty-five. He turned against Moreau in the Le Mans debacle of 1865 and died in 1875, two years after Moreau.

64. Mottais, 31.

65. *Ibid.*, 32.

66. Catta, *Moreau*, I, 483.

67. Moreau may not have given André the appointments or the title. In his March 20, 1844, letter announcing André's death, Moreau writes that it was the General Council who appointed André, on André's return from Africa, to be Moreau's "Assistant and Counseller in the various transactions of my administration." See Mottais, 44. The Council, of course, may simply have voted on Moreau's nomination of André and not instigated the appointment themselves.

68. Mottais, 37.

69. *Chronicles*, 265, qtd. in Mottais, 44.

70. Vanier, qtd. in Mottais, 46.

Introduction, Part III

1. Catta, *Moreau*, I, 9.

2. Although the lower room remains today in the same state it was in Moreau's day, the upper room has been refurbished into a large one-room apartment lighted by large windows.

3. Moreau's trials in establishing the Good Shepherd Sisters at Le Mans are covered in depth by three chapters in Catta, *Moreau*, I, 142-276.

4. Moreau, *Circular Letters*, I, 11. The number, however, includes boarders who probably account for more than half the one hundred.

5. Morin, 15.

6. Moreau, *Circular Letters*, I, 23.

7. *Ibid.*, I, 30.

8. Bennoune, 31.

9. *Ibid.*, 35.

10. Catta, *Moreau*, I, 461.

11. Moreau, *Etrennes Spirituelles*, qtd. in Catta, *Moreau*, I, 470.

12. Ironically Le Boucher left the Community four years after he entered it. Victor Drouelle, Le Boucher's replacement, was born at Conlie in 1812. Already ordained when he joined Moreau's band of auxiliary priests in 1837, he was sent to Algeria in 1840. Serving in various administrative roles in the Community, he died in Paris in 1875, two years after Moreau's own death. He was instrumental in the downfall and humiliation of Moreau in 1868.

13. Brother Louis (Victor Marchand) was born in 1812 at St. Thomas de Courceriere. He entered Holy Cross in 1839 and was professed before he went to Algiers in May, 1840. He died tragically September 16, 1841, at Mustapha in Algeria at the age of thirty-eight. Swimming in the Mediterranean with some of the children from the orphanage, he died of apoplexy. Catta reports the name of the drowned brother as "humble Brother Aloysius." See Catta, *Moreau*, I, 486. We cannot say how the Cattas knew that the drowned brother was "humble" except that brothers are stereotypically expected to be "humble." Bother Alphonsus (Francis-Mary Tulou) was first known as Brother Francis of Assisi. Born in 1798 in La Chapelle des Fougeretz, he entered at Ruillé in 1827. Professed in 1837, he went to Algeria as a carpenter in 1840. He returned to Le Mans in June, 1842, and died there March 24, 1853. Brother Victor (John Huard) was born in 1812 in Larchamp, the same town where André Mottais had been born in 1800. He became a novice in 1839, a year before being sent to Algeria as a refectorian. He left the Community in April, 1842. Brother Eulogius (Antoine Boisard) was born in 1808 at Orléans. He entered Holy Cross in 1839 but left in 1842, a year and a half after having been sent to Algeria. Brother Ignatius (Theodore Feron), son of Nicholas Feron and Mary Ferouelle, was born in 1820 at Lignières la Doucelle. Entering Holy Cross in 1839, he went to Algeria in 1840, returned to France in 1842, and returned to Algeria in 1850 as a teacher. After serving in Rome, he returned to Le Mans in 1855 but was dismissed in 1857. Brother Liguori (Louis Guyard), the son of Francis Guyard and Anne Granger, was born in 1819 at Parné. He entered Holy Cross in 1838, went to Algeria in 1840, returned to France in 1842, went once again to Algeria in 1844, but left the Community in 1846.

14. The Cattas praise Haudebourg's letters but not André's. They quote liberally from Haudebourg, but print only one paragraph from André, and that is a paragraph praising a priest. See Catta, *Moreau*, I, 482. Mary-Victor Haudebourg was born September 16, 1811, to John Mary Haudebourg and Victoire Bouillard, in La Ferté Bernard. He was already a priest when he joined

Moreau's auxiliary band in June of 1840. Sent as a novice to Algiers in September, 1840, he returned to Le Mans the following June and was professed in August of 1842. He left the Community in 1851.

15. Mottais, 41.

16. Mottais, 42A. See Introduction, Part II, note 67.

17. On this last point see Maddix in Mottais, 83.

18. Mottais, 42A.

19. Mottais, 28. See Introduction, Part II, and Mottais, 23.

20. Moreau mentions a brother-director but does not name him in his first circular letter (page 5). Five years later there is some indication (in circular letter #9) that the brother-director is Brother Leopold who is living, however, at Saint-Berthevin, near Laval, not at Le Mans. See Moreau, *Circular Letters*, I, 24. Leopold (Pierre-Nicholas Putiot) was not a member of the old guard (André, Etienne, Vincent) at Ruillé. He entered the Brothers of St. Joseph in 1830 and was not professed until 1842. He died at Le Mans in 1864 at the age of fifty-nine.

21. Catta, *Moreau*, I, 367. One would think that baptism (the only sacrament Christ received) is the "truest" expression of religion.

22. For example, of the twenty-five religious living at Le Mans in 1840, the names of twelve priests are given as important members of the growing community, but not a single brother is named. See Catta, *Moreau*, I, 429.

23. Moreau's little discipline is preserved by the Marianite Sisters in the sacristy of their Solitude in Le Mans. On Sorin's humiliation of a sister, see Costin, 26. On Sorin's humiliation of a student, see O'Connell, 380. On Sorin's demotion of Father William Corby, see O'Connell, 673.

24. Lafayette, 1.

25. De Gouges, 1. What is interesting about De Gouges' document is that she apparently wrote it alone and thus suffered alone for its rhetoric. Lafayette, on the other hand, enjoyed Thomas Jefferson's help in drafting the more serene *Declaration of the Rights of Man*.

26. *Ibid.*, 1.

27. Today, the religious men of Holy Cross recognize the equality of members. In a report from their Inter-Societal Committee on the Consecrated Life, the sentiment is expressed cogently. "The present Code of Canon Law calls Catholics to a communion seemingly based upon an equality more like solidarity and order than authority and rank: 'In virtue of their rebirth in Christ there exists among all faithful a true equality.'" See Committee report, 19. By "rebirth in Christ" Canon Law probably means the sacrament of baptism. The only problematic word in the committee's sentence is "seemingly."

28. Catta, *Moreau*, I, 369.

29. Catta, *Moreau*, I, 380.

30. Moreau, *Circular Letters*, I, 44.

31. Catta, *Moreau*, I, 429.

32. Animosity between clerics and laymen in the men's community of Holy Cross peaked during World War II when the members decided they could no longer tolerate a unified governance on regional or local levels. With Rome's approbation, the men split into distinct provinces: those for brothers separate from those for priests. Rome, however, insisted that brothers be given a choice to stay within a priests' province, and dozens decided to remain in the clerical provinces. After the split came about, Holy Cross flourished until the Second Vatican Council when in the 1960s it, like most religious communities, suffered a decline in membership.

Chapter One

1. Kundera notes Robespierre is a hero because the bloodshed he fostered did not recur in French history. Had Robespierre been the designer of a recurring Reign of Terror, his heroicity would have faded into infamy. See Kundera, 4.

2. Sagan, 484.

3. Schama, 846.

4. Bruneau, *Odysee*, 57.

5. Bruneau, *Odysee*, 5.

6. Bruneau, *Odysee*, 57.

7. Letter of Marie-Joseph Tourneux to author, December 31, 1997.

8. Gatian gives the precise time of his birth in a letter to Sorin. See Klawitter, ed., 299.

9. Henry Clement Monsimer and Rosalie Marie Espitallier had four children: Marie Leone (1875–1916), Eugene D. (1878–1964), Henry Xavier (1885–1927), and Louis Frederick (1888–1966). The grandchildren are numerous. The Monsimer family tree has been thoroughly researched by Tourneux.

10. Flandrin, 55.

11. *Ibid.*, 71.

12. *Ibid.*, 90.

13. Qtd. in Flandrin 169.

14. Flandrin, 200.

15. Qtd. in Flandrin, 206.

16. Moule was one of fifteen priests and four sisters tried and executed on the same day in Laval. Among the Jacobins who condemned them was one who had been a seminarian with Jacques Dujarié at Domfront. See Catta, *Dujarié*, 22.

Chapter Two

1. It was the final point in Moreau's June 20, 1835, letter to Bishop Bouvier: "To aim at one day establishing the novitiate at Le Mans."

2. Catta, *Moreau*, I, 314, n. 114.

3. *Ibid.*, I, 315.

4. *Ibid.*, I, 346.

5. *Ibid.*, I, 342.

6. *Ibid.*, I, 311.

7. See André Mottais' letter to Bouvier, November 14, 1834.

8. *Ibid.*

9. Bruneau, *Odyssée*, 12. Exact dates for the births of the siblings are Perrine on May 29, 1819, Constant on January 24, 1822, and Felicité-Jeanne on May 28, 1823.

10. Conversation of author at Gennes with Mme. Tourneux, July 7, 1996.

11. Brother Chrysostom (Céleste Maillard) came to Ste. Croix at age nineteen in August, 1840, one year after Gatian. He received a teaching diploma in 1843 and left Holy Cross six years later. Brother Hilaire (Pierre Beury) was born in 1817 and entered Holy Cross in 1835. He served in Algeria but left Holy Cross from there in 1846. He returned to the Community circa 1853 and died at Angers in 1890. As there is no Brother John of the Cross listed for this time in the General Matricule, the brick layer that Gatian refers to is probably Brother John (Jean-Baptiste Hilaire Diard) who was a fellow novice aged eighteen. He left Holy Cross in February, 1842, after Gatian was already in America.

12. O'Connell, 220.

13. Corbinière, 112.

14. James M. Maurice de Long d'Aussac de St. Palais enjoyed a long tenure as bishop of Vincennes, twenty-eight years. He recruited in Europe three times and deputized Joseph Kundek to recruit in Germany for the German Catholic settlements at Ferdinand and Jasper, Indiana. Another result of Kundek's efforts was the arrival of Benedictine monks in 1854 to found St. Meinrad.

15. Joseph Kundek to Leopodine Society, October 12, 1846, qtd. in Kleber 15-16, qtd. in Taylor, 131.

16. Rudolph, 26

17. *Ibid.*, 29.

18. *Ibid.*, 27.

19. Morin, 25.

20. *Ibid.*, 25.

21. *Ibid.*, 26.

22. Mottais, 28.

23. True to form, the Cattas in their definitive life of Moreau do not even name the six brothers sent to America, but they wax eloquent over the brothers' priest-superior. See Catta, *Moreau*, I, 500.

24. Brother Baptiste (John Verger) was born at Ahuillé (Sorin's birthplace also) on December 1, 1797, making him almost a year younger than Brother Vincent. His parents were Stephen Verger and Jacquine Déoré. He came to Ruillé on December 7, 1821, and became a novice the following year on November 1. He was professed on August 19, 1838, and died at Mauléorier in 1855. Baptiste may have been at Mauléorier to prepare for teaching the coming year. The school closed in 1866.

25. Mottais, 29.

26. Brother Antonin was born May 13, 1805, in Domfront. He came to Ruillé on May 17, 1828, just days before his 23rd birthday. He was sent to Rome in 1852 as a gardener. Returning from Rome in 1859, he lived on until 1882, dying at the age of 77.

27. *Council of Administration*, notes for 1844.

28. Sorin *Memo* in O'Reilly, qtd. in Morin, 33-34.

29. Sorin, *Circular Letters*, I, 56-58.

30. Sorin, *Chronicles*, 41.

31. Gatian was a novice at this time, and the date of his first vows is unknown. On August 27, 1843, he did renew vows of poverty and chastity for three years. On August 21, 1844, he renewed them again to 1847. On August 30, 1846, he renewed perpetual vows of obedience and stability, and he renewed

limited vows of poverty and chastity. On August 21, 1848, he vowed obedience forever and poverty for one year. See Gatian's matricule card, IPA.

Chapter Three

1. Corbinière, 85.

2. *Ibid.*, 125.

3. *Ibid.*, 140.

4. *Ibid.*, 153-154.

5. *Ibid.*, 155.

6. Sorin, *Chronicles*, 9.

7. "Canal fever" caught Indiana in the 1830's, and the territory went on a construction spree that left it thirteen million dollars in debt with work stopping by 1841 on all projects except the Wabash and Erie Canal to Terre Haute. See Larson, 37.

8. Hodge, 6. The population of the entire Indiana Territory by 1841 reached 700,000. See O'Connell, 68.

9. Law, 76. By 1813, Governor Harrison had tamed the Shawnee nation a few years after meeting Tecumseh on the banks of the Wabash.

10. Cauthorn, 114.

11. Sorin letter to Moreau, October 14, 1841, GA.

12. Qtd. in *Life and Life-Work*, 228. Although the buildings have long been destroyed, the bell from the church remains in the foyer at the Administrative Center of the Midwest and Indiana Provinces, Notre Dame.

13. Grannan, 15.

14. Sorin letter to Moreau, October 14, 1841, GA.

15. Morin, 110.

16. Sorin letter to Moreau, October 17, 1841, GA.

17. Klawitter, ed., 3.

18. *Ibid.*, 4.

19. *Ibid.*, 11.

20. *Ibid.*, 7.

21. Klawitter, ed., 14.

22. *Ibid.*, 45-56.

23. Gollar, 254.

24. *Ibid.*, 252.

25. Morin, 153. Francis Xavier was still known at the time as Brother Mary. Brother Peter (James Tully), born in Ireland in 1808, left the Community in 1847. Brother Francis (Michael Disser), born in 1825 in Alsace, left in 1846. Brother Patrick (Michael Connelly) was born in 1797 in Ireland. He was a farmer and died at Notre Dame in 1867. Brother William (John O'Sullivan) was born in Ireland in 1815. A carpenter, he left the Community in 1847. Brother Basil (Timothy O'Neil), born in Ireland in 1810, left the Community in 1850.

26. Sorin, letter to Moreau, December 5, 1842, qtd. In Moreau, *Circular Letters*, I, 60.

27. The original owner of the property, the irascible priest Stephen Badin, had, however, called it "Our Lady of the Lakes." It has been suggested that the lakes were actually one, with an island (where Columba Hall stands today), until Sorin had the brothers blow up a dam to drain the swamps around the island, but an appendage to Brother John's 1843 letter clearly states that there were two lakes on the property, not one. The appended paragraphs were written later than John's February letter to Moreau, but they are still an early indication that the lakes were two on a property named Our Lady of the "Lake," not "Lakes." In a letter to Sorin dated November 15, 1842, Bishop Hailandière himself had referred to the property as "Our Lady of the

Lake," before the first group had even gotten to the location. So the title had already been planted in the missionaries' minds.

28. Morin, 160.

29. Brother Joseph (Charles Rother) was the candidate waiting for the group in 1841 at Black Oak Ridge. He left the Community in 1850. Brother John (Frederick Steber) was born in 1815 in Trieste. He was Sorin's fair haired boy. Sorin sent him in 1843 to retrieve a second colony from Le Mans. There, Moreau gave him permission to study for the priesthood. He left the Community in 1846. Brother Thomas (James William Donoghue) was born in 1824 in New Orleans. He left in 1852. Brother Paul (Jean-Bray de la Hoyde) was born in 1816 in Ireland. He died at Notre Dame in 1844, the first of the men recruited in America to die in the Community. He is the first man named in the act of incorporation for the Brothers of St. Joseph in South Bend (January 15, 1844), along with Brother Augustine (Jeremiah O'Leary), Brother Mary Joseph (Samuel O'Connell), and Brother André (Michael Walsh). Brother Ignatius (Thomas Everard) was born in 1817 in Ireland. He worked for many years at the Holy Cross orphanage in New Orleans and died at Notre Dame in 1899. Brother Celestine (Lawrence Kirwin) was born in 1821 in Ireland. He left the Community in November, 1843, from Notre Dame. Samuel O'Connell became Brother Mary Joseph. For information on him see note 4 for Chapter 4. Peter Berel became Brother Francis de Sales. Born in France in 1805, he worked at the New Orleans orhanage. He died at Le Mans in 1862.

30. John writes that a "boarder" accompanied them, but this student (Lawrence Kirwin) was at one time a novice named Brother Celestine and may have been in the process of rethinking his religious vocation when the group left St. Peter's. See previous note.

31. See deed in University of Notre Dame archives.

32. Stabrowski, 1.

33. *Ibid.*, 3.

34. A second had arrived by themselves in June, 1843, consisting of two priests, a seminarian, and five Marianite sisters. En route they missed Brother John

(Frederick Steber) who had been sent from Notre Dame to accompany them.

35. Klawitter, ed., 67.

36. *Ibid.*, 137.

37. Sorin letter to Moreau, August 23, 1848, Notre Dame: IPA.

38. *Council of Professors*, notes for January 12, 1844, Notre Dame: IPA.

Chapter Four

1. Mace, I, 15.

2. Mace, II, 868.

3. Morin, 34.

4. Brother Mary Joseph was born Samuel O'Connell in Ireland in 1819. He joined the Holy Cross group in December, 1842, and went to Notre Dame with Brother Vincent a few months later. He was the first postulant to become a novice at Notre Dame. After teaching in Vincennes, he replaced Anselm at Madison in 1845. When he returned to Madison the following year with Brother Francis (Michael Disser), the new pastor, Maurice de St. Palais, sent them away. Mary Joseph left the community a few months later (November, 1846).

5. *Particular Council* notes, Notre Dame. Celestine left the young Community, or rather was forced out, three months after Anselm's June, 1843, letter to Sorin.

6. Klawitter, ed., 29.

7. August Mary Martin, chaplain at the Royal College in Rennes, arrived in America in 1839. He met the first Holy Cross colony at Logansport, Indiana, where he was pastor of St. Vincent de Paul Church. He was appointed Vicar General of the Vincennes diocese in 1842 and was the first bishop of Natchitoches, Louisiana. He was Sorin's closest confidant among the Vincennes clergy: they shared perceptions of Hailandière. See O'Connell, 11.

8. Ibid., 29.

9. See Vincent letter for April 10, 1842, in Klawitter, ed., 8.

10. Hailandière's bad qualities are not covered in Alerding's history of the Vincennes diocese, but Alerding was bishop of Fort Wayne when he wrote the book. See Brown, I, 481.

11. Klawitter, ed., 31.

12. *Ibid.*, 31.

13. See O'Connell, 219-220.

14. Klawitter, ed., 31.

15. *Ibid.*, 14.

16. *Ibid.*, 36.

17. *Ibid.*, 36.

18. Prejudice is not automatically washed out of a novice's soul. Even adult religious were tainted: see the May 22, 1885, letter by Brother Oswald living in New Orleans. Notre Dame: IPA.

19. Klawitter, ed., 42.

20. *Ibid.*, 43.

21. *Ibid.*, 56.

22. *Ibid.*, 69.

23. St. Michael's Church since August, 1842, had as its pastor Julian Delaune who opened the school September 26, 1843, first in the church, then in the church basement. Delaune was pastor until 1846 when he left Madison to direct Sorin's ill fated college in Kentucky. He died in Paris on May 4, 1846, at the age of thirty-seven.

24. See O'Connell, 220.

25. Klawitter, ed., 84.

26. Malaria was common on the frontier. See Hanners, 30.

27. Klawitter, ed., 91.

28. *Ibid.*, xxi-xxii.

29. Sorin's *Chronicles* in translation use the word "bathing" for "swimming."

30. Sorin, *Chronicles*, 57.

31. The original land for the sixty acre cemetery was purchased in 1837 by the city of Madison. The cemetery is bound by State Road 7, Vine Street, a creek (Crooked Creek), and the foothills of Hanging Rock Hill. If Anselm's grave were inundated in the great Ohio River flood of 1937, it would probably have been inundated by the creek rather than the river.

32. Robert Newland of Indianapolis found the marker lying flat under three inches of dirt and grass. The stone is large and heavy, 66 inches high and 17 1/2 inches wide. The top has decorative work and a cross in an arch, but some top decoration has been broken off.

33. In addition to the inscription, the postcard reads: "Pilgrimage to this cemetery where the above inscription marks the resting place of one of the group who founded N.D. Bro. Anselm was drowned. Marius." The postcard is half typed, half script, the memorial from the stone being the typed part.

Chapter Five

1. Klawitter, ed., 103.

2. All minute books are held in the Indiana Province Archives (IPA) at Notre Dame, Indiana. There are seven council books remaining from the brothers' earliest years at Notre Dame, and the books cover various years. The "Council of Administration" minute book contains seventy-four entries, from October 31, 1842, to July 23, 1845. The minute book for the "Particular Council of the Brothers" contains thirty-eight entries from September 5, 1842, to June 29, 1847. The third book contains the minutes for the "Council of Trades." It contains fifty-two entries from September 7, 1845, to November 21, 1846. The Minor Chapter book has 324 entries, from

March 22, 1847, to June 12, 1854. It is by far the most complete and the most interesting of all the minutes books. The fifth volume continues the Minor Chapter minutes from April 10, 1855, to August 27, 1857. The General Chapter book has but a single entry: September 9, 1845. The final volume (for "Monthly Chapter") has but five entries, from an unspecified date in 1849 to June 5, 1850. All are original manuscripts, except for volume five, Minor Chapter Minutes 1855–1857: only a typescript remains of these minutes. There is no mention of Gatian in the minutes of the "Particular Council of the Brothers" until August 14, 1843, when he sits in the council with Sorin, Vincent, and Lawrence. All of the seven council books end in a summer, except the volume for the Council of Trades, which ends in November 1846, and the General Chapter which met only once, in September, 1845.

3. Particular Council notes, IPA, 18.

4. Minor Chapter notes, IPA, 20.

5. *Ibid.*, 23.

6. Klawitter, ed., 104.

7. See O'Connell, 257.

8. Klawitter, ed., 104.

9. *Ibid.*, 104. Since Gatian later uses the phrase "playing the fool" in reference to himself during a chapel service, the phrase probably means making eye contact or staring. See Gatian's *Chronicles*, entry for January 10, 1849.

10. MacKenzie, ed., 168.

11. *Ibid.*, 191.

12. *Ibid.*, 174.

13. *Ibid.*, 174.

14. *Ibid.*, 174.

15. Trans. MacKenzie, 195.

16. Trans. MacKenzie, 126.

17. This personal journal is the *Chronicles* by Gatian that will be examined more fully in the next chapter.

18. Qtd. in MacKenzie, 206.

19. Because of its relevance to the person of Jesus Christ, religious celibacy is often related to the matter of Jesus' own sexuality. The gospels are silent on the subject, but the Apocrypha does include "The Secret Gospel of Mark," which predates our present Gospel of Mark, both composed from an Ur text dated to 70 CE. This text includes the story of a young man who spends a night alone with Jesus. See Barnstone, 342.

20. Klawitter, ed., 114.

21. Gatian's attack on Sorin's flaws is unsolicited, quite different from Brother Vincent's rendering of Sorin's faults, a rendering elicited by Sorin himself who needed a spiritual monitor, a custom in religious communities well into the twentieth century. O'Connell does not understand the monitor system and attributes to Vincent "a mild paternalism." See O'Connell, 265. Vincent was actually acting at Sorin's request.

22. See O'Connell, 270.

23. Klawitter, ed., 96.

24. *Ibid.*, 98.

25. Klawitter, ed., 111-113.

26. *Ibid.*, 113. Maurice de St. Palais became bishop of Vincennes when Hailandière resigned. Born in France of considerable wealth, he traced his family to the Crusaders.

27. Gatian maintains in his November 21, 1846, letter to Moreau that the matter of safety was decided "four weeks ago," but no council minutes record such a deliberation. The only two Councils with minutes that survive from October, 1846, are the Particular Council of Brothers and the Minor Chapter. Neither records the debate. Gatian may possibly be referring to informed debates at the dining table, for example, or debates at recreation periods.

28. Klawitter, ed., 119.

29. *Ibid.*, 120.

30. *Ibid.*, 120.

31. *Ibid.*, 121.

32. *Ibid.*, 123. Sister Mary of the Cenacle was named superior of the sisters on September 10, 1846, at the end of the annual retreat. Sister Mary of the Five Wounds, who had been superior, became mistress of novices. See Costin, 26.

33. See, for example, his official letter of monition to Sorin, dated February 29, 1847, in Klawitter, ed., 137-138. See also note 16, above.

34. Klawitter, ed., 125.

35. Meeting notes for the Council of Administration (IPA) stop with July 23, 1845. Minor Chapter notes (IPA) begin with March 22, 1847. The lapse of almost two years between Council and Chapter does not mean there were no meetings of the former. The notes are lost. That Gatian was excluded from Chapter membership is noted in a letter from Moreau to Sorin dated December 15, 1847: Moreau leaves to Sorin's discretion the exclusion of Gatian from membership in the Chapter and remarks that he hopes God will inspire Sorin to lead Gatian to a better disposition. See Moreau letter to Sorin, December 15, 1847, GA.

36. Klawitter, ed., 150.

37. *Ibid.*, 151.

38. *Ibid.*, 151.

39. *Ibid.*, 151

40. *Ibid.*, 153.

41. *Ibid.*, 156.

42. *Ibid.*, 125.

43. *Ibid.*, 107-108.

44. *Ibid.*, 133. O'Connell suggests that the primary reason that the bishop wanted the novitiate moved to Indianapolis is that it would be closer to him and easier to supervise. See O'Connell, 183.

45. *Ibid.*, 140. By June 29, 1847, the novitiate had been or was soon to be relocated to Indianapolis as there is an entry in the minutes for the meeting of the Particular Council of Brothers on that day that some complaints had been made against Brother James (Thomas Shelly) so "it was decided he should be sent to Indianapolis with the Novices." (See Particular Council notes, IPA, 24). It is the final entry in the entire book. There is no indication what Brother James did to merit the punishment, but it was obviously necessary to get him into a new location without dismissing him from the Community entirely. He may have had a personality conflict with another brother. At the time of his transfer to Indianapolis James was fifty years old, having been born in 1797 in County Kilkenny, Ireland. He was as old as Brother Vincent. Known as Brother Maximus at his reception in 1845, he changed his name to James in 1847. He was a gardener and died at Notre Dame on October 6, 1870.

46. Minor Chapter, notes for May 24, 1847, 9. The only problem with identifying the council book entry as the Boder plan is that Joseph's letter announcing the plan is dated May 23, one day before the council meeting. It would be impossible for a letter to travel from Indianapolis to South Bend in one day. Of course, Joseph may have misdated the letter, but since he sent two letters dated May 23, the likelihood of his misdating both is slighter, although it is possible he was distracted and slip-shod about dating both letters. Another plan to cover the debt had come in Joseph's letter of February 24, 1847, but that is a full two months before the Council meeting of May 24, and Sorin would never have waited a month to present a solution to the debt problem. Anyway, the language of the minutes gives every indication that the scheme is fresh. There are five other Joseph letters between February 24 and May 23, but none contains a scheme to resolve the debt. It is possible that Sorin lost a letter from Joseph because there are no letters posted in April, 1847, a curious gap in a rich period of Joseph's correspondence.

47. Minor Chapter, notes for June 24, 1847, 13. Brother Stephen (Finton Moore) was born in 1811 in County Queens, Ireland. He entered the Community of Holy Cross in September, 1844, and was professed August 30,

1846. He died at Notre Dame February 2, 1869. His cemetery cross, which is probably incorrect, lists his age as 60.

48. Klawitter, ed., 171.

49. *Ibid.*, 183.

50. *Ibid.*, 208.

51. *Ibid.*, 275.

52. *Ibid.*, 293.

53. *Ibid.*, 172.

54. A letter dated November 18, 1847, from Brother Vincent to Moreau was read in the Minor Chapter explaining why Gatian was expelled from the Chapter. See *Minor Chapter, Notes*, 27. This letter has not survived.

55. *Minor Chapter, Notes*, October 24, 1847.

Chapter Six

1. Klawitter, ed., 218.

2. *Ibid.*, 218.

3. The Girondins were actually more complex than nineteenth century historians (like Lamartine) assessed them. See Schama, 583.

4. Klawitter, ed., 218.

5. *Ibid.*, 219.

6. A note for April 4, 1845, from the Council of Professors indicates that Hays was put into Gatian's class. Gatian was the secretary for this council at this time. A note for February 18, 1846, indicates that John Hays is to stay in Gatian's class. Hays may himself have asked to be taken out of Gatian's class, but the notes do not indicate a reason for the question of Hays' placement.

7. *Council of Professors, Notes*, 14.

8. The Notre Dame Archives show that John Hays matriculated in 1844, left in August, 1846, and returned as a Manual Labor School student in October, 1846. He worked in the Secretary's Office in 1846 and 1847, probably for Gatian. The US Census for 1850 records him as an apprentice at Notre Dame (when Gatian was sent off to California). A final record shows him re-entering January 20, 1853, and leaving in June, 1853. He thus outlasted Gatian at Notre Dame. Information courtesy of Peter Lysy, Notre Dame Archives, e-mail, September 5, 2000. There was a Hays family assoicated with the brothers at Black Oak Ridge in 1842 (see Morin 141), but there is no record of any Hays boy from this family attending Notre Dame. As early as 1820 in Fort Wayne, there was an Indian agent named John Hays. He had lived previously for twenty-seven years in Cahokia, one of the oldest settlements in Illinois. Arriving in Fort Wayne on July 14, 1820, he soon found the situation with the Miami and alcohol uncontrollable. (See Robertson 229.) He left within five months. In May, 1822, he returned briefly, but after a winter battling rheumatism, he resigned his post and the following summer moved permanently to Cahokia where he lived out his final years. This Indian agent could not, of course, have been the father of the John Hays at Notre Dame. The census rolls for Indiana in 1850 contain the name "John Hays" sixteen times. The census of free inhabitants for Monroe Township (Allen County) for June 4, 1860, lists one John Hays. (See Jackson.)

9. Klawitter, ed., 219.

10. *Ibid.*, 219.

11. Brother Basil (Timothy O'Neil) was born in Ireland in 1810. He entered the community at Black Oak Ridge in November, 1842, and went to Notre Dame one week later with Gatian and Sorin. After teaching in Fort Wayne, he was sent to Brooklyn in October, 1848. Six months later he was assigned to New Orleans, but he left the community in 1850.

    To identify Brother Aloysius is a bit more difficult. The first Brother Aloysius in the Holy Cross General Matricule joined in the 1840's: James O'Hanlon, who was born in 1805 in Ireland and entered the community in August, 1845. He left the community one month later but returned in 1855 taking again the name Aloysius (Louis de Gonzague). He was the first man in Holy Cross to be named Aloysius. He died at Notre Dame in 1860. Obviously, this is not the Aloysius who was sent to Brooklyn with Basil. In 1845 Sorin sent an Aloysius along with a Brother Francis to teach in Vincennes, from which city this Aloysius wrote two letters. In the first letter he tells Sorin that he opened school on September 29, 1845, with Brother Francis, but he wants to return to Notre Dame because he is sick. His next letter (January 14, 1846) says that he had made up his mind "to return to New York as soon as the weather will permit." (See Klawitter, ed., 101.) "Return" means he has been in New York already, but it is probably not his home because he speaks in the letter of waiting for Sorin's orders on the best way to travel. This is a full year before Sorin and the New York bishop started negotiations for the Brooklyn school. Aloysius is forty-one years old, and Sorin had sent him out to teach (as a novice) within one month of his entering the community.

However, the Brother Aloysius teaching in Brooklyn in 1849 mentioned repeatedly in Gatian's Brooklyn letters is Robert Sidley who entered the Community in March, 1848, at age eighteen. According to the General Matricule, he took the name Aloysius and made his novitiate at Indianapolis under Alexis Granger. He left the Community in August, 1852. In a typed matricule entitled "Brothers Who Took the Habit in U.S" (Midwest Province Archives), Robert Sidley's dates of entry and leaving match those for Sidley in the General Matricule. Based on Gatian's letters, Robert Sidley is the Brother Aloysius who taught in Brooklyn. He is the Aloysius whom O'Connell labels "Irish-born." See O'Connell, 240. Gatian refers to Aloysius as "Louis de Gonzague" near the end of his second letter. See Klawitter, ed., 253. The confusion between Aloysius and Louis de Gonzague is solved when we remember that the full name of the saint was Aloysius Gonzaga. Thus at times Robert Sidley is "Aloysius," when people use the Latinate form of the name, and at other times he is "Louis de Gonzague" when people use the French form.

12. Klawitter, ed., 239.

13. *Ibid.*, 241.

14. One has to question this surgical procedure, if indeed Gatian is to be taken at his word. Surgery was still rather primitive, and the reattachment of an ear is a modern phenomenon. Gatian possibly means that the ear was partially detached, and the doctor simply sewed it back in place.

15. Brother Thomas (James William Donoghoe) was born in New Orleans in 1824. He entered Holy Cross at Black Oak Ridge in 1841 and went to Notre Dame with Brother Vincent in 1843. He left the community in September, 1852.

16. Klawitter, ed., 159.

17. *Ibid.*, 263.

18. The deafness was probably temporary, due to frostbite or a bad cold contracted on the perilous journey from Notre Dame because in later years Gatian in his correspondence never refers to any problem with deafness.

19. *Ibid.*, 263. When we realize that at the time Notre Dame had only thirty-six students in total enrollment, we can sympathize more with brothers in Brooklyn facing over fifty boys in each room. See Gatian, *Chronicles*, March 24, 1848, for student enrollment at Notre Dame.

20. *Ibid.*, 270.

21. *Ibid.*, 286.

22. Brother Michael (James Flynn) was born in 1810 in Ireland. He entered the community in 1845 and took final vows in 1848. After a teaching career, he worked in the Notre Dame laundry and the lime yard. In 1860 he was Notre Dame fire chief. He died in 1884.

23. Klawitter, ed., 289.

24. *Ibid.*, 294.

25. *Ibid.*, 295.

26. *Ibid.*, 295.

27. Merrick, 171.

28. Qtd. in Adler, 67.

29. Qtd. in Flandrin, 189.

30. See Gatian, *Chronicles*, April 9, 1847: "A particular friendship has subsisted between three pupils since the beginning of the year." The phrase "particular friendship" was long used in religious communities to characterize one-on-one friendship that estranged the duo from the other members of the community and was a prelude to exclusivity and possible sexual involvement.

31. Gatian, *Chronicles*, April 9, 1847. Brother Charles Borromeo (August Thébaut) was born in 1818 in France. He is believed to have entered at Ste. Croix in 1846. He was sent to America where he received the habit on March 19, 1847. One month later Gatian records Charles Borromeo's infatuation with "Mr. Hobeck," a thirty-six year old man whom Sorin had brought from Louisville in 1845 as a postulant. "Hobeck" does not appear in any Holy Cross matricule, but he apparently died in 1847. (See Gatian, *Chronicles*, April 9, 1847.) Brother Charles Borromeo was professed in 1848. He was recalled to Le Mans in 1858. He went secretly to New Orleans in 1870 and died at Notre Dame in 1893 at age seventy-five, four months after Brother Vincent.

32. Klawitter, ed., 299.

33. The orphanage sat on Chartres Street, right on the Mississippi levee, down river from the heart of the city. The buildings remained until 1950 when they were demolished.

34. Klawitter, ed., 307.

35. Brother Theodulus (Francis Barbé) was born in France in 1818. He came to America in 1846 and was sent to New Orleans in 1849 where he was appointed director of the orphanage after Brother Vincent left. He died of yellow fever in New Orleans in 1853. Brother Louis is Brother Aloysius (Robert Sidley). See note above.

36. Sister Georgia Costin recounts the incident dramatically. See Costin, 78.

37. Klawitter, ed., 319. Brother Francis de Sales (Peter Berel) was born in France in 1805, just eight years after Vincent. He taught later in France and died in 1862 at Le Mans.

38. *Ibid.*, 328-329.

39. See O'Connell, 313.

40. Sorin, *Chronicles*, 274.

41. Vincent's most striking portrait hangs in the Brother Vincent Pieau Center, Austin, Texas. The artist, Francis Miller, was born in Columbus, Ohio, in 1855 and died in New York City in 1930. He was trained in New York, Paris, and Berlin. Miller's concept of Brother Vincent matches what we know of the subject through letters and tradition: Vincent is a calm person, a wise man, with a kind sense of humor. In the painting Vincent is an old man with a full gray beard. He sports a pillbox hat under which his eyes burrow into the viewer. The gentlest of smiles completes his face.

Chapter Seven

1. Sorin, *Chronicles*, 90.

2. *Ibid.*, 90-91.

3. Monsimer, letter to Sorin, August 15, 1851, Notre Dame: IPA. Another way to get Gatian off the Notre Dame campus in 1849 may have been to assign him to begin a new school. The Monthly Council notes for 1849 read, "Br. Gatien shall be sent in South Bend as soon as possible to begin there a regular school at least a French class." (*Monthly Council 1849–1850*, ND: IPA, 1.) Unfortunately this note does not give a month or day for the meeting. The next note is dated December 12, 1849, and the third note is dated April 3, 1850, so no conclusions can be reached about the exact dating for the note on Gatian's starting a school in South Bend other than to say it would have been in 1849 before December 12.

4. Cullen, 4.

5. Gatian, *Chronicles*, entry for January 10, 1849.

6. For a possible route of the St. Joseph Company in their last month on the road, see Cullen, 17-19.

7. Lawrence letter qtd. in Cullen, 20. "Placer" has been suggested to be a word meaning a place where "gold is found mixed with alluvial detritus." See *A Memorial and Biographical History*, 180.

8. Cullen, 20.

9. Gatian, letter to Sorin, September 15, 1850, IPA.

10. *Ibid.*

11. Qtd. in Cullen, 24.

12. *Ibid.*, 25.

13. Efforts to find the grave have been futile. Brother Franklin Cullen's efforts to locate the grave in the 1980's led him to conclude that the area of the camp and the grave are now under water since a flood control project on the South Fork of the American River has inundated the area. "In all probability he [Placidus] was buried in the cemetery just outside their cabin." (Franklin Cullen, CSC, letter to author, June 13, 1993.) Another possibility may be the Blair's-Winkelman Cemetery (also known as the "Old Johnson Cemetery") off Hassler Road near Camino. One grave is dated to 1851, and there are many unmarked graves. Brother Lawrence said the St. Joseph Company pitched camp three quarters of a mile from Johnson's trading post. If Placidus died at the camp, the brothers may very well have taken him that short distance to a cemetery on the Johnson ranch. Unfortunately, a fire in 1910 destroyed all official death records in the El Dorado County Recorder's office.

14. Gatian, letter, November 29, 1850, IPA. The William Lucas referred to was a man who joined the St. Joseph Company in California.

15. Gatian, letter to Sorin, November 29, 1850, IPA.

16. *Ibid.*

17. In the 1850 federal census Brother Lawrence appears twice (December 19 and December 27) under "Minage" on the typescript because the typist in 1972 read the accented "e" ("é") as a dotted "i." For the second entry, Brother Lawrence is listed as having $4000 in real estate. (Information from Sacramento Public Library)

18. The future of the St. Joseph Company laymen can be found in Cullen, 27. Campeau left California in 1859 and settled in Nebraska. He died there in

1890. Woodworth may have settled in Cincinnati. No trace of Dowling remains.

19. Cullen, 30.

20. Moreau, *Circular Letters*, I, 258.

21. Moreau, letter to Sorin, September 30, 1850, IPA.

22. Others who condemned Sorin for the venture were Louis Baroux (Holy Cross priest who had been ministering to the Native Americans at Pokagon) and Sister St. Francis Xavier. Their reactions can be read in Cullen, 30. Cullen remarks, the "letter that must have borne a particularly sharp sting came from his [Sorin's] friend, Sister St. Francis Xavier." She, of course, knew nothing about the Gatian matter. See Cullen, 30.

23. O'Connell, 260.

24. The exact date of Gatian's departure from Holy Cross is unknown, but the General Matricule gives it as September, 1850. Gatian's September 15, 1850, letter to Sorin certainly indicates at least his inclination to be going. However, Moreau's reference to him as "Gatian" in his September 30 letter to Sorin indicates that Moreau was unaware of Gatian's having left the religious life.

25. Dry Town, Calaveras County, is ten miles south of Placerville, but there is no present day Jacksonville twenty-three miles north of Dry Town. There is a Jackson ten miles south of Dry Town, but if Urbain passed through that town to get to Dry Town, he would have been south or east or west of it, an itinerary that does not make much sense since he was heading south out of Grass Valley (north of Placerville). The "Jacksonville" in his letter has probably disappeared or undergone a name change. In any event, in January he was in Grass Valley north of Placerville, and then he went to Dry Town south of Placerville, After meeting up with Campeau, he headed 250 miles north to Shasta County by the time of his August 15, 1851, letter to Sorin. The towns he names (Dry Town, One Horse Town) have since disappeared, been renamed, or were quaint metaphors at the time for mining camps.

26. Qtd. in Cullen, 7.

27. Giles, 53.

28. Monsimer, letter to Sorin, August 15, 1854, IPA.

29. *Ibid.*

30. If we were to try to reconstruct Urbain Monsimer, we would have to rely on the descendants of his half-brothers and half-sisters because both of Urbain's brothers who shared his same father and mother died unmarried and childless.

31. Monsimer, postscript to letter by Henry Kennedy to Sarah Kennedy, March 2, 1851, Archives, Sisters of the Holy Cross, St. Mary's, Notre Dame.

32. Sarah Kennedy joined the Sisters of the Holy Cross at St. Mary's on June 2, 1859, at age fifteen, the daughter of Henry Kennedy and Rosanna Brady. She took the religious name Sister Columba and was a music teacher throughout her life. She died October 27, 1879, and is buried at St. Mary's. Record of Apostolic Services, Archives, Sisters of the Holy Cross, St. Mary's, Notre Dame.

33. We should remember, however, that some nineteenth century proposals of marriage were different in tenor from those a century later. At the end of Cooper's novel *The Pioneers*, a Frenchman on the verge of leaving America proposes marriage to the local governor's daughter: "It was evident that he had made the offer as a duty which a well-bred man owed to a lady in such a retired place, before he left the country, and that his feelings were but very little, if at all, interested in the matter." See Cooper, 424. Urbain's postscript, on the other hand, is more romantic than social because he followed up on his sentiments for four years. In the nineteenth century, Edgar Allan Poe married his thirteen year old cousin Virginia Clem, and the match was apparently satisfactory.

34. Urbain repeats a message of love to the Kennedy "children" in a letter to Sorin dated November 19, 1854.

35. In a letter dated November 1, 1854, to Sorin we learn that Urbain may have made attempts to date women as Urbain notes that he has never been to a ball "and do not calculate to commence here" in Placerville. He adds, "Besides I do not know of any young lady worth accompanying thither or to

any other place in this great country of gold, crime and infamy." See Monsimer, letter to Sorin, November 1, 1854, IPA.

36. Monsimer, letter to Sorin, April 14, 1858, IPA.

37. In fact, Holy Cross would not staff a school in California until 1941 when brothers went to St. Anthony's High School in Long Beach. See "A Chronological Listing of the Schools, Activities, Etc. Conducted by the Brothers of Holy Cross in the United States," MPA.

38. Monsimer, letter to Sorin, April 23, 1860, IPA.

39. *Ibid.*

40. The blasphemy that Urbain dates to January 6, 1848, was the incident he recounts in his Chronicles for January 7, 1848. It was a Saturday because the community was reciting the Litany of the Blessed Virgin, a Saturday devotion, when Gatian began "playing the fool." The problem heightened at supper that night when Gatian had to be restrained by six men and removed from the dining hall. Gatian's real sin against John Hays was sexual harassment by which Gatian, as a teacher, expected affections from a student that the student was unwilling to give. It was an abuse of power that Gatian ultimately fails to recognize was the cause of his downfall.

41. We know his first destination was New York because he writes as much in his final letter. How he got to New York is unknown. Brother Franklin Cullen suspects he went by way of Panama, a much gentler journey by water instead of bouncing across the entire continent in a wagon and a train. See Cullen, 29.

42. The registry office in Saulges contains the following record of Urbain's death. "29 juillet, 1860: Décès de Urbain Jean-Baptiste Monsimer, célibataire, au Préau, né le 3 avril 1826, fils de Urbain Monsimer et de défunte Rose Reneaudeau."

43. Howard, qtd. in Schaal, 19.

Works Cited

Adler, Laure. *Secrets d'Alcôve*. Paris: Hachette, 1983.

Alerding, Herman J. *A History of the Catholic Church in the Diocese of Vincennes.* Indianapolis: Carlon and Hollenbeck, 1883.

Barnstone, Willis, ed. *The Other Bible*. San Francisco: Harper & Row, 1984.

Bennoune, Mahfoud. *The Making of Contemporary Algeria, 1830–1987*. Cambridge: Cambridge University Press, 1988.

Bosher, J.F. *The French Revolution*. New York: Norton, 1988.

Brown, Sr. Mary Borromeo. *History of the Sisters of Providence of Saint Mary-of-the-Woods*. 2 vols. New York: Benziger Brothers, 1949.

Bruneau, Denis. *L'Odyseé d'un jeune Mayennais aux Etats-Unis de 1841 à 1860, Urbain Monsimer (Frère Gatien C.S.C.)*. Angers: 1991.

Catta, Etienne, and Tony Catta. *Basil Anthony Mary Moreau*. Trans. Edward L. Heston, CSC. 2 vols. Milwaukee: Bruce, 1955.

Catta, Tony. *Father Dujarié*. Milwaukee: Bruce, 1960.

Cauthorn, Henry S. *A History of the City of Vincennes, Indiana from 1702–1901*. Terre Haute: Moore & Langen, 1902.

"Chronological Listing of the Schools, Activities, Etc. Conducted by the Brothers of Holy Cross in the United States." Notre Dame: Midwest Province Archives, n.d.

Chronicles of Notre Dame de Sainte-Croix. Rome: Archives of the Congregation of Holy Cross, n.d.

Cooper, James Fennimore. *The Pioneers*. New York: Signet, 1964.

Costin, CSC, Sister Georgia. *Priceless Spirit: A History of the Sisters of the Holy Cross, 1841–1893.* Notre Dame: University of Notre Dame Press, 1994.

_____. "Time Line for Mission of New Orleans." Monograph. St. Mary's, Notre Dame: Bertrand Hall Archives, n.d.

Council of Administration, 1842–1845, Notes. Notre Dame: Indiana Province Archives.

Council of Professors, 1844–1846, Notes. Notre Dame: Indiana Province Archives.

Cullen, CSC, Franklin. *Holy Cross on the Gold Dust Trail.* Notre Dame: Indiana Province Archives, 1989.

De Gouges, Olympe. "Declaration of the Rights of Woman and Female Citizen." In Darline Gav Levy, et al., eds. Urbana: University of Illinois Press, 1989. 92-96.

De la Corbinière, Clémentine. *The Life and Letters of Sister St. Francis Xavier (Irma Le Fer de la Motte).* Saint Mary-of-the-Woods: Providence Press, 1934.

Dionne, CSC, Gérard. Review of Thomas Maddix, *Naming the Options.* Rpr. Mottais, p 84-101.

Duboscq, Genviève. *My Longest Night.* Trans. Richard S. Woodward. New York: Arcade, 1994.

Dunn, CSC, William. *Saint Edward's University: A Centennial History.* Austin: Saint Edward's University Press, 1986.

Flandrin, Jean-Louis. *Families in Former Times: Kinship, Household and Sexuality in Early Modern France.* Trans. Richard Southern. London: Cambridge University Press, 1979.

Gervais, CSC, Bernard. "Matricule Generale." Rome: Archives, Congregation of Holy Cross, n.d.

Giles, Rosena. *Shasta County, California: A History.* Oakland, Biobooks, 1949.

Gollar, C. Walker. "Early Protestant-Catholic Relations in Southern Indiana and the 1842 Case of Roman Weinzaepfel." *Indiana Magazine of History.* (September 1999): 233-254.

Grannan, Apollinaris. *History of St. Peter's Parish, Montgomery, Indiana.* Vincennes: Kramoc, 1968.

Gudde, Erwin. *California Gold Cam* Berkeley: University of California Press, 1975.

Hanners, John. "The Great Wizard of the North." *Traces of Indiana and Midwestern History.* (Spring 1990): 26-35.

Hodge, J. *Vincennes in Pictures and Story.* N.c.: n., 1902.

Inter-societal Committe on the Consecrated Life. *Report.* Congregation of Holy Cross, 2002.

Jackson, Ronald V., ed. *Indiana 1850 Census Index.* Bountiful, Utah: Accelerated Indexing Systems, n.d.

Klawitter, CSC, George. *Adapted to the Lake: Letters by the Brother Founders of Notre Dame, 1841–1849.* New York: Peter Lang, 1993.

Kleber, Albert. *Ferdinand, Indiana, 1840–1940.* St. Meinrad: 1940.

Kundera, Milan. *The Unbearable Lightness of Being.* Trans. Michael H. Heim. New York: Harper & Row, 1984.

Lafayette, Marquis de. "Declaration of the Rights of Man." Versailles: Baudoin, 1789.

Laprés, CSC, Raymond. "Brother André : First Brother of St. Joseph, First Brother of Holy Cross." *Bulletin des Frères de Sainte-Croix* (October 1952): 103-121. Rpr. Mottais, *Writings*: 54-66.

Larson, John L. "Ruins and Old Routes." *Traces of Indiana and Midwestern History.* (Spring 1990): 36-47.

Law, Judge. *The Colonial History of Vincennes under the French, British and American Governments.* Vincennes: Harvey, Mason & Co., 1858.

Life and Life-Work of Mother Theodore Guerin. New York: Benziger Brothers, 1904.

Mace, Georges. *Un Département Rural de l'Ouest: La Mayenne.* 2 vols. Mayenne: Floch, 1982.

MacKenzie, Norman. *The Early Poetic Manuscripts and Note-books of Gerard Manley Hopkins.* New York: Garland, 1989.

Maddix, CSC, Thomas. "Breaking the Historical Amnesia: A Fresh Look at the Originating Vision of the Brothers of St. Joseph." In *Naming the Options: A Study of the Mission of the Brothers of Holy Cross During a Period of Comfort and Discomfort.* PhD diss. 1989. Rpr. Mottais, 75-92.

Memorial and Biographical History of Northern California. Chicago: Lewis Pub., 1891.

Merrick, Jeffrey, ed. *Homosexuality in Early Modern France.* New York: Oxford University Press, 2001.

Minor Chapter, 1847–1854, Notes. Notre Dame: Indiana Province Archives.

Monsimer, Urbain (Brother Gatian). *Chronicles. 1847–1849.* Notre Dame: Indiana Province Archives.

Monthly Council of the Brothers, 1849–1850, Notes. Notre Dame: Indiana Province Archives.

Moreau, Basil. *Circular Letters.* 2 vols. Trans. Edward L. Heston. N.c.: n.p., 1943.

Morin, CSC, Garnier. *Holy Cross Brothers: From France to Notre Dame.* Notre Dame: Dujarié Press, 1952.

Mottais, André. *Writings.* Ed. Edmund Hunt, CSC, and George Klawitter, CSC. *Brother André Mottais, Pioneer of Holy Cross: "Remove my name every time it appears."* 2nd ed. Austin: St. Edward's University, 1999.

O'Connell, Marvin. R. *Edward Sorin.* Notre Dame: University of Notre Dame Press, 2001.

O'Dwyer, CSC, Ephrem. *The Curé of Ruillé*. Notre Dame: Ave Maria Press, 1941.

O'Reilly, CSC, Aiden. *Brother Aiden Extracts*. Unpublished notes. Notre Dame: Midwest Province Archives, n.d.

Particular Council of the Brothers, 1842–1947 Notes. Notre Dame: Indiana Province Archives.

Pernoud, Georges, and Sabine Flaisser. *The French Revolution*. New York: Capricorn Books, 1970.

Pétion, Jérôme. *Memoirs*. Paris: C.A. Dauban, 1866.

"Questions for Self-Examination." London: Palmer, 1861.

Robertson, Nellie. "John Hays and the Fort Wayne Indian Agency." *Indiana Magazine of History*. (Sept. 1943): 221-236.

Rudolph, L.C. *Hoosier Faiths*. Bloomington: Indiana University Press, 1995.

Sagan, Eli. *Citizans & Cannibals: The French Revolution: The Struggle for Modernity, and the Origins of Ideological Terror*. New York: Rowman & Littlefield, 2001.

Schaal, Carol. "Nothing Ventured, Nothing Gained." *Notre Dame Magazine*. (Summer 1992): 17-20.

Schama, Simon. *Citizens: A Chronicle of the French Revolution*. New York: Alfred A. Knopf, 1989.

Sorin, Edward. *Circular Letters*. 2 vols. Notre Dame: 1894.

_____. *The Chronicles of Notre Dame du Lac*. Trans. John M. Toohey. Ed. James T. Connelly. Notre Dame: Notre Dame Press, 1992.

Stabrowski, CSC, Donald. "Brickmaking at Notre Dame." Notre Dame: Indiana Province Archives, 1991.

Taylor, Robert M. and Connie A. McBirney. *Peopling Indiana: The Ethnic Experience*. Indianapolis: Indiana Historical Society, 1996.

Vanier, CSC, Philéas. "Brother André's Project." In *Canon Dujarié*. Rpr. Mottais, *Writings*: 46-53.

_____. *Canon Dujarié*. Montréal: 1948.

_____. *Recueil Documentaire*. Rome: Archives of the Congregation of Holy Cross.

0-595-29830-3